A
Survival Kit
for the
Special
Education
Teacher

Roger Pierangelo

**THE CENTER FOR APPLIED
RESEARCH IN EDUCATION**
West Nyack, New York 10995

Library of Congress Cataloging-in-Publication Data

Pierangelo, Roger.
    A survival kit for the special education teacher / Roger Pierangelo.
      p. cm.
    ISBN 0-87628-870-0
    1. Handicapped children—Education.   2. Special education.   I. Title.
LC4015.P52 1994   93-44763
371.91—dc20   CIP

Printed in the United States of America

10   9   8   7   6   5

ISBN 0-87628-870-0

**THE CENTER FOR APPLIED RESEARCH
IN EDUCATION**
West Nyack, New York 10994

On the World Wide Web at http://www.phdirect.com

Prentice-Hall International (UK) Limited, *London*
Prentice-Hall of Australia Pty. Limited, *Sydney*
Prentice-Hall Canada Inc., *Toronto*
Prentice-Hall Hispanoamericana, S.A., *Mexico*
Prentice-Hall of India Private Limited, *New Delhi*
Prentice-Hall of Japan, Inc., *Tokyo*
Simon & Schuster Asia Pte. Ltd., *Singapore*
Editora Prentice-Hall do Brasil, Ltda., *Rio de Janeiro*

This book is dedicated to my wife Jackie and children Jacqueline and Scott who gave me the purpose to expand my horizons, the support to undertake this project and the understanding while I was writing the book.

I also dedicate this book to my parents who gave me a truly loving foundation from which to grow, my sister Carol who has been more special to me than she realizes and my brother-in-law Dr. George Giulaini, whose invaluable guidance, support and direction greatly contribed to my professional opportunities and experiences and was always there when I needed him.

About the Author

Dr. Roger Pierangelo has over 25 years of experience as a regular classroom teacher, shool psychologist in the Herricks Public School system in New Hyde Park, N.Y., administrator of special education programs, full professor in the graduate special education department at Long Island University, private practitioner in psychology, member of Committees on Special Education, evaluator for the N.Y. State Education Department, Director of a private clinic, and consultant to numerous private and public schools, PTA and SEPTA groups.

Dr. Pierangelo earned his B.S. from St. John's University, M.S. from Queens College, Professional Diploma from Queens College and Ph.D. from Yeshiva University. Currently he is working as a psychologist both in the schools and in private practice, teaching at the college level, and serving as director of a private clinic.

Dr. Pierangelo is a member of the American Psychological Association, New York State Psychological Association, Nassau County Psychological Association, New York State Union of Teachers, and Phi Delta Kappa.

Acknowledgments

The students in my classes, 1968-73 while I was a teacher in the Roslyn Public Schools, Roslyn, N.Y. who were with me when it all started.

Harriet Brodie, special education teacher in the Herricks Public Schools, Herricks, N.Y. for her sensitivity, insight, professional experience and outstanding contributions for sections 32, 33, and 34 of this book.

John Okulski, Principal of Garden City High School, Garden City, N.Y. whose kindness, sensitivity, and willingness to go the extra step and common sense with children were a great inspiration for me over the years.

Ollie Simmons whose smiling face and sense of humor always made the workday begin on a positive note.

Bill Smyth, a very special person and guidance counselor in the Herricks Public School System, New Hyde Park, N.Y. whose life experiences, guidance, stories, genuineness, and humor always helped me maintain a positive outlook on life and who is always willing to do what is "best for kids."

Susan Kolwicz, my editor, who made this unbelievable undertaking a most enjoyable and professional experience. Working with someone like Susan as an editor is every writer's dream.

About This Survival Kit

PURPOSE OF THE GUIDE

This unique guide has been developed to help all teachers survive the pressures of working with exceptional children and derive greater rewards from the experience. Many texts are filled with theories, but very little practical advice has been made available. From my 15 years of teaching special educators, 25 years in psychology and education, 13 years in private practice, and 17 years on Committees on Special Education, I have come to realize the need that all teachers have for a wide variety of information that can be accessed at a moment's notice. This book is organized to give teachers that practical advice. It also presents a global concept of special education that allows teachers to fulfill the requirements for any role that they may encounter.

Filled with practical tools and suggestions, the guide takes special education teachers through the various stages required to understand the processes of referral, parent intakes, evaluation, interpretation, diagnosis, remediation, prescription, placement, recommendations, parent conferences, Committee on Special Education referrals, individual educational plans, classroom management, curriculum, materials, and practical educational law. It also contains many useful tables, charts, and helpful handouts for parents.

It is the responsibility of any special education teacher to keep abreast of the latest techniques, laws, tools, and evaluative measures that exist in the field. Having one book that provides all the necessary survival skills can only facilitate the process of teaching exceptional children.

WHO CAN USE THIS GUIDE

This type of book can be very useful not only for special education teachers but for regular classroom teachers, administrators, college students, and parents of exceptional children. The information contained here offers all these individuals answers to many everyday questions involving their students, children, and teaching learning techniques.

HELPFUL AND UNIQUE FEATURES

This book, which contains the most up-to-date information possible, is a unique guide for special education teachers because of several features:

- Its developmental, step-by-step approach takes readers through a variety of topics and procedures necessary for a realistic as well as complete awareness of exceptional children.

- Written in an easy-to-read format, the book draws on the author's extensive experience to present a wealth of tried-and-true suggestions.

- The material is presented in a way that allows readers to make an easy transition to classroom applications.

- The focus is on the more practical and commonly required issues, avoiding any material that may be obscure and meaningless.

- Many illustrations reinforce the concepts presented throughout the guide, including charts and tables on subjects of special interest to educators.

- Numerous practical tips give teachers the opportunity to share with parents on a variety of topics.

- Useful information can be immediately applied to the variety of roles that special educators may fill.

- The *Survival Kit* concudes with invaluable parent conference handouts, examples of psychoeducational reports, common abbreviations, and glossaries of special education terminology.

Roger Pierangelo

Table of Contents

Part 1

Clinical Issues for Special Educators

Section 1

Introduction: Responsibilities and Roles of the Special Education Teacher

The special education teacher in today's schools plays a critical role in the proper education of exceptional students. The teacher is unique in that he or she can fill many different roles in the educational environment. For instance, the special education teacher can be assigned as

1. A teacher in a self-contained special education classroom in a regular school. This would involve working with a certain number of disabled students in a special education setting. This type of setting allows for the use of *mainstreaming*, the involvement of a disabled child in a regular classroom for a part of the regular school day, as an educational tool when a student is ready for this type of transitional technique. The teacher in a self-contained classroom can often draw on the resources of a teaching assistant.

2. The resource teacher in a *categorical resource room*, a resource room in a special school that deals with only one type of exceptionality, or a *noncategorical resource room*, a resource room usually found in the regular mainstream school where many exceptionalities are educated at one time. Such a role necessitates close involvement with each child's homeroom teacher and the transfer of practical techniques and suggestions to facilitate the child's success while in the regular setting.

3. The special education teacher can also be an educational evaluator on the child study team (CST) or pupil personnel team (PPT), a school-based support team that discusses and makes recommendations on high-risk students. This role requires a complete and professional understanding of testing and evaluation procedures, and diagnosis and interpretation of test results.

4. A member of the *Committee on Special Education* (CSE), a district-based committee mandated by federal law whose responsibilities include the classification, placement, and evaluation of all disabled children within the district. This role involves interpreting educational test results, making recommendations, and diagnosing strengths and weaknesses for the individual educational plan, a list of goals, needs, and objectives required for every disabled student.

5. A member of a *multidisciplinary team* educating secondary students in a departmentalized program.

3

6. A *consultant teacher*, a special education teacher assigned to work with a disabled child right in the mainstreamed class.

7. An *itinerant teacher*, a special education teacher hired to visit various schools in several districts and work with special children. This provides the child with the required auxiliary services and allows a district to meet requirements without having a program of their own.

8. As a *private practitioner* who deals with the evaluation and remediation of children as an auxiliary service after school.

Whatever the role, you will always encounter a variety of situations that require practical decisions and relevant suggestions. Moreover, no matter what role you play in special education, there is always a need to be able to understand fully symptomology, causality, evaluation, diagnosis, prescription, and remediation as well as communicating vital information to professionals, parents, and students.

Section 2

The Clinical or Case Study Method

The *clinical* or *case study method* is a process by which we collect all available evidence—social, psychological, educational, environmental, behavioral, and medical—that may help us understand an individual child and the possible *etiology* or *cause* of his or her difficulties.

However, there are several intervention strategies that the school should try before beginning the clinical case study process which may eventually lead to the Committee on Special Education. If these strategies are attempted and the school administrators believe that it has exhausted all options, then and only then should it begin the process of referral and evaluation. Some of the options that should be explored first follow.

SUGGESTED PREREFERRAL STRATEGIES

Pupil Personnel Team Discussions

This procedure should be used so that several staff members are able to view the symptoms and provide a variety of preventive suggestions prior to evaluation.

Team Meeting with Teachers

Sometimes a group meeting with all the child's teachers can prevent the need for further involvement. One or several teachers may be using techniques that could benefit the others in working with the child. By sharing information or observations, it is possible to identify patterns of behavior reflective of some particular condition or disability. Once this pattern is identified, it may be handled in a variety of ways without the need for more serious intervention.

Parent Interviews

Meeting the parent(s) is always recommended for the child who is having some difficulty in school. This initial meeting can be informal and just for the purpose of clarifying certain issues and gathering pertinent information that may help in the classroom. If testing or serious intervention is required, then a more formal and in-depth meeting may have to take place.

Classroom Management Techniques

There are times when the real issue may not be the child, but the style of the classroom teacher. If that is the case, then help for the teacher can come in the form of classroom management techniques. These practical suggestions may be offered by an administrator, psychologist, or any team member who feels comfortable with this situation and can also be realistic and diplomatic. Many classroom techniques and modifications can be tried before taking more serious steps. (Modifications and suggestions are discussed in later chapters.)

Help Classes

Some children may just require a temporary support system to get them through a difficult period. Some schools provide extra nonspecial education services, such as help classes that may be held during lunch or after school. These classes are designed to assist the child by clarifying academic confusion that, if not addressed, could lead to more serious problems.

Resource Room Assistance

This option can be tried prior to any CSE review only when the school district offers such services for nonspecial education students. Some schools provide resource room for students who are having academic problems that are not severe enough to warrant classification. If this option is available, then the school may want to try to see if this type of support works.

Reading Evaluation

This evaluation can be recommended when reading is the specific area of concern and the need for a complete and comprehensive reading diagnostic battery is called for by the team. Some symptoms that may necessitate this type of evaluation are

- Inability to develop a sight word vocabulary by second grade
- Consistent inability to remember what is read
- Tendency to lose place while reading
- Inadequate development of word attack skills

Remedial Reading or Math Services

These types of services do not require a review by the CSE. Remedial reading or math classes are not special education services and can be instituted as a means of alleviating the child's academic problems.

Recommendation for In-School Counseling

Sometimes children may experience a *situational* or *adjustment* disorder (a temporary emotional pattern that may occur at any time in a person's life without a prior history of problems) resulting from separation, divorce, health issues, assignment to a new district, and so on. When this pattern occurs, it may temporarily interfere in the child's ability to concentrate, remember, and attend to tasks. Consequently, a drop in academic performance is noted. If such a pattern occurs, the school psychologist may want to institute in-school counseling with the parent's involvement and permission. This recommendation should be instituted only with issues that can be resolved in a relatively short period of time. More serious issues may have to be referred to outside agencies or professionals for longer treatment. When such a recommendation is made, the psychologist will provide a minimum of three names from which the parents may choose.

Daily/Weekly Progress Reports

Sometimes children who have fallen behind academically "hide" from the real issues by avoiding reality. The use of daily progress reports for a week or two at first, and then weekly reports, may provide the child with the kinds of immediate gratification to get back on track. These immediate reports offer a child a greater sense of hope and control in getting back to a more normal academic pattern.

Intellectual Evaluation

This evaluation may be a first step in determining whether or not the child's present problems reflect a severe discrepancy between ability and achievement. It should also be used if group intelligence test scores are questionably lower than the ability observed by the teacher(s). This option may also place unrealistic expectations on the part of the parents, child, or teachers.

Hearing Test

This evaluation should be one of the first factors recommended by the team if such a test has not been undertaken within the last six months to a year. Be aware that inconsistencies in test patterns from year to year indicate a chronic pattern. Some symptoms that might indicate an updated audiological examination are

- Child turns head when listening.
- Child asks you to repeat frequently.
- Child consistently misinterprets what he or she hears.
- Child does not respond to auditory stimuli.
- Child slurs speech, speaks in a monotone voice, or articulates poorly.

Vision Test

As with the hearing exam, results of the vision screening should also be considered first by the PPT. Again, if a vision screening has not been done within six months to a year, then request this immediately. Possible symptoms that may necessitate such an evaluation are

◆ Turning head when looking at board or objects
◆ Excessive squinting
◆ Frequent rubbing of eyes
◆ Holding books and materials close to face or at unusual angles
◆ Frequent headaches
◆ Avoiding close work of any type
◆ Covering an eye when reading
◆ Consistently losing place when reading

Disciplinary Action

This recommendation is usually made when the child in question needs a structured boundary set involving inappropriate behavior. It is generally used in conjunction with other recommendations if a pattern exists since such patternal behavior may be symptomatic of a more serious problem.

Medical Exam

Try to rule out any possibility of a medical condition causing or contributing to the existing problems. If the PPT feels that there is any possibility of such involvement, then a recommendation should be made. This recommendation may be chosen when the need for a more complete medical work-up is evident. The team reviews available records, and in light of the presenting problems and symptoms, makes the necessary outside recommendations to the parents, that is, neurological examination, ophthalmological examination, and so on.

Change of Program

This recommendation usually occurs when a student may be placed in a course that is not suited to his or her ability or needs. If a student is found to have a low IQ and is in an advanced class and failing, then the student's program should be changed to include more modified classes or more restrictive classes such as special education. If the recommendation for a more restrictive setting is being considered, then it necessitates a review by the CSE. In cases of possible special education, the PPT is only a recommending body that does not make decisions of classification and placement to a special education setting.

Consolidation of Program

There are times when reducing a student's course load is necessary. If a child is "drowning" in school, then his or her available energy level may be extremely limited. In such cases you may find that he or she is failing many courses. Temporary consolidation or condensing the program allows for the possibility of salvaging some courses since the student's available energy does not have to be spread so thin.

PINS Petition

A PINS petition, or "person in need of supervision," is a family court referral. This referral can be made by either the school or the parent and is usually made when a child under the age of sixteen is out of control in terms of attendance, behavior, or some socially inappropriate or destructive pattern.

Referral to Child Protective Services

A referral to Child Protective Services (CPS) is indicated for all educators if there is a suspicion of abuse or neglect. The school official or staff do not have a choice if such suspicion is present. Referrals to this service may result from physical, sexual, or emotional abuse or educational, environmental, or medical neglect.

INITIATING THE CLINICAL OR CASE STUDY METHOD

Once the school believes that all options have been attempted, then the next step involves a more in-depth look at potential causes.

Every child who is referred for evaluation should receive careful diagnosis before recommendations are made. The case study begins by obtaining a description of the symptoms that bring the child to the attention of the diagnostic team. Teachers need to be aware of "signals" or of symptoms suggesting the possible presence of a more serious problem so that earlier identification and possible treatment are possible. The earlier the high-risk child is identified, the better the *prognosis* or *outcome*. Patterns of behavior indicate problems and should not be overlooked. Children do not grow out of inappropriate *patterns of behavior or patterns of serious symptoms*, they just become more seriously disturbed.

The clinical or case study method involves a global approach to the identification and treatment of a child. It is made up of several parts, all of which need to be accomplished to develop a realistic and productive outcome. Leaving any of the parts out could lead to a misdiagnosis or poor treatment. The parts of the case study method are

- ◆ The initial referral
- ◆ The rating scale

- ◆ The observation
- ◆ The pupil personnel team
- ◆ Parent intake
- ◆ Evaluation
- ◆ Diagnosis
- ◆ Recommendations
- ◆ Referral to the Committee on Special Education
- ◆ Individual educational plans
- ◆ Meeting with teachers
- ◆ Meeting with parents

The first step in the clinical or case study method for the special education teacher is to be aware of certain patterns of behavior in children that may be indicative of more serious problems. There are many patterns that teachers and parents should be aware of that indicate the presence of a potentially high-risk student. Some of these patterns may be exhibited in school and others at home. In either case appropriate communication between home and school will increase chances that proper attention can be instituted.

SCHOOL SYMPTOMS EXHIBITED BY HIGH-RISK STUDENTS

A high-risk student is usually someone who is experiencing possibly severe emotional, social, environmental, or academic stress. As a result of this intense turmoil, many symptoms are generated in a dynamic attempt to alleviate the anxiety. They can show up in many different behavior patterns. Some of the more common ones that can be exhibited by either elementary or secondary students while in school are

1. A history of adequate or high first quarter grades followed by a downward trend leading to failures in the final quarter.

   This type of pattern is usually indicative of students with low energy levels. The low energy level is usually the result of emotional conflicts draining the students of the necessary energy for academic performance. As a result such a student tends to "burn out" early and has very little left for consistent performance. If this pattern exists, it is something that needs to be addressed. It will not change with pressure.

2. A history of excessive absences.

   This pattern, if not the result of real medical issues, is usually reflective of the protective defense exhibited by students in conflict.

   Avoidance, flight and denial are 3 of the major defenses that are employed by students of high risk. In order to reduce their tension, these students usually become impulsive in their actions without thought of implications. Either cutting or avoidance tend to become an immediate "solution" for their problem. However, they do not have the insight or judgment to realize that this pattern will increase their stress. Their only concern is the reduction of their tension.

3. A history of excessive lateness.

   A student who is depressed will usually have a difficult time falling asleep or getting up in the morning to the point where it interferes in their ability to make it to school in time. While this may occur as isolated situations with most students, a pattern of missing early classes may be reflective of a more pervasive depressive pattern.

   It can also be a symptom of disorganization or a chaotic family structure which may be adding to the child's stress.

4. Frequent inability to separate from parent at the start of the school day. While this can be normal behavior in very young children, it becomes a more serious symptom after age six or seven.

5. High achievement scores and high school abilities index with a history of low academic performance.

   Bright, high risk students may exhibit this pattern because it is easier to sustain their low energy levels for short tasks such as Achievement Tests or IQ Tests. However, when the demands require sustained concentration and performance over a long period of time, this type of student cannot maintain the necessary energy.

6. Consistent failure in two or more quarters of at least two subjects.

7. A history of parent "coverage" for inappropriate behavior, poor work performance, poor attitude, failures, or absences.

   When a child is involved in this type of "protection" it tends to create an attitutde of learned helplessness. The child in this case does not learn how to deal with frustration or seek solutions. As a result, the child may be more impulsive in his or her behavior because of the knowledge that he will be "saved" by others if something should occur. This can be a very serious pattern as the pressures of school increase and the child is unable to resolve them by him- or herself.

8. Student wandering the halls after school with no direction or purpose.

   Many students from dysfunctional families will use school as a primary source of security, protection and comfort. While many students stay after school for a purpose the child who wanders may be a student in distress.

9. A history of constant projection onto others as a reason for a lack of performance, handing in work, failures, or cutting.

10. A history of feeling powerless in the student's approach to problems.

11. Recent stress-related experiences, for example, divorce, separation, death of a parent, or parent's loss of employment.

12. A history of constant visits to the nurse.

13. Social withdrawal from peers with an emphasis on developing relationships with adults.

There may be other patterns as well. However, keep in mind that the *frequency, duration,* and *intensity* of the symptoms is crucial in determining a pattern of high risk. (More will be said about these concepts later in this chapter.) Once a pattern is identified as possible indications of "high risk," it is then important for teachers to understand how problems may interfere with the child's ability to learn. Children with serious problems are not "stubborn" or "lazy." The real reasons for a lack of academic production or inappropriate behavior may lie in their dynamic state of tension and how it affects their ability to learn in the classroom.

HOW EMOTIONAL PROBLEMS AFFECT A CHILD'S ABILITY TO FUNCTION IN THE CLASSROOM

When children are experiencing serious emotional turmoil, the tension that is generated usually results in symptoms. These symptoms become the first signal noticed by teachers. Therefore, it is very important for teachers to understand the difference between symptoms and problems. If this is not fully understood, a great deal of frustration will occur in trying to extinguish the symptom on both the part of the child and the teacher.

The identification of symptoms as an indication of something more serious is another first step in helping children work out their problem or problems.

SYMPTOMATIC BEHAVIOR POSSIBLY INDICATING MORE SERIOUS PROBLEMS

Examples of typical symptomatic behavior that may be indicative of more serious concerns may include the following:

- Exhibits impulsiveness
- Lies constantly
- Frequently hands in incomplete work
- Exhibits awkwardness
- Gives many excuses for inappropriate behavior
- Appears fearful of adults
- Constantly blames others for problems
- Appears fearful of new situations
- Panics easily
- Exhibits verbal hesitancy

- Exhibits distractibility
- Is hypoactive
- Has short attention span
- Is hyperactive
- Overreacts
- Fears criticism
- Becomes physical with others
- Rarely takes chances
- Exhibits intrusive behavior
- Is moody
- Cannot focus on task
- Defies authority
- Procrastinates
- Appears anxious
- Squints
- Is not able to generalize
- Turns head while listening
- Appears insecure
- Exhibits disorganization
- Has trouble starting work
- Exhibits inflexibility
- Tires easily
- Exhibits irresponsibility
- Exhibits controlling behavior
- Has poor judgment
- Criticizes others easily
- Exhibits symptoms of denial
- Forgets easily
- Daydreams
- Is painfully shy
- Is unwilling to venture a guess
- Is overly social
- Is unwilling to reason
- Seems to be a slow starter
- Exhibits social withdrawal
- Engages in arguments frequently
- Criticizes oneself constantly
- Destroys property

- Bullies other children
- Is lazy
- Needs constant reassurance
- Exhibits inconsistency
- Has poor reading skills
- Cannot spell at grade level
- Argues with others

HOW TO DETERMINE THE SEVERITY OF A POTENTIAL PROBLEM

While many of these symptoms may indicate a problem, several guidelines should be used to determine the severity of the situation:

1. *Frequency of symptoms*—Consider how often the symptoms occur. The greater the frequency, the greater chance of a serious problem.
2. *Duration of symptoms*—Consider how long the symptoms last. The longer the duration, the more serious the problem.
3. *Intensity of symptoms*—Consider how serious the reactions are at the time of occurrence. The more intense the symptom, the more serious the problem.

If you suspect serious problems, they cannot be ignored. The more immediate the response to such symptoms, the greater chance of success with the child.

The greater the frequency, duration, and intensity of the symptoms, the greater the energy drain on the part of the child. Symptoms that are ways to relieve tension are usually indications of conflicts, fears, and other problems within the child. All conflicts require energy, and the greater the number of conflicts or the more serious the conflict exhibited, the greater expenditure of energy required. Since everyone has a certain amount of available energy, the energy required to deal with these conflicts must come from somewhere. Therefore, conflicts tend to drain energy away from other processes such as concentration, memory, attention, and so on. That is usually why children with emotional problems exhibit the following typical avoidance behaviors either in the classroom or at home.

- Forgets on a selective basis
- "Forgets" to write down assignments day after day
- Takes hours to complete homework
- Finishes homework very quickly
- Cannot seem to get started with homework
- Frequently brings home unfinished classwork
- Consistently leaves long-term assignments until the last minute

- Complains of headaches, stomachaches, and other physical problems before or after school
- Exhibits "spotlight behaviors" for attention

Perhaps the first things parents notice when children are experiencing problems with learning are avoidance symptoms. These are techniques that children use to avoid what they perceive as a failure or an ego-deflating situation. Children will often exhibit these symptoms at home and at school to avoid loss of parental approval, peer humiliation, or fear of failure. In this way, children do not have to

Show their parents that they are not capable
Deal with possible parental anger and frustration
Come face to face with their own inadequacy
Deal with peer pressure and possible ridicule

Avoidance behaviors are common "tools" utilized by children who are experiencing problems in learning. Some of the more common ones are as follows:

COMMON AVOIDANCE BEHAVIORS

FORGETS ON A SELECTIVE BASIS This symptom is exemplified by the child who knows the batting averages of all baseball players, the words from most songs on the radio, the times of most television shows, but "forgets" to bring home his or her math book. The selectivity of the forgetfulness usually centers on areas of learning that may be creating frustration.

FORGETS TO WRITE DOWN ASSIGNMENTS DAY AFTER DAY This symptom may continue even after repeated requests or threats. The avoidance of a perceived failure experience is accomplished through the use of this behavior.

TAKES HOURS TO COMPLETE HOMEWORK In this case, the child seems to labor or procrastinate over the work. Frequent trips to the kitchen for food, or to the bathroom, or to get a drink, or sharpen a pencil, will delay the possibility of perceived failure. This symptom also occurs if a child is under tension and cannot concentrate for long periods of time. The child will tend to "burn out" quickly and daydream the night away.

FINISHES HOMEWORK VERY QUICKLY In this type of symptom the child's major objective is to get the ego-threatening situation (homework) over as quickly as possible. Every attempt is made to "rush" through the assignments with little if any care or patience. Getting it over as quickly as possible almost makes it seem as if it never existed.

CANNOT SEEM TO GET STARTED WITH HOMEWORK When a child's anxiety level is very high, it makes it very difficult to "start the engine." Like a cold engine on a winter day, you can turn the key and it revs, but it never turns over. An anxious child acts in the same way. The child may spend a great deal of time getting "ready" for the homework by arranging books, sharpening pencils, getting the paper out, opening the textbooks, getting a glass of water, going to the bathroom, and so on, but never really starting the assignments.

FREQUENTLY BRINGS HOME UNFINISHED CLASSWORK This symptom is frequently exhibited by students for several reasons. One reason is a low energy level and therefore problems dealing with tasks involving sustained concentration. The second reason may involve the concept of learned helplessness and may arise when a parent constantly sits next to a child when he or she is doing homework. The child becomes conditioned to this assistance and is helpless without it. Since someone sitting next to the child is not re-created in the classroom, the child procrastinates with the classwork so that he or she can bring it home and have someone help with it.

The third reason may involve the child's need for attention. Bringing home unfinished classwork necessitates some parents' need to sit with them and complete the work. This "captive audience" of parent attention is reinforced when a parent tries to leave. The child stops working or complains that he or she can't do it. Consequently, the parent remains seated next to the child. Bringing home unfinished classwork extends the period of attention the child may receive from the parent. However, these types of situations usually become more tense and negative as the hours progress and the parent's patience waivers.

CONSISTENTLY LEAVES LONG-TERM ASSIGNMENTS UNTIL THE LAST MINUTE Avoidance of school-related tasks, especially long-term ones, is a frequent symptom of children with low energy levels. It would be like avoiding paying a big bill when you have very little money. You may "hide" the bill or forget it exists. Magical thinking is a frequent dynamic mechanism of children who are highly anxious.

COMPLAINS OF HEADACHES, STOMACHACHES, AND OTHER PHYSICAL PROBLEMS BEFORE OR AFTER SCHOOL Very high tension levels over an extended period of time may result in somatic (bodily) complaints, such as headaches and stomachaches. These complaints, while real to the child, may indicate an avoidance of an uncomfortable or ego-deflating situation. When a child has a pattern of these types of complaints, especially before and after school, the teacher needs to see this "signal" as a symptom of a more serious problem.

EXHIBITS "SPOTLIGHT" BEHAVIORS "Spotlight" behaviors are any behaviors that bring the focus of attention to the child, for example, calling out, laughing out loud, getting up out of seat, annoying other children. When this occurs it is usually a release of tension. Some children use "spotlight" behaviors to alleviate the tension of academic inadequacy and may even hope to get into trouble to leave the room. In this way they will not have to deal with possible academic failure. Another reason for "spotlight" behaviors is control. However, keep in mind that the more controlling a child is, the more out of control they feel. The third reason for "spotlight" behaviors is for the sole purpose of gaining the teachers attention. However, in this way, the child, not the teacher, is determining when he or she gets attention. It is better for the teacher to pay spontaneous and random attention to such a child when he or she is not expecting it. In this way you may reduce the impulsive need for seeking out attention.

ENERGY DRAIN AND ITS EFFECT ON BEHAVIOR AND LEARNING

Normal Development and Division of Energy

Everyone has a certain amount of psychic energy to use in dealing with the everyday stresses of life. In normal development there is a certain amount of stress, but because of an absence of major conflicts which tend to drain energy, the individual has more than enough to keep things in perspective. Consequently, the division of energy and the symptoms that result (more often than not) when a child is relatively "conflict free" is illustrated by the chart on page 18.

High Tension Level and Division of Energy

However, when serious conflicts arise, the available energy must be "pulled" to deal with the conflicts like white blood cells to an infection. Since energy must be drained away, there is less available energy to keep things in perspective. In this case, the resulting symptoms and behaviors take on a different look. (See the chart on page 19.)

When a parent or teacher observes a pattern of behaviors similar to the following, that adult should automatically become aware that some serious problem may exist. These symptoms are not the problems but an outgrowth of a serious problem. It is therefore very important for the teacher or team to try to identify what the problem or problems are so that treatment can take place.

Normal Development and Division of Energy

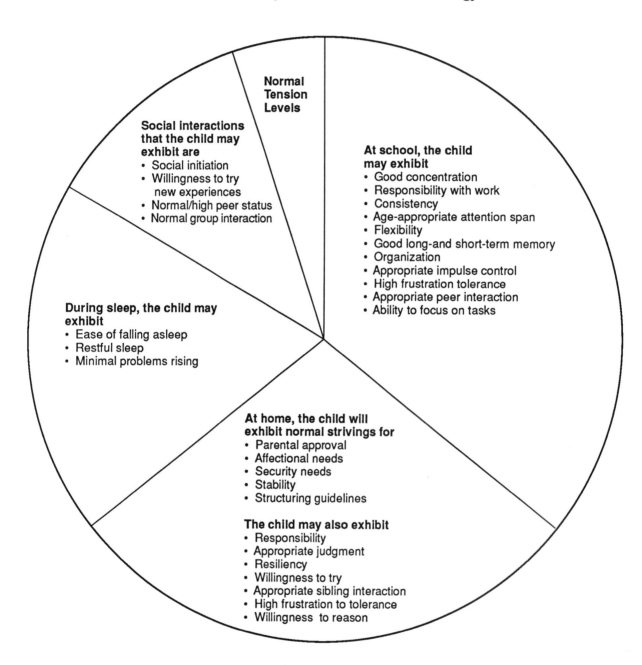

Normal Tension Levels

Social interactions that the child may exhibit are
- Social initiation
- Willingness to try new experiences
- Normal/high peer status
- Normal group interaction

At school, the child may exhibit
- Good concentration
- Responsibility with work
- Consistency
- Age-appropriate attention span
- Flexibility
- Good long-and short-term memory
- Organization
- Appropriate impulse control
- High frustration tolerance
- Appropriate peer interaction
- Ability to focus on tasks

During sleep, the child may exhibit
- Ease of falling asleep
- Restful sleep
- Minimal problems rising

At home, the child will exhibit normal strivings for
- Parental approval
- Affectional needs
- Security needs
- Stability
- Structuring guidelines

The child may also exhibit
- Responsibility
- Appropriate judgment
- Resiliency
- Willingness to try
- Appropriate sibling interaction
- High frustration to tolerance
- Willingness to reason

High Tension Level and Division of Energy

At home, the child may exhibit
- Oversensitivity
- Tantrums
- Forgetfulness
- Restlessness
- Daydreaming
- Unwillingness to venture out
- Verbal self-abuse
- Unwillingness to reason
- Denial

At school, the child may exhibit
- Inability to focus on task
- Disorganization
- Distractibility
- Impulsivity
- Poor memory
- Inflexibility
- Short attention span
- Irresponsibility
- Inconsistency
- Poor judgment
- Unwillingness to reason

High anxiety levels may result from
- Consistent school failure
- Peer rejection
- Learning disabilities
- Parental expectations
- Sibling performance
- Style of teacher versus style of student
- Separation/divorce
- Death in the family
- Health-related problems
- Constant parental tension (for example, loss of job)
- Change in environment

Social interactions that the child may exhibit are
- Social withdrawal
- Unwillingness to try new relationships
- Low peer status

During sleep, the child may exhibit
- Trouble falling asleep
- Restless sleep
- Resistance to rising
- Frequent nightmares

Part

The Special Education Process

Section 3

Screening and Referral Process

REFERRAL FORMS

Usually the first time a psychologist, special education teacher, or pupil personnel team becomes aware of a problem is when the classroom teacher fills out a referral form on a specific child.

Purpose and Types

The major purpose of such a form is to alert other school professionals that a student is exhibiting difficulties in the classroom that may require further attention. These referral forms usually appear in two forms: an *open-ended referral form* and **a** *structured referral form*. An open-ended referral form my look like the following:

SAMPLE A: OPEN-ENDED REFERRAL FORM

Name: Matthew Jones   *Date of Referral:* November xx, 19xx

Grade: 4

Teacher: Mrs. Brown

Why are you referring this child?

Matthew is experiencing severe academic difficulties in the classroom. He procrastinates, is easily distracted, refuses to hand in work, has a short attention span, and has difficulty with social skills. The other children tolerate him but are losing patience. I have contacted the mother and she has mentioned that these problems have been around for some time.

I have estimated his ability to be at least average and his academic performance is well below grade level in all areas. He further exhibits low frustration tolerance, an unwillingness to attempt new concepts, self-criticism, and intolerance for those around him.

I am very concerned about Matthew's deterioration this year and would like some advice on how to handle the situation.

Has parent been notified of this referral?   yes_____ no_____

Administrator's signature_____   Date_____

This type of referral form allows teachers to fill in what they consider the most important issues about this child. However, the information given to the team may not be the type of information necessary for an overall indication of severity, history, and nature of the symptoms presented.

A structured referral form, on the other hand, may look like the following:

SAMPLE B: STRUCTURED REFERRAL FORM

Name: *Date of Referral:*

Grade:

Teacher:

Please answer the following questions using behavioral terms:

What symptoms is the child exhibiting that are of concern at this time?

What have you tried that has worked?

What have you tried that does not seem to work toward alleviating these symptoms?

What are the child's present academic levels of functioning?

What is the child's social behavior like?

Have the parents been contacted? yes_____no_____ If no, why not?

Further comments:

As you can see from this type of form, the teacher is guided through a series of questions that define the specific areas determined as important by the pupil personnel team. Room is also given at the end for any further comments that the teacher feels are necessary to the understanding of the child.

Regardless of the type of form used, special education teachers should begin to look for signals in the symptoms being presented and should ask themselves the following questions at the time of the referral:

25

Questions to Consider Concerning the Referral

What are the comments from past teachers?

Never assume that the child is always the problem. Obtaining comments from past teachers may give a different picture and may also help pinpoint the changes that have led to the referral. A child who has had positive teacher feedback for the past four years and all of a sudden begins to deteriorate may have experienced something over the summer, may be affected by changes at home, or may be having a personality conflict with the teacher.

What is going on at home?

Many symptoms in school may be the result of tension or problems emanating from the home. If confused as school-related problems, the true issue will be overlooked and you will be treating symptoms, not problems. Home-related issues affect every child and some more than others. A brief conversation by the classroom teacher can possibly find out *situational disturbances* (brief, but intense, patterns of tension resulting from loss of a job, death of a relative, separation, and so on) that may be causing the child to have difficulty focusing or performing in school.

What are the achievement test scores and what patterns do they reflect?

Group achievement tests can be good indicators of certain types of patterns. While individual achievement tests should be used only when evaluating a disabled child, group tests may offer evidence of learning problems, emotional patterns, and the onset of other problems, especially if one year is so different from prior ones.

What does the developmental history look like?

A child's developmental history can be like a fingerprint in determining possible causes or influences that may be contributing to the present problem. A thorough intake that covers all areas of a child's history is a crucial factor in the proper diagnosis of a child's problems. A look at developmental milestones, traumatic experiences, hospitalizations, prior testing, and other areas offer us a closer look at the total child.

When was the last time both vision and hearing were checked?

These two factors should be ruled out immediately as having any influence on the presenting problem. If the child has not been evaluated in either area within at least one year, or symptoms indicate possible visual or auditory involvement, such as squinting, eye fatigue, or failure to hear directions, then a retest is indicated.

Regardless of the type of form used, the referral form should be considered a list of signals that need to be investigated. It is important that you communicate the difference between symptoms and problems to the teacher and indicate that the purpose of an evaluation, if required, is to pinpoint the specific types of problems that are manifested by the pattern of symptoms exhibited by the child.

SAMPLE A: TEACHER REFERRAL FORM

Student's Name: *Referring Teacher:*

Address:

Sex: *Age:*   *Date of Birth:*   *Date of Referral:*

Parents:

Grades Repeated:

Current Academic Performance Levels:

Math: Reading: Spelling:

Any observable behavioral or physical limitations:

Reasons for referral:

List specific academic and behavioral strengths:

List academic and behavioral weaknesses:

What have you tried to remedy the problem?

Has (have) parent(s) been notified of this referral? yes____ no____

What was the reaction?

SAMPLE B: TEACHER REFERRAL FORM

Student's Name: *Referring Teacher:*

Address:

Sex: *Age:*   *Date of Birth:*   *Date of Referral:*

Parents:

Why is this pupil being referred?

How have you attempted to deal with these problems?

Have you discussed this referral with the student? What was his or her reaction?

What is the child's perception of the situation?

Current performance estimates (below, on, or above grade level)

Reading_____ Math_____ Spelling_____

Describe the child's current social behavior with peers:

Any relevant history that may assist in the understanding of this child?

Has (have) the parent(s) been contacted about this referral? yes____ no____

What was the reaction?

RATING SCALES

There may be times when we need to refine the information received on a referral form into something more objective. This can be accomplished through the use of a personal interview with the teacher or a *rating scale*.

Purpose

Rating scales are useful tools for quantifying a behavior or characteristic. Having a teacher answer yes or no to "Is the child overly active" means very little. Having that same teacher rate the child's activity level across a five-point scale allows for a better measure of the problem. Classroom teachers have the best long-term observational opportunities and will provide an excellent view of a child's status if given the right tool. However, since the terms presented may be open to interpretation (for example, "impulsivity" may be defined by various people very differently) you may want to sit with the teacher first and discuss the behaviors to be observed. This will operationalize the scale and provide a more consistent interpretative tool. It may also be helpful to sit with the classroom teacher and fill out the scale together. This will allow you to ask pertinent questions as you go along the scale and may enhance the interpretative quality of the tool.

It should also be noted to the teacher that the purpose of the rating scale is to help identify the source of the problem and should not be used as an indication of inferior ability, potential, or unwillingness to learn. If the teacher fully understands the nature of symptoms, these misinterpretations can be avoided.

You may want to keep in mind that if the rating scale is too short, it will not provide an adequate overall picture of the child. And if it is too long, it may be seen as a burden by the teacher. The rating scale is an excellent tool in the case study procedure and can begin to narrow down the specific areas of concern. There are many types of rating scales that focus on different academic, behavioral, social, self-help, developmental, and perceptual areas.

Types

Further, a rating scale can be developed using almost any kind of rating criteria. Examples of three-point scales may include categories such as

- Always, Sometimes, Never
- Excellent, Satisfactory, Needs to Improve
- Often, Seldom, Never

However, a three-point scale is limited and may make quantifying observable data more difficult. Behavior is not always so specific and may require more subtle choices. Consequently the more useful rating scales may use a five-point set of categories such as

- ◆ Of Primary Concern, Of Some Concern, Of Little Concern
- ◆ Of No Concern, Does Not Apply to This Child
- ◆ Always, Most of the Time, Sometimes, Almost Never, Never

Examples

The following is an example of how a rating scale can be used to qualify a series of observations by the classroom teacher and shed some light on the severity of the symptoms.

SAMPLE A: STUDENT RATING SCALE

1-Always   2-Most of the Time   3-Sometimes   4-Seldom   5-Never

Academic Behavior

1. Has trouble comprehending what he/she reads   _____
2. Uses adequate word attack skills   _____
3. Loses his/her place while reading   _____
4. Slows down when reading aloud   _____
5. Exhibits good sight word vocabulary   _____
6. Shows adequate math computational skills   _____
7. Understands word problems   _____
8. Applies mathematical skills in solving problems   _____
9. Exhibits appropriate handwriting for age   _____
10. Exhibits adequate spelling skills for age   _____

Classroom Behavior

1. Exhibits impulsivity   _____
2. Exhibits distractibility   _____
3. Gets along with peers   _____
4. Follows rules of a game   _____
5. Willing to reason   _____
6. Conforms to boundaries and rules in the classroom   _____
7. Attends to task   _____
8. Completes homework   _____
9. Completes classwork in allotted time   _____
10. Listens carefully   _____
11. Becomes easily frustrated   _____
12. Cooperates with others   _____

Language Behavior

1. Exhibits adequate vocabulary   _____
2. Exhibits limited verbal fluency   _____
3. Exhibits faulty articulation   _____

SAMPLE B: PUPIL BEHAVIOR RATING SCALE

Please rate the following behaviors according to the following scale:

Rating

1. The behavior does not apply to this child and is never observed.
2. The behavior is rarely exhibited.
3. The behavior occurs some of the time.
4. The behavior occurs most of the time.
5. The behavior always occurs.

____Is anxious

____Is disruptive

____Fights frequently

____Is unhappy

____Is withdrawn

____Is moody

____Is distractible

____Is impulsive

____Does not complete work

____Has short attention span

____Daydreams

____Is argumentative

____Is disorganized

____Is easily confused

____Spells poorly

____Reads poorly

____Has limited reading comprehension

____Has faulty articulation

____Uses poor grammar

____Has problems judging time

____Has poor fine motor skills

____Is slow in completing tasks

____Exhibits poor logical reasoning and thinking

____Has poor number concepts

____Tires easily

____Defies authority

____Fears criticism

____Is critical of others

____Is controlling

____Is painfully shy

____Is a slow starter

____Is inconsistent

____Is hyperactive

____Is hypoactive

____Fears new situations

____Procrastinates

____Rarely takes chances

____Is overreactive

____Has problems with writing

____Has problems with math

____Uses vocabulary poorly

____Has poor expressive language-ability

____Has inadequate word attack skills

____Has poor balance and coordination

____Has poor gross motor skills

____Has tracing and drawing difficulties

____Has difficulty with abstract concepts

____Has problems with auditory memory tasks

OBSERVATION SCALES

Observing children in different settings is a necessary part of the screening and referral process. This part of the process offers another perception of the child. A child who has been referred should be observed in a variety of settings, including the classroom, playground, gym, and lunchroom.

Purpose

Basic behaviors need to be observed, for example, attention, focus, aggressiveness, compliance, flexibility, rigidity, oppositional behavior, shyness, controlling behavior, distractibility, impulsivity, social interaction, and so on.

Questions to Consider When Observing

Is there a difference between the nature of behaviors in a structured setting, for example, a classroom, and an unstructured setting, for example, a playground?

This factor may shed light on the child's need for a more structured environment in which to learn. Children who do not have well-developed internal control systems need a highly structured environment to maintain focus and appropriate behavior. Some children cannot shift between structured and unstructured and back again. They may not possess the internal monitor that regulates conformity and logical attendance to rules. These children may be more successful in a structured play setting set up by teachers during the lunch hour.

Does the child seem to respond to external boundaries?

This factor is important to the teacher since it is a monitor of potential learning style. If a child who lacks internal controls does conform to external boundaries, for example, time-out or teacher proximity during worktime, then this factor needs to be taken into consideration when prescribing classroom management techniques. When the child conforms to such boundaries, then his or her behavior is a message for what works for that child.

What is the child's attention span during academic tasks?

Attention span at different ages is measured normally in minutes or hours. You should become aware of the normal attention span for children of all ages and compare the child's behavior over several activities and days to see if a pattern of inattention is present. If the attention span is very short for someone of his or her age, then modifications to work load, for example, shorter but more frequent assignments, may have to be included.

Does the child require constant teacher supervision or assistance?

A child who requires constant teacher supervision or assistance is a child who may be exhibiting a wide variety of possible symptomatic behavior that may be resulting from but is not limited to attention deficit disorder, processing problems, emotional difficulties involving need for attention, need for control, high anxiety, internal stress, limited intellectual capacity, hearing problems, and so on. All these areas need to be investigated, and a good evaluation should determine the root of such behavior. However the key is always the frequency, intensity and duration of such symptoms.

Does the child interact appropriately with peers?

Observing children at play can tell us a great deal about self-esteem, tension levels, social maturity, physical development, and many other factors. Social interaction is more common in children over the age of six or seven while parallel play is still common in younger children. Appropriate social interaction gives us insight into the child's own internal boundaries and organization. A child who always needs to control may really be masking high levels of tension. The more controlling a child is, the more out of control that the child is feeling. A child who can conform appropriately to group rules, delay his or her needs for the good of the team, and conform to various changes or inconsistencies in rules is probably a child who is very self-assured and has low anxiety levels. The opposite is most always typical of children at risk. However, one should always consider developmental stages since certain behaviors, such as control, may be more typical at early ages.

Is the child a high- or low-status child?

Observing a child in different settings allows us the opportunity to see the social status of the child and the impact of that status on the child's behavior. Low-status children are often seen as those with learning disabilities, who are more apt to feel insignificant and therefore fail to receive positive social cues that help reinforce feelings of self-esteem. Having the psychologist begin a counseling group of five or six low-status children enables them to feel empowered with feelings of connection.

Examples

The *unstructured checklist* that allows the observer to fill in any information that he or she feels is important.

SAMPLE A: UNSTRUCTURED OBSERVATION CHECKLIST

Name of Student Observed: Observer:

Date of Observation:

Place of Observation:

Behaviors to Observe	Classroom	Playground	Lunchroom	Gym
1. Impulsivity				
2. Attention to task				
3. Attention span				
4. Conformity to rules				
5. Social interaction with peers				
6. Aggressiveness				
7. Level of teacher assistance required				
8. Frustration levels				
9. Reaction to authority				
10. Verbal interaction				
11. Procrastinates				
12. Organizational skills				
13. Developmental motor skills				

As seen by the foregoing example, any of a number of general areas can and should be observed. This is an informal working scale for your own information. However, keep in mind that it can also serve to fulfill the Committee on Special Education's requirement for a classroom observation that must be part of the packet when a review for classification is required. The spaces provided allow for comments and notes which may shed some light on the child's overall pattern and severity of symptoms.

The following is an example of a *structured form.*

SAMPLE B: CLASSROOM OBSERVATION REPORT FORM

Student's Name/ID #_____

Date of Birth_____ Dominant Language_____

Dates of Observation_____ Length of Observation_____

Observer_____

Position_____

Classroom Observed_____ Location_____

Teacher's Name_____

Subject Area Being Taught_____

Task—Individual

A. When assigned task, the student

1. Initiates task without need for teacher's verbal encouragement
2. Requests help to start task
3. Complains before getting started on a task
4. Demands help in order to start on a task
5. Actively refuses to do task despite teacher's encouragement
6. Passively retreats from task despite teacher's encouragement

B. While working on task, the student

7. Works independently
8. Performs assigned task without complaints
9. Needs teacher's verbal encouragement to keep working
10. Needs teacher in close proximity to keep working
11. Needs physical contact from teacher to keep working
12. Seeks constant reassurance to keep working
13. Is reluctant to have work inspected
14. Belittles own work

C. At the end of assigned time, the student

15. Completes task
16. Takes pride in completed task
17. Goes on to next task
18. Refuses to complete task

Social Interaction

The student

20. Establishes a relationship with one or two peers
21. Shares materials with peers

© 1994 by The Center for Applied Research in Education

22. Respects property of peers
23. Gives help to peers when needed
24. Accepts help from peers when needed
25. Establishes a relationship with most peers
26. Teases or ridicules peers
27. Expresses prejudiced attitudes toward peers
28. Physically provokes peers
29. Physically hurts peers
30. Seeks to be attacked by peers
31. Participates appropriately in group activities
32. Postpones own needs for group objectives
33. Withdraws from group
34. Overly assertive in group
35. Disrupts group activities (e.g., calling out, provocative language, etc.)
36. Exhibits aggressive behavior within group not amenable to teacher intervention

Relationship to Teacher

The student

37. Tries to meet teacher's expectations
38. Functions adequately without constant teacher encouragement
39. Interacts with teacher in nondemanding manner
40. Responds to teacher without haggling
41. Tests limits, tries to see how much teacher will allow
42. Seeks special treatment from teacher
43. Responds to teacher's criticism without fear
44. Responds to teacher's criticism without verbal anger
45. Responds to teacher's criticism without physical outburst (e.g., temper tantrums)
46. Defies teacher's requirement
47. Scorns or ridicules teacher's support
48. Responds with anger when demands are thwarted by teacher
49. Blames and accuses teacher ("not helping," "not liking me")
50. Abuses teacher verbally (no apparent cause)
51. Abuses teacher physically (no apparent cause)
52. Requires close and constant supervision because behavioral controls are so limited

Comments

PUPIL PERSONNEL TEAMS/CHILD STUDY TEAMS

Many schools are moving toward a more global approach to the identification of potential high-risk students. This concept, known variously as the pupil personnel team, child study team, school-based support team, and so on, is one way of accomplishing this task.

Purpose

The members of this team work as a single unit in determining the possible etiology, contributing factors, educational status, prognosis, and recommendations for a student. The concept of bringing together many disciplines to help work on a case is the major objective of the PPT. In this way you have many experts covering many fields and disciplines rather than a single individual trying to determine all of the factors.

Membership of the Pupil Personnel Team

This team is usually made up of the following individuals:

- ◆ Administrator
- ◆ Psychologist
- ◆ Nurse
- ◆ Classroom Teacher
- ◆ Social Worker
- ◆ Special Education Teacher
- ◆ Guidance Counselor
- ◆ Reading Teacher
- ◆ Speech and Language Teacher

The members of this team usually meet on a regular basis, once or twice a week depending upon the case load. This is a local school–based support team and should not be confused with the Committee on Special Education, which is a district-based team with a parent member. The pupil personnel team does not have a parent member and is not required to do so as is the CSE.

Questions to Consider When the PPT Receives a Referral

When a PPT first receives a referral from a teacher, it must consider many issues. These may include the following:

Has this child ever been referred to the PPT?

Prior referral may indicate an *historical disturbance* or long-term problem and therefore a more serious situation, especially if the same pattern exists. *Situational disturbances* with no prior problems usually have a better prognosis.

Do we have any prior psychological, educational, language, or any other appropriate evaluations?

This information is very important so that child is not put through unnecessary testing. These reports also offer the team another perspective on the problem.

Is anyone familiar with other family members?

Family patterns of behavior may help define contributing factors to the child's problem. It may also offer the team some experience on the best approach to take with this family.

Are there any medical issues we need to be aware of at this time that might impact on this case?

These issues are crucial, and the existence of medical problems should always be determined first. Difficulties with hearing, eyesight, taking medication, severe allergies, and so on may be significant contributors to poor performance and may be masked as "unmotivated," "lazy," or "stubborn."

What do the child's report cards look like? What patterns are exhibited?

Some children have trouble starting off in a new situation and play catch-up the entire year. Others do well the first marking period and slowly decline to a pattern of poor grades. Others exhibit the roller-coaster effect with children consistently receiving grades from failing to passing. Knowing the child's report card "style" may help with the type of support, remediation, and program offered.

What are the child's group achievement test scores?

Achievement test scores can offer much useful information about a child's patterns. If the team suspects a learning disability, then the areas affected should be consistently low from year to year. Many fluctuations of scores and wide ranges of results may indicate more emotional involvement than a learning disability. A child who is not functioning in the classroom but consistently receives achievement scores within the ninetieth percentile may not be functioning because of reasons other than learning disabilities.

If no prior testing is available, is there any group IQ test information available to give us some general idea of ability?

While group IQ tests should never be used to determine a high-risk child's true intellectual potential, they may offer a general idea of ability. Unfortunately, however, children with learning and emotional problems may lack the energy or motivation to take such tests adequately; since it is being given to the group, these children's behavior toward the test can be easily hidden or not observed.

Has anyone observed this child?

This piece of information is required if the team plans to refer the child to the CSE. In any case observation should always be a piece of the contributing information presented to the PPT. One member, usually the psychologist, social worker, guidance counselor, or special education teacher, should observe the child in a variety of situations prior to the first PPT meeting. It is very important for the team to know how this child functions in structured and unstructured settings. (More specific information on observation is presented in the next section.)

Do we have samples of the child's classwork?

Samples of classwork over a period of time offer a clearer overview of the child's abilities and attitude toward classwork. This also gives several team members an opportunity to observe possible academic symptoms that may first appear in written work.

Has the parent been notified of the teacher's concerns?

The team should not be the one to notify the parent that a problem may exist. It is the responsibility of the classroom teacher to alert the parents that he or she is concerned and would like a closer look by the PPT. A parent does not have a legal right to refuse such a request since it is considered a normal school procedure. The parent should also be notified by the teacher that someone from the team will be in touch with them to gather more information and to review any findings.

At this point a parent intake may be required to gather more information that may enhance the diagnosis of the problem or problems. This procedure is discussed at length in the next chapter.

Options of the Pupil Personnel Team

In the meantime, the PPT may be discussing the next logical step at a series of meetings that may take up to several weeks depending on delays, conflicts, procedures, organizational ability of the team, and so on. Once the PPT has all the necessary information gathered on the child, including

- Evaluations
- Observations
- Rating scales
- Parent intake
- Work samples
- Academic records

- Group achievement scores
- Medical records
- Past teacher reports and the like

it can determine a direction. There are several directions and recommendations that can be instituted during this process by the PPT, including the following.

PSYCHOEDUCATIONAL EVALUATION Utilize this recommendation when a child's academic skill levels (reading, math, writing, and spelling) are unknown or inconsistent, his or her learning process shows gaps (e.g., memory, expression), or a referral is made to the CSE. This is done to rule out or rule in a discrepancy between intellectual potential and academic achievement required for the classification of language development or to determine strengths and weaknesses in academic and processing levels. Some symptoms that might suggest this recommendation are

- Consistently low test scores on group achievement tests
- Indications of delayed processing when faced with academic skills
- Labored handwriting after grade 3
- Poor word recall
- Poor decoding (word attack) skills
- Discrepancy between achievement and ability
- Consistently low achievement despite remediation

LANGUAGE EVALUATION This recommendation usually occurs when the child is experiencing significant delays in speech or language development, problems in articulation, or problems in receptive or expressive language. Some symptoms that might warrant such an evaluation are

- Difficulty pronouncing words through grade 3
- Immature or delayed speech patterns
- Difficulty labeling thoughts or objects
- Difficulty putting thoughts into words

PSYCHOLOGICAL EVALUATION Use this recommendation when the child's intellectual ability is unknown or there is a questionable factor in his or her inability to learn. Also use this recommendation when referring to the CSE for a potential learning, emotional, or intellectual problems. The psychological evaluation can rule out or rule in emotionality as a primary cause of a child' s problem. Ruling this factor out is required before the diagnosis of language development can be determined. Some symptoms that might signal the need for such an evaluation are

- High levels of tension and anxiety exhibited in behavior
- Aggressive behavior

◆ Lack of motivation or indications of low energy levels

◆ Patterns of denial

◆ Oppositional behavior

◆ Despondency

◆ Inconsistent academic performance ranging from very low to very high

◆ History of inappropriate judgment

◆ Lack of impulse control

◆ Extreme and consistent attention-seeking behavior

◆ Pattern of provocative behavior

REFERRAL TO CSE FOR A MEETING TO DISCUSS THE RECOMMENDATION FOR EVALUATION DENIED BY PARENT(S) If a parent refuses to sign a release for testing and the teachers feel strongly that such a procedure is in the best interests of the child, then a review by the CSE is possible to resolve this dispute. If available, both parents should be urged to attend a meeting prior to this referral so that some agreement or compromise can be worked out. While it may be difficult for both parents to attend due to work schedules, family responsibilities, or unwillingness to face the problem, the school should make every attempt to have at least one parent present. Whatever the recommendation instituted by the pupil personnel team, it should be done with all the most recent available information on a child. Such recommendations may have tremendous implications and should never be taken lightly.

DEALING WITH PARENT INTAKES AND INTERVIEWS

The next step in the process involves a complete social history which can be regarded as a description of the family life situation. In some cases this part of the process may not be possible to obtain because of a number of variables such as parent's work restrictions, inability to obtain coverage for younger siblings, resistance, or apathy.

While the intake in many schools is done by the social worker or psychologist, it is important that you understand the process in case you are called upon to do the intake. There are several things to consider before the meeting.

Things to Consider

1. Always make the parent(s) feel comfortable and at ease by establishing a *receptive environment*. If possible, hold the meeting in a pleasant setting, using a round table or any table instead of a desk, and offer some type of refreshment to ease possible tension of the situation.

2. Never view the parent(s) as an adversary even if they are angry or hostile. Keep in mind that the anger or hostility is a defense because they may not be aware of what you will be asking or they have encountered a series of negative school meetings over the years. Since this may be an opportunity for parents to "vent," or express, their concerns, do not get defensive, and be understanding without taking sides.

3. Inform them every step of the way about the *purpose of the meeting and the steps involved in the referral process.* Reassure them that no recommendation will be made without their input and permission.

4. Inform them to the purpose of testing and what you hope to gain from the process. Be *solution oriented* and offer realistic hope even if past experiences have resulted in frustration. Remind the parent that children can be more motivated, resilient, and successful at different stages.

5. Make sure the parents know that if the testing reveals a significant discrepancy between ability and achievement, then the case needs to be reviewed by the CSE. This is an important piece of information to convey to the parents since it involves their rights to due process.

6. Go over the *release form* and explain each test and its purpose. The more information parents have, the less fearful they will be. Explain that their signature requires that the testing be completed 30 days from the date signed and will not take months before they are made aware of the findings.

7. You may want to offer them a pad and pen so that they can write down information, terms, or notes on the meeting. Further indicate that they should feel free to call you with any questions or concerns they may have.

8. Reassure the parents about the *confidentiality* of the information gathered. Indicate the individuals on the team who will be seeing the information and the purpose for their review of the facts.

Parent Consent for Evaluation

Therefore, the purpose of a parent intake may be twofold: to gather information and to secure a release for testing. A release form may look like the following:

Examples of Parent Intake Forms

PARENT CONSENT FOR EVALUATION

To the Parent/Guardian of:_____

Birthdate:_____

School:_____

Grade:_____

We would like to inform you that your child _____
is being referred for individual testing which will help us in his/her educational planning.
Referral was made for the following reasons:

_____

_____

_____

Testing results will help us in determining your child's educational needs and in planning
the most appropriate program. The evaluation procedures and/or tests may include the following:

Intelligence:_____

Communication/Language/Speech:_____

Physical:_____

Behavior/Emotional:_____

Academic:_____

Vocational:_____

Other:_____

It is necessary that the School District CSE have your written permission to evaluate your
child. You have had the opportunity to discuss the need for this testing and the possibilities for special educational services with the school principal/designee. The evaluation(s)
will be conducted by the multidisciplinary team who will share the results of said evaluation with you at a building level meeting. Both this meeting and a CSE meeting will be held
within 30 school days of receipt of this notice.

I grant permission for the evaluation(s) mentioned above

_____

I do not grant permission for the evaluation(s) mentioned above

_____

Date_____

Parent's
Signature_____Date_____

Administrator/Designee_____

© 1994 by The Center for Applied Research in Education

A parent intake form should contain necessary but not intrusive questions. The questions should be specific enough to help in the diagnosis of the problem, but not so specific as to place the parent in a vulnerable and defensive position. An example of an intake form is as follows:

IDENTIFYING DATA

Name of Client: Matthew Jones

Address: 12 Court Street

Phone: 675-7863

Date of Birth: 03/04/82

Age: 9

Siblings: Brothers—names and ages: Brian 15

Sisters—names and ages: Karen 4

Mother's Name: Jill   Father's name: Ben

Mother's Occupation: Medical Technician

Father's Occupation: Accountant

Referred by: Teacher

Grade: 4

School: Holland Avenue

DEVELOPMENTAL HISTORY

Length of Pregnancy: Full term—22-hour labor.

Type of Delivery: Forceps.

Complications: Apgar score 7, Jaundice at birth.

Lengthy Hospital Stays: None.

Falls or Injuries: None.

Allergies: Early food allergies, none recently.

Medication: None at present.

Early Milestones (e.g., walking, talking, toilet training).

According to parent, Matthew was late in walking and talking in comparison to brother. He was toilet trained at age three. Parent added that he seemed to be slower than usually in learning things.

Traumatic Experiences: None.

Previous Psychological Evaluations or Treatment (Please explain reasons and dates): None. However, parent indicated that it was suggested by first grade teacher, but the teacher never followed through.

Any Previous Psychiatric Hospitalizations? No.

Sleep Disturbances: Trouble falling asleep, somnambulism at age five but only lasted a few weeks. Talks a great deal in his sleep lately.

Eating Disturbances: Picky eater, likes sweets.

Last Vision and Hearing Exams and Results: Last eye test in school indicated 20/30. Last hearing test in school was inconclusive. Parent has not followed through on nurse's request for an outside evaluation.

Excessively High Fevers: No.

Childhood Illnesses: Normal ones.

ACADEMIC HISTORY

Nursery School Experience: Matthew had difficulty adjusting to nursery school. The teacher considered him very immature and his skills were well below those of his peers. He struggled through the year.

Kindergarten Experience (adjustment, comments, etc.): Matthew's difficulties increased. According to the parent he had problems with reading and social difficulties. His gross and fine motor skills were immature.

First Grade Through Sixth Grade (teacher's comments, traumatic experiences, strength areas, comments, etc):

According to past teachers Matthew struggled through the years. He was a nice boy and polite and at times tried hard. But in the later grades 2 and 3 his behavior and academics began to falter. Teachers always considered referral but felt he might grow out of it.

Subjects That Presented the Most Difficulty: Reading, math, spelling.

Subjects That Were the Least Difficult: Science.

Most Recent Report Card Grades (if applicable):

Matthew has received mostly NEEDS TO IMPROVE on his report card.

SOCIAL HISTORY

Groups or Organizations: Tried Boy Scouts but dropped out. Started Little League but became frustrated.

Social Involvement as Perceived by Parent: Inconsistent. He does not seem to reach out to kids and lately he spends a great deal of time alone.

Hobbies or Interests: Baseball cards, science.

Once the intake is over again reassure the parent about the confidentiality of the material and the purpose.

EXAMINING SCHOOL RECORDS

The school usually has a wealth of information about all children, distributed among a number of people and a number of records. Gathering this information after a referral and prior to evaluation may reduce the need for testing and will provide a very thorough picture of the child and his or her abilities and patterns. Investigating the following areas will contribute to the overall "picture" of the child.

Prior Teacher Reports

Comments written on report cards or in permanent record folders may provide a different view of the child under a different style of teaching. Successful years with positive comments may be a clue to the child's learning style and may provide you with information about the conditions under which the child responds best.

Reports of Prior Parent-Teacher Interviews

Prior conferences between previous teachers and parents may provide you with information that may be important in understanding the child's patterns and history.

Cumulative School Record

This particular file may contain information from standardized achievement test results, group IQ results, teacher comments dating back to kindergarten, records from previous schools, individual reading test results, and family information.

Group IQ Test Information

This information is usually found in the permanent record folder. Many schools administer a test such as Otis Lennon, Henmon Nelson in grades 3, 6, and 9, so look carefully. Within the past year or so the term school abilities index has replaced the term "IQ" or intelligence quotient.

Standardized Test Scores

These scores should be analyzed for patterns of strengths and deficiencies. The older the child, the greater the number of scores that can be compared.

Report Card Grades

These materials can be reviewed for comments and patterns of productive and difficult years.

Attendance Records

These records should be reviewed for patterns of lateness or absence. If such patterns exist, the reasons should be investigated to rule out medical causes (hospital stays, illnesses), psychological causes (dysfunctional family patterns, school phobia, etc.), or social causes (peer rejection or isolation).

Number of Schools Attended

There are times when a child will be enrolled in several schools in several years. The reasons for the many moves should be investigated and may add to the child's adjustment difficulties.

Prior Teacher Referrals

Investigate school records for prior referrals from teachers. There are times when a teacher will refer but no action may have been taken due to time of year, parent resistance, delay in evaluation procedures, and so on. These referrals may still be on file and may reveal information that can be useful.

Medical History in the School Nurse's Office

Investigate these records for indications of visual or hearing difficulties, prescribed medication that may have an affect on the child's behavior (e.g., antihistamines), or medical conditions in need of attention or that can be contributing to the child's present situation.

Whatever the situation, the special education teacher should review the vast amount of available records in the school building.

UNDERSTANDING THE CHILD'S BEHAVIOR DURING TESTING

The evaluation of a student involves many areas of input and observation. A critical period of observation takes place at the time of testing when the special education teacher has a firsthand opportunity to view the child under these types of conditions. It should be noted that the way a child approaches different types of evaluations may be very similar to the style he or she uses in the classroom. There are many behaviors that should be observed when administering tests. Recording these observations will greatly facilitate report writing. Some suggestions of behaviors to be observed follow.

Adjustment to the Testing Situation

 ◆ What was the child's initial reaction?
 ◆ How did the child react to the examiner?
 ◆ Were there any initial signs of overt tension?

How children adjust to the testing situation can vary greatly. Several factors need to be considered when the child first encounters the testing situation. These include

1. Children's *initial adjustment* to the testing situation can vary greatly. The key to any adjustment period is not necessarily the initial reactions but the duration of the period of maladjustment. Children are usually initially nervous and uptight but relax as time goes on with the reassurance of the examiner. However, children who maintain a high level of discomfort throughout the sessions may be harboring more serious problems that need to be explored.

2. *Examiner variables* (conditions that may affect test outcome that are directly related to the examiner, for example, examiner style, gender, tension, expectations) may need to be considered, especially if test results vary greatly from examiner to examiner.

3. Overt *signs of tension* (observable behaviors indicative of underlying tension) may affect the outcome of test results. Some overt signs of behavior often manifested by children include constant leg motion, little or no eye contact with the examiner, consistent finger or pencil tapping, and *oppositional behaviors* (behaviors that test the limits and guidelines of the examiner), such as singing or making noises while being tested, keeping jacket on or a hat almost covering his or her face, and so on. If this type of tension is extreme, you may want to explore the possibility that the results may be minimal indications of ability.

Reaction Time

 ◆ Were responses delayed, blocked, irregular?
 ◆ Was there any indication of negativism?
 ◆ Were responses impulsive or well thought out?

The speed in which a child answers questions on a test can indicate several things:

1. The child who impulsively answers incorrectly without thinking may be a child with high levels of anxiety which interfere with his or her ability to delay and concentrate.

2. The child who is negative or self-defeating, for example, "I'm so stupid, I'll never get any of these right," may be exhibiting a very low level of self-confidence or hiding a learning problem.

3. The child who blocks or delays may be a child who is afraid of reaction or criticism and is using these techniques to ward off what he or she perceives as an ego-deflating situation.

Nature of Responses

- Are some nonsensical, immature, childlike?
- Are they inconsistent?
- Does child ask to have responses repeated?
- Is the child critical of his or her responses?

The types of response a child gives during an evaluation may indicate the following:

1. A child who continuously asks to have questions repeated may have hearing difficulties. This deficit should always be ruled out first along with visual acuity prior to a testing situation.

2. The child who asks to have questions repeated may be having problems processing information and may need more time to understand what is being asked.

Verbalizations

- Is the child verbose?
- Is he or she spontaneous in responding?
- Does he or she have peculiarities of speech?

The verbal interaction with the examiner during an evaluation can be very telling. This factor may indicate the following:

1. Some children with high levels of anxiety may tend to vent this through constant verbalizations. This may be a factor when these verbalizations begin to interfere and the child has to be constantly reminded to focus on the task at hand.

2. Verbal hesitations may be due to immature speech patterns, expressive language problems, poor self-esteem, or lack of understanding of the question due to limited intellectual capacity.

Organizational Approach Used During Testing

- ◆ Does the child plan and work systematically?
- ◆ Does the child make false starts?
- ◆ Does the child make use of trial-and-error methods?

The manner in which a child handles individual tasks and organizes his or her approach may indicate the following:

1. A child who sizes up a situation and systematically approaches a task using trial and error may be a child with excellent internal organization, the ability to delay, and low levels of tension and anxiety. However, some children with emotional problems may also perform well on short-term tasks because they see it as a challenge and can organize themselves to perform over a relatively short period of time. Their particular problems in organization and consistency may come when they are asked to perform this way over an extended period.

2. Children with chaotic internal organization may appear as if they know what they are doing but the overall outcome of a task indicates a great deal of energy input with very low production. It's almost like "spinning wheels" and the energy output is a cover for not knowing what to do.

3. Some children may become less organized under the stress of a time constraint. The factor of style under time restrictions is one aspect in determining the child's overall learning style.

4. Children with attention deficit hyperactive disorder may also exhibit a confused sense of organization. However, there are other factors as well as attentional ones that go into the diagnosis of this disorder.

Adaptability During Testing

- ◆ Does the child shift from one test to the next?
- ◆ Is the child's interest sustained in all types of test items?

The ability of a child or adult, for that matter, to adapt or shift from one task to another without difficulty is a very important factor in determining learning style and may be one predictor for successful outcome of a task. Other factors include

1. Adaptability in life is one crucial aspect to adjustment. The ability to shift without expending a great deal of energy offers the person more available resources for the next task. A child who is rigid or does not adapt well is using up much of his or her available energy, thus reducing the chances of success on the subsequent task.

2. Sustaining interest may also be a direct result of available energy. A child who loses interest quickly may be immature, overwhelmed, or preoccupied. Some of these reactions may be normal for the early ages. However, as the child gets older such reactions may be symptomatic of other factors such as learning problems, emotional issues, and limited intellectual capacity.

Effort During Testing

- Is the child cooperative?
- Does the child give evidence of trying hard?
- Does the child become frustrated easily?

The effort that a child puts into a testing situation may be reflective of the effort exhibited within the classroom and may indicate the following:

1. A child who is oppositional or uncooperative may be a child who needs to control. Always keep in mind that the more controlling a child is, the more out of control the child feels. Control on the part of a child is aimed at securing predictability so that he or she can deal with a situation even though energy levels may be lowered by conflict and tension. If they can control a situation or person, they know what to expect. Due to their tension levels, they do not adapt well and are easily thrown by new situations or people.
2. A child who tries hard to succeed may do so for several reasons. He or she may enjoy success and find the tasks normally challenging. This type of child is normally not thrown by a mistake and can easily move to the next task without difficulty.

In conclusion, always keep in mind that *all behavior is a message*, and the way a child interacts with the examiner may be clues to learning style or problem areas. If you can "hear" a child's behavior by being aware of significant signs, you may come to a better understanding of the child's needs.

REPORTING TEST RESULTS TO PARENTS AND TEACHERS

An important skill for special education teachers is their ability to report test results to other professionals or parents in such a way that these people walk away with an understanding of the causes, specific areas of student strengths and weaknesses, and practical recommendations to alleviate the situation. Many times parents will leave a conference having been "bombarded" with jargon and statistics and understand nothing.

Things to Consider

Reporting results so that they are understood may be accomplished in the following ways:

1. When setting up the appointment with a parent never begin to explain the results over the phone, even if the parent requests a "quick" idea of how the child performed. If the parent does request this "summary," gently say that the type of information that you have is better explained and understood in person. If you sense further anxiety, try to reassure the parent that you will meet as soon as possible. It is important to see the parent(s) visually so that you can further explain areas in which they seem confused or uncomfortable. The face-to-face contact also makes the conference a more human approach. Hearing results from our doctor over the phone may not be as comforting as in person.

2. Again as with an intake, make the parent(s) feel comfortable and at ease by setting up a receptive environment. If possible, hold the meeting in a pleasant setting, use a round table—or any table—instead of a desk, and offer some type of refreshment to ease possible tension of the situation.

3. It may be helpful to refresh the parent's memory about the reasons for the evaluation and the symptoms that brought the child to the attention of the team. Explain the tests that comprised your test battery, why they were used, and what specific types of information you hoped to arrive at by using these measures.

4. Go over strength areas first, no matter how few there may be. You can also report positive classroom comments, and any other information that may help set the tone for acceptance of problem areas.

5. Provide a typed outline of the tests and scores for the parent to take with them if the report is not ready. If possible, have the report typed and ready to hand them. It looks more professional and may help alleviate problems that may occur when reports are sent home and the parents read it without a professional present.

6. Explain in simple terms any statistical terms you may be using, for example, percentiles, stanines, mental ages, and the like. In fact, you may want to define these terms on the same sheet with the scores so that parents have a key when they go back and review the scores.

7. Again, as with the intake, offer the parents a pad and pen so that they can write down information, terms, or notes on the meeting. Indicate that they should feel free to call you with any questions or concerns they may have.

8. Put aside a sufficient amount of time for difficult conferences. You do not want to run out of time. The parents should leave in a natural, not rushed, manner.

9. Take time to explain the differences between symptoms and problems. This explanation can go a long way in alleviating parent's frustration.

10. It is helpful for parents to hear how the problems or deficiencies you found were contributing to the symptoms in the classroom and at home. It is reassuring for parents to know that what they were seeing were only symptoms, even though they may have been quite intense, and that the problems have been identified and recommendations are available. Offer them as much realistic hope as possible.

11. Be as practical and specific as possible when offering suggestions on how parents can help at home. Offer them printed sheets with step-by-step procedures for any recommendation that you make. Parents should not be teachers and should never be given general recommendations that require their interpretation. This may aggravate an already tense situation at home. Offer them supportive materials that they can use with the child. For many parents, working with their child can be positive, but in some cases, for example, low parental frustration levels, you may want to shy away from this type of interaction.

12. If the case is going to be reviewed by the Committee on Special Education, take some time to alleviate the parents' fears by explaining the process and what they can expect. Indicate that your report is part of the packet that will be presented and that they are entitled to a copy of all materials. Some school districts charge for copies, so indicate that fact if it is a policy.

13. Again reassure the parent about the confidentiality of the information gathered. Indicate the individuals on the team who will be seeing the information and the purpose for their review of the facts. Also indicate that to send out this information, you would always need permission from them in the form of a signed release.

Part

Evaluation Measures, Interpretation, and Analysis

Section 4

How to Analyze a Student's Intellectual Profile

INTELLECTUAL EVALUATIONS—INTRODUCTION

The special education teacher's evaluation of a child should cover several areas, including intellectual levels, academic, processing, and language skills, background history, academic history, present levels of classroom functioning, and behavioral manifestations. All these factors play an important role in diagnosing the real problems and determining the child's best learning style.

The first area to explore may be the child's intellectual ability and potential. While this test is usually completed by a psychologist, it is very important that the special education teacher become familiar with how to determine

- ◆ Indications of greater potential
- ◆ Different diagnostic patterns exhibited on this test
- ◆ Learning disabilities
- ◆ Academic strengths and weaknesses
- ◆ Modality (channel) strengths and weaknesses
- ◆ Processing strengths and weaknesses

The psychologist has several tests from which to choose in the measurement of intelligence. The *Wechsler Scales* are three separate tests that measure a variety of intellectual areas and compute a Verbal, Performance, and Full-Scale IQ for children and adults ages 4 1/2 and up. The verbal areas are considered auditory-vocal tasks (auditory input–vocal output) while the performance areas are visual-vocal and visual-motor tasks (visual input and vocal or motoric output). The three tests are

- ◆ Wechsler Preschool and Primary Scale of Intelligence
- ◆ Wechsler Intelligence Scale for Children—III

◆ Wechsler Adult Intelligence Scale—Revised

Another intellectual measure utilized by psychologists is the *Stanford-Binet Intelligence Scale*. This test is an individual intelligence test and is a measure of global or general intelligence that results in a mental age and IQ. This test is generally used with younger children and with more intellectually limited youngsters.

Other measures are sometimes used, but chances are that the preceding measures are the most common ones that you will encounter. Once this information is obtained, the psychologist can determine several things and report back to parents and teachers the following information:

1. The child's present overall levels of intellectual ability
2. The child's present verbal intellectual ability
3. The child's nonlanguage intellectual ability
4. Indications of greater potential
5. Possible patterns involving learning style, for example, verbal comprehension and concentration
6. Possible influence of tension and anxiety on testing results
7. Intellectual ability to deal with present grade level academic demands
8. The influence of intellectual ability as a contributing factor to a child's past and present school difficulties, for example, limited intellectual ability found in retardation

THE WECHSLER SCALES OF INTELLIGENCE

There is a great deal of important information on the intelligence test that is usually overlooked by special education teachers. Many times the only information communicated is the IQ score. This score is perhaps the least important factor from the results and may not be very accurate depending upon the scatter (variability of the results) of the subtest scores.

The most widely used individual intelligence tests in education are the earlier-mentioned: *Wechsler Preschool and Primary Scale of Intelligence (WPPSI)*, ages 1/2–6 1/2; the *Wechsler Intelligence Scale for Children—III (WISC—III)*, ages 6 1/2–16 1/2; and the *Wechsler Adult Intelligence Scale—Revised (WAIS—R)*, ages 16 1/2 and over. All three scales result in three IQ measures: Verbal IQ, Performance IQ, and Full-Scale IQ. The resulting IQ scores fall into several classification ranges:

Intelligence Classifications and IQ Ranges

IQ Range	Classification	Percent Included
130 and over	Very Superior	2.2
120–129	Superior	6.7
110–119	High Average	16.1
90–109	Average	50.0
80–89	Low Average	16.1
70–79	Borderline	6.7
69 and below	Intellectually Deficient	2.2

Each test has twelve subtests, six verbal and six performance. The WPPSI consists of eleven subtests, the WISC—III has thirteen, and the WAIS—R has eleven. A description of all the subtests found on the three scales follows.

Verbal and Performance Subtests

VERBAL SUBTESTS

Information. Measures general information acquired from experience and education, remote verbal memory, understanding, and associative thinking. The socioeconomic-cultural background and reading ability of the student may influence the subtest score. (This subtest is part of the WPPSI, WISC—III, and WAIS—R.)

Similarities. Measures abstract and concrete reasoning, logical thought processes, associative thinking, and remote memory. (This subtest is part of the WPPSI, WISC—III, and WAIS—R.)

Arithmetic. Measures mental alertness, concentration, attention, arithmetic reasoning, reaction to time pressure, and practical knowledge of computational facts. This is the only subtest directly related to the school curriculum. Scores are greatly affected by anxiety. (This subtest is part of the WPPSI, WISC—III, and WAIS—R.)

Vocabulary. Measures a child's understanding of spoken words, learning ability, general range of ideas, verbal information acquired from experience and education, and kind and quality of expressive language. This subtest is relatively unaffected by emotional disturbance, but it is highly susceptible to cultural background and level of education. It is also the best single measure of intelligence in the entire battery. (This subtest is part of the WPPSI, WISC—III, and WAIS—R.)

Comprehension. Measures social judgment, common-sense reasoning based on past experience, and practical intelligence. (This subtest is part of the WPPSI, WISC—III, and WAIS—R.)

Digit Span. Measures attention, concentration, immediate auditory memory, auditory attention, and behavior in a learning situation. This subtest correlates poorly with general intelligence. (This subtest is part of the WPPSI, WISC—III, and WAIS—R.)

Sentences. Measures attention, concentration, immediate auditory memory, auditory attention, and behavior in a learning situation. (This subtest is part of the WPPSI.)

PERFORMANCE SUBTESTS

Picture Completion. Measures visual alertness to surroundings, remote visual memory, attention to detail, and ability to isolate essential from nonessential detail. (This subtest is part of the WPPSI, WISC—III, and WAIS—R.)
Picture Arrangement. Measures visual perception, logical sequencing of events, attention to detail, and ability to see cause-effect relationships. (This subtest is part of the WISC—III, and WAIS—R.)
Block Design. Measures ability to perceive, analyze, synthesize and reproduce abstract forms, visual-motor coordination, spatial relationships, and general ability to plan and organize. (This subtest is part of the WPPSI, WISC—III, and WAIS—R.)
Object Assembly. Measures immediate perception of a total configuration, part-whole relationships, and visual-motor spatial coordination. (This subtest is part of the WISC—III and WAIS—R.)
Coding. Measures ability to associate meaning with symbol, visual-motor dexterity (pencil manipulation), flexibility, and speed in learning tasks. (This subtest is part of the WISC—III.)
Digit Symbol. Measures ability to associate meaning with symbol, visual-motor dexterity (pencil manipulation), flexibility, and speed in learning tasks. (This subtest is part of the WAIS—R.)
Symbol Search. Measures visual discrimination. (This subtest is part of the WISC—III.)
Mazes. Measures ability to formulate and execute a visual-motor plan, pencil control and visual-motor coordination, speed and accuracy, and planning capability. (This subtest is part of the WPPSI and WISC—III.)
Animal House. Measures ability to associate meaning with symbol, visual-motor dexterity, flexibility, and speed in learning tasks. (This subtest is part of the WPPSI.)
Geometric Design. Measures a child's pencil control and visual-motor coordination, speed and accuracy, and planning capability. This subtest is part of the WPPSI.)

Indications of Greater Potential

Let's take a look at some of the factors that need to be analyzed and see the types of information that can be uncovered with some investigation.

Once a child has finished taking an IQ test and received a score, it is crucial to determine whether or not that score is truly reflective of his or her potential ability or is an underestimate of that ability. If expectations, educational plans, placement, and so on are going to be determined on this child, then the child's true intellectual potential must be considered as a very important factor. At this point the special education teacher may want to secure a copy of the **protocol** (the booklet or sheet on which the answers to a test are written) from the psychologist. Having this information at hand may facilitate calculations and diagnosis. There should be no problem with this request since you are allowed to see this information as part of the diagnostic team and as long as the psychologist is reassured of the purpose (to get a better understanding of learning style, approach to tasks, modality strengths and weaknesses, etc.) and that the copy will be returned to his or her files as soon as you are finished. However, if there is some resistance, you may have to accomplish this in his or her office. Either way, don't hesitate to complete this area of diagnosis since it is a crucial piece of the overall puzzle.

Once you have the protocol in front of you, you will notice many things about the test. The cover of the protocol contains a great deal of useful information. The first thing we want to look at is the pattern of scaled scores (scores converted from raw scores for purposes of interpretation and a common standard) that appear next to the raw score (the number of correct responses on a given test) on the front of the protocol. The scale scores can range from a low of 1 to a high of 19, with 10 considered the midpoint. However, several scaled scores may constitute a specific range (e.g., scaled scores of 8, 9, 10, and 11 are considered average) as can be seen by the accompanying chart:

Relationship of IQ Scores to Percentiles

IQ	Range	Scaled Score	Percentile
145	Very Superior	19	99.9
140	Very Superior	18	99.6
135	Very Superior	17	99
130	Very Superior	16	98
125	Superior	15	95
120	Superior	14	91
115	Above Average	13	84
110	Above Average	12	75
105	Average	11	63
100	Average	10	50
95	Average	9	37
90	Average	8	25
85	Low Average	7	16
80	Low Average	6	9
75	Borderline	5	5
70	Borderline	4	2
65	Mentally Deficient	3	1
60	Mentally Deficient	2	0.4
55	Mentally Deficient	1	0.1

To get a better idea of the value of a scaled score simply multiply it by 10, and that will give you a "rough" idea of the correlated IQ value.

It is from these scaled scores that our investigation of greater potential begins. The IQ results from the Wechsler Scales may not always indicate an individual's true intellectual potential. To determine if the resulting scores are valid indicators of an individual's true ability, refer to the following scatter guidelines.

SCATTER GUIDELINES

1. Check for *intertest scatter.* Intertest scatter is scatter or variability between subtests. You check for verbal intertest scatter and performance intertest scatter by first finding the range of scores from low to high. If the range is greater than three points than the possibility of intertest scatter exists.

    Example

Information	8
Similarities	15
Arithmetic	6
Vocabulary	13
Comprehension	10
Digit Span	5

    In the illustration, the range of scores is from 5 (Digit Span) to 15 (Similarities). Since the range is greater than three points, intertest scatter may exist. When intertest scatter is present it may indicate an unevenness of performance. For a resulting IQ score to be considered valid, the pattern should reflect subtest scores with a range of three or less. The reason for this scatter can be a variety of reasons including emotional factors, processing problems, and neurological factors. However, intertest scatter is only one signal, but if it exists jot it down on your work sheet.

2. Check for *intratest scatter.* Intratest scatter is variability in performance within a subtest. You will need to see the test protocol to establish this type of scatter. Since IQ tests are made with questions of increasing difficulty, one would expect a subject to answer easier ones and miss on the more difficult questions. Sometimes the opposite exists, where a subject will continuously miss easier questions and be able to respond correctly to harder ones. When this occurs in several subtests, intratest scatter may exist, indicating greater potential. The more subtests that reflect intratest scatter, the greater the potential.

3. Check for verbal-performance scatter. The normal range difference of scores between the two levels should be under 12–15 points. Such a pattern would indicate a more consistent pattern of performance. A difference of more than 12–15 points between Verbal IQ and Performance IQ is an indicator of scatter and uneven performance possibly resulting from one or several factors, for example, emotionality or processing difficulties.

4. Check for vocabulary-similarities scatter. For the next factor you must first find the mean verbal scaled score (the average of all the verbal scaled scores added together). First, add up *all* the verbal scaled scores given and divide by the number of subtests. This will provide you with the mean scaled score. If the Vocabulary and/or Similarities scaled scores are more than three points higher than this mean, then another type of scatter may exist. *Vocabulary* and *Similarities* have the greatest correlation with intelligence on the Wechsler Scales. If an individual is able to score significantly higher on these subtests than the others, then the possibility exists that greater potential is present regardless of the scores on other subtests.

DIAGNOSTIC PATTERNS ON THE WECHSLER SCALES

The patterns of scaled scores can sometimes reflect a certain type of diagnostic pattern. Therefore, it may be useful to begin developing a "feel" for a child by understanding his or her patterns of scores. Some of the more common diagnostic patterns may include the following:

Diagnostic Pattern 1—Slow Learner

Definition. A slow learner is a child whose intellectual ability consistently falls within the low-average (80–89) range over repeated measures and whose scaled score pattern reveals the absence of any scatter or greater potential. The diagnosis of a slow learner is sometimes mistaken for a learning disabled (LD) child who may also score in the 80s on an intellectual measure. However, several factors differentiate these two populations:

1. A slow learner may not be able to meet grade level expectations regardless of the type of support received, while the expectation of the LD child is that he or she will be able to attain grade level performance with assistance.
2. While both populations may obtain IQ scores within the 80 range, the LD child's pattern will usually reflect greater potential.

The diagnostic pattern for the slow learner on the Wechsler Scales may be reflected in the following ways:

Verbal		**Performance**	
Information	7	Picture Completion	8
Similarities	8	Picture Arrangement	7
Arithmetic	8	Block Design	6
Vocabulary	8	Object Assembly	7
Comprehension	7	Coding	8
Digit Span	7	Symbol Search	7

Verbal Mean = 45 divided by 6 = 7.5 rounded off to 8

Performance Mean = 43 divided by 6 or 7.2 rounded off to 7

Verbal IQ—85   Performance IQ—82   Full-Scale IQ—83

NOTE

1. There is an absence of intertest scatter: the range of verbal scaled scores and performance scaled scores is not greater than three points.

2. If one were to look at the protocol, there would likely be no indication of intratest scatter.

3. The Verbal IQ and the Performance IQ are only three points apart, indicating the absence of verbal-performance scatter.

4. The Vocabulary subtest scaled score and/or the Similarities subtest scaled scores are not significantly greater than the mean verbal scaled score. The mean verbal scaled score is 8, and neither subtest is more than three points from the mean.

5. A history of IQ scores within this range are also necessary for this diagnostic pattern. A child scoring in the 80s with the foregoing factors present would not be a slow learner if a separate individual IQ test taken a year or so earlier showed significantly greater potential.

The importance of defining this category lies in reducing the child's frustration with unrealistic expectations and work load. The teacher needs to be very aware of such a pattern so that goals and work requirements closely meet the ability levels of the child.

Diagnostic Pattern 2—Educable Mentally Retarded

Definition. The definition for educable mentally retarded requires a score within the mentally deficient range, no indications of greater potential, and a low score on a measure of adaptive behavior (Adaptive Behavior Scale). The absence of any one of these factors may prevent such a diagnosis.

The diagnostic pattern for an educable mentally retarded child on the Wechsler Scales may be reflected in the following ways:

Verbal		**Performance**	
Information	5	Picture Completion	6
Similarities	5	Picture Arrangement	6
Arithmetic	5	Block Design	5
Vocabulary	5	Object Assembly	5
Comprehension	6	Coding	7
Digit Span	6	Symbol Search	6
		Mazes	5

Verbal Mean = 32
divided by 6 = 5.3
rounded off to 5

Performance Mean = 40
divided by 6.6 rounded to 7

Verbal IQ—73   Performance IQ—74   Full-Scale IQ—71

NOTE

1. There is an absence of intertest scatter: the range of verbal scaled scores and performance scaled scores is not greater than three points.
2. If one were to look at the protocol, there would likely be no indication of intratest scatter.
3. The Verbal IQ and the Performance IQ are only one point apart, indicating the absence of verbal-performance scatter.
4. The Vocabulary subtest scaled score and/or the Similarities subtest scaled scores are not significantly greater than the mean verbal scaled score. The mean verbal scaled score is 5 and neither subtest is more than three points from the mean.
5. Scores on measures of adaptive functioning are low.
6. There is a history of IQ test measures within the same range and no indications of significantly greater potential.

Diagnostic Pattern 3—Trainable Mentally Retarded

Definition. A trainable mentally disabled child is one whose IQ scores fall well within the low levels of the mentally deficient range. These children would also score low on a measure of adaptive behavior. While intelligence tests are sometimes administered for purposes of classification, a better measure for a student in this category is a social maturity scale such as the Vineland or Syracuse.

The diagnostic pattern for the trainable mentally retarded child on the Wechsler Scales may be reflected in the following ways:

Verbal		**Performance**	
Information	2	Picture Completion	2
Similarities	2	Picture Arrangement	2
Arithmetic	1	Block Design	2
Vocabulary	2	Object Assembly	1
Comprehension	2	Coding	2
Digit Span	2	Mazes	2

Verbal Mean = 11   Performance Mean = 9
divided by 6 = 1.8 rounded to 2   divided by 6 = 1.5 or rounded to 2
Verbal IQ—54   Performance IQ—50   Full-Scale IQ—48

NOTE

1. There is an absence of intertest scatter: the range of verbal scaled scores and performance scaled scores is not greater than three points.
2. If one were to look at the protocol, there would likely be no indication of intratest scatter.

3. The Verbal IQ and the Performance IQ are only four points apart, indicating the absence of verbal-performance scatter.

4. The Vocabulary subtest scaled score and/or the Similarities subtest scaled scores are not significantly greater than the mean verbal scaled score. The mean verbal scaled score is 2, and neither subtest is more than three points from the mean.

5. Scores on measures of adaptive functioning are low.

6. There is a history of IQ test measures within the same range and no indications of significantly greater potential.

Diagnostic Pattern 4—Emotionally Disabled

Definition. Emotionally disabled children are those whose present dynamic state is so tense and draining that their emotions greatly affect their ability to function commensurate with their potential. This pattern has also been evident for a long period of time. While other measures are used to provide evidence for this diagnosis, certain patterns on the intelligence test may signal the presence of this area of dysfunction.

The diagnostic pattern for the emotionally disturbed child on the Wechsler Scales may be reflected in the following ways:

Verbal		**Performance**	
Information	7	Picture Completion	12
Similarities	15	Picture Arrangement	5
Arithmetic	4	Block Design	10
Vocabulary	14	Object Assembly	4
Comprehension	6	Coding	11
Digit Span	5	Symbol Search	3

Verbal Mean = 51 divided by 6 = 8.5 rounded to 9   Performance Mean = 45 divided by 6 or 7.5 rounded to 8

Verbal IQ—95   Performance IQ—90   Full-Scale IQ—92

NOTE

1. There is extreme intertest scatter: the range of verbal scaled scores and performance scaled scores are both greater than three points.

2. If one were to look at the protocol, there would likely be many indications of intratest scatter and great variability of performance.

3. The Verbal IQ and the Performance IQ may or may not be discrepant. In this particular case, they are not. However, in many cases, they are because the child's energy level is sporadic and sustained concentration is difficult. Therefore, after several subtests, the child may give up. In addition, performance tests are sometimes more motivating than the verbal tests that are more school related in their content and that may account for some scatter in the results.

4. The Vocabulary subtest scaled score and/or the Similarities subtest scaled scores are significantly greater than the mean verbal scaled score. The mean verbal scaled score is 9, the Similarities score 15, and the Vocabulary 14. The assumption here is that no matter how low your IQ, if these two scores are significantly higher than the rest, then greater potential is present because it is not possible to guess your way to a high score.

Diagnostic Pattern 5—Learning Disabled–Visual Motor

Definition. This is a child who may exhibit serious difficulties in any developmental skill involving eye-hand coordination, spatial relationships, visual-motor dexterity, ability to see cause-effect relationships, and pencil control.

The diagnostic pattern for the learning disabled child with visual-motor deficits on the Wechsler Scales may be reflected in the following ways:

Verbal		Performance	
Information	12	Picture Completion	13
Similarities	11	Picture Arrangement	6
Arithmetic	13	Block Design	7
Vocabulary	10	Object Assembly	5
Comprehension	10	Coding	6
Digit Span	10	Mazes	6

Verbal Mean = 66 divided by 6 = 11

Performance Mean = 43 divided by 6 = 7.2 rounded to 7

Verbal IQ—106   Performance IQ—82   Full-Scale IQ—92

NOTE

1. There is an absence of verbal intertest scatter: the range of verbal scaled scores and performance scaled scores is not greater than three points, indicating that this area should be considered a valid indicator of the child's true ability.

2. If one were to look at the protocol, there might be an indication of intratest scatter on the performance areas.

3. In this pattern, the Verbal IQ and the Performance IQ would be significantly different. However, there is no guarantee that verbal subtests might not be low as well. A child whose confidence and self-esteem are low, and lacks the willingness to venture a guess or expand upon an answer may suffer.

4. The Vocabulary subtest scaled score and/or the Similarities subtest scaled scores are not significantly greater than the mean verbal scaled score. The mean verbal scaled score is 11, and neither subtest is more than three points from the mean. However, the real discrepancy here is the difference between the Verbal test scores which are auditory-vocal (auditory channel input and vocal output) and the Performance test scores which are visual-vocal–visual-motor (visual input and vocal output and visual input and motoric output).

Diagnostic Pattern 6— Language Impaired

Definition. This child may exhibit serious difficulties in receptive or expressive language abilities. He or she may have trouble labeling, naming, retrieving, remembering, and expressing ideas and concepts.

The diagnostic pattern for the language-impaired child on the Wechsler Scales may be reflected in the following ways:

Verbal		**Performance**	
Information	7	Picture Completion	10
Similarities	6	Picture Arrangement	12
Arithmetic	7	Block Design	13
Vocabulary	7	Object Assembly	13
Comprehension	6	Coding	14
Digit Span	7	Mazes	12

Verbal Mean = 40 divided by 6 = 6.6 rounded to 7   Performance Mean = 74 divided 12.3 rounded to 12

Verbal IQ—81   Performance IQ—118   Full-Scale IQ—100

NOTE

1. There is an absence of intertest scatter: the range of verbal scaled scores and performance scaled scores is not greater than three points.
2. If one were to look at the protocol, there would likely be no indication of intratest scatter.
3. The Verbal IQ and the Performance IQ are only two points apart, indicating the absence of verbal-performance scatter.
4. The Vocabulary subtest scaled score and/or the Similarities subtest scaled scores are not significantly greater than the mean verbal scaled score. The mean verbal scaled score is 6, and neither subtest is more than three points from the mean.

Diagnostic Pattern 7—Gifted

Definition. The gifted child is among those children identified by professionally qualified persons who, by virtue of outstanding abilities are capable of high performance. This includes a demonstrated achievement and/or potential ability in general intellectual ability, specific academic aptitude, and creative and productive thinking.

The diagnostic pattern for the gifted child on the Wechsler Scales may be reflected in the following ways:

Verbal		Performance	
Information	17	Picture Completion	17
Similarities	18	Picture Arrangement	18
Arithmetic	16	Block Design	17
Vocabulary	16	Object Assembly	18
Comprehension	16	Coding	19
Digit Span	15	Symbol Search	17

Verbal Mean = 98 divided   Performance Mean = 106
by 6 = 16.3 rounded to 16   divided by 6 = 17.6 rounded to 18
Verbal IQ—138   Performance IQ—142   Full-Scale IQ—142

NOTE

1. There is an absence of intertest scatter: the range of verbal scaled scores and performance scaled scores is not greater than three points.
2. If one were to look at the protocol, there would likely be no indication of intratest scatter.
3. The Verbal IQ and the Performance IQ are only two points apart, indicating the absence of verbal-performance scatter.
4. The Vocabulary subtest scaled score and/or the Similarities subtest scaled scores are not significantly greater than the mean verbal scaled score. The mean verbal scaled score is 6, and neither subtest is more than three points from the mean.

HOW TO DETERMINE MODALITY OR CHANNEL STRENGTHS AND WEAKNESSES ON THE WECHSLER SCALES

A *modality* or *channel* is the avenue through which information comes to us. There are six modalities or channels:

◆ Visual modality—information received through the eye
◆ Auditory modality—information received through the ear
◆ Kinesthetic modality—information obtained through a variety of body movements and muscle feelings.
◆ Tactile modality—information obtained through the sense of touch via the fingers and skin surfaces.
◆ Gustatory modality—information obtained through the sense of taste
◆ Olfactory modality—information obtained through the sense of smell

The Verbal subtests of the Wechsler Scales are considered auditory-vocal tasks and the Performance subtests visual and visual motor.

One of the major purposes of an evaluation is to determine **learning style**, the various factors that contribute to an individual child's ability to learn. One of the factors involved in learning style is determining which modality is a strength and which is a weakness. One way to determine this on the Wechsler Scales is by comparing the difference in IQs between the Verbal areas and the Performance areas. If the difference in these scores is greater than 12–15 points, then a stronger and weaker modality may be evident.

HOW TO DETERMINE PROCESS STRENGTHS AND WEAKNESSES ON THE WECHSLER SCALES

An important piece of information obtained from the results of the Wechsler Scales are the patterns of performance exhibited by the child on each subtest. Since each subtest area measures a different process, determining the child's overall strengths and weaknesses adds to our information on learning style. To determine these factors we must use the mean verbal scaled score, average of all the scaled scores for the verbal subtests, and the mean performance scaled score, average of all the scaled scores for the performance subtests. Once this is determined, we then subtract each verbal scaled score from the mean verbal scaled score and each of the performance scaled scores from the mean performance scaled score. Any subtest that is greater than three points from the mean may be considered a significant strength, and any subtest that is greater than three points below the mean is considered a significant weakness. Let us take a look at an example:

Verbal		**Performance**	
Information	7	Picture Completion	12
Similarities	15	Picture Arrangement	5
Arithmetic	4	Block Design	10
Vocabulary	14	Object Assembly	4
Comprehension	6	Coding	11
Digit Span	5	Symbol Search	3

Verbal Mean = 51 divided by 6 = 8.5 rounded to 9   Performance Mean = 45 divided by 6 or 7.5 rounded to 8

Verbal IQ—95   Performance IQ—88   Full-Scale IQ—91

In the following example the mean verbal scaled score is 9. If we subtract each verbal subtest from that we get the following:

Subtest	Mean Scaled Score		Scaled Score	Deviation from the Mean		
Information	9	minus	7	equals	-2
Similarities	9	minus	15	equals	+6
Arithmetic	9	minus	4	equals	-5
Vocabulary	9	minus	14	equals	+5
Comprehension	9	minus	6	equals	-3
Digit Span	9	minus	5	equals	-4

When we look at these results of the verbal subtests, we notice that two subtests (Similarities and Vocabulary) are significant strengths, and two subtest (Arithmetic and Digit Span are significant weaknesses. Therefore, we find that the process of abstract reasoning (Similarities) and word knowledge (Vocabulary) are strengths, and the process of arithmetic reasoning (Arithmetic) and auditory sequential memory (Digit Span) are weaknesses.

Now if we do the same for the Performance subtests (mean scaled score of 8), we get the following results:

Subtest	Mean Scaled Score		Scaled Score	Deviation from the Mean		
Picture Completion	8	minus	12	equals	+4
Picture Arrangement	8	minus	5	equals	-3
Block Design	8	minus	10	equals	+2
Object Assembly	8	minus	4	equals	-4
Coding	8	minus	11	equals	+3
Mazes	8	minus	3	equals	-5

In this example we have one significant process strength (Picture Completion) and two significant process weaknesses (Object Assembly and Mazes). Therefore, we find that the process of visual alertness and memory (Picture Completion) is a significant strength; the processes of whole relationships and visual-motor spatial coordination (Object Assembly) and visual-motor dexterity (Mazes) are significant weaknesses. Such patterns are important since certain trends may be indicative of specific disorders.

OTHER FORMS OF ANALYSIS USING THE WECHSLER SCALES

There are some other forms of analysis that are possible using the Wechsler Scales. For instance, on the WISC—III there are four separate subscales derived from the scores. These scores are calculated from certain subtests. They are

Verbal Comprehension (VCI)—Information, Similarities, Vocabulary, and Comprehension.

Perceptual Organization (POI)—Picture Completion, Picture Arrangement, Block Design, and Object Assembly

Freedom from Distractibility (FDI)—Arithmetic and Digit Span

Processing Speed (PSI)—Coding and Symbol Search

Other forms of analysis specific to all three Wechsler Scales—WPPSI, WISC—III, and WAIS—R—are derived from a combination of several subtests. Finding a pattern of strengths or weaknesses among these subtests can enhance your diagnosis and help support the evidence for a specific learning style.

Abstract and Conceptual Thought—Similarities, Comprehension, and Block Design

Memory—Coding, Digit Span, and Arithmetic

Receptive and Expressive Language—Similarities, Vocabulary, and Comprehension

Visual-Perceptual Organization—Picture Arrangement, Mazes, and Object Assembly

Social Judgment and Common Sense—Comprehension and Picture Arrangement

Sequential Reasoning—Arithmetic, Mazes, Digit Span, and Comprehension

Psychomotor Speed and Coordination—Picture Arrangement, Block Design, Object Assembly, Mazes, Symbol Search, and Coding.

These scores are found on the front of the WISC—III protocol and should be reviewed for possible factors influencing learning style. Even though these subscales are not found in the WPPSI or WAIS—R manuals, research has found their use in interpreting these two tests encouraging.

Section 5

How to Effectively Determine a Student's Academic Strengths and Weaknesses

The special education teacher should possess a knowledge of evaluation measures, their purpose, and who is primarily responsible for the measurement of a particular area among the various professionals on staff. The factors that may determine the test used include chronological age, type of disability, mental age, personal preference of the evaluator, language ability, and time allotted.

A crucial phase in the case study process includes the determination of academic strengths and weaknesses. Such a determination leads to the development of prescription and remediation and is extremely important in the development of individual educational plans. Further, because multiple causation is frequently responsible for learning problems, each possibility should receive consideration and investigation. This part of the case study is used to organize diagnostic data and relate it to the things the school can do.

OBJECTIVES OF AN EDUCATIONAL EVALUATION

The objectives of the educational evaluation are as follows:

1. To help determine the child's stronger and weaker academic skill areas. The evaluation may give us this information which is very useful when making practical recommendations to teachers about academic expectations, areas in need of remediation, and how to best input information to assist the child's ability to learn.

2. To help the teacher gear the materials to the learning capacity of the individual child. A child reading two years below grade level may require modified textbooks or greater explanations prior to a lesson.

3. To develop a learning profile that can help the classroom teacher understand the best way to present information to the child and thus increase the child's chances of success.

4. Along with other information and test results, to help determine if the child's academic skills are suitable for a regular class or so severe that he or she may require a more *restrictive educational setting* (an educational setting or situation best suited to the present needs of the student other than a full-time regular class placement, e.g., resource room, self-contained class, and special school).

73

Whatever achievement battery the special educator chooses, it should be one that covers enough skill areas to make an adequate diagnosis of academic strengths and weaknesses.

The academic investigation begins with the special educator's selection of a *test battery* (a series of tests). This selection is the personal choice of the evaluator as long as certain areas are covered by the procedure. The special educator should be aware that specific achievement areas need to be covered by the test battery:

SPECIFIC SKILL AREAS

Reading

Vocabulary—the ability to understand words

Decoding—the ability to analyze words phonetically

Encoding—the ability to express oneself verbally

Sight word recognition—the ability to automaticaly recognize and correctly verbalize words

Reading comprehension— the ability to understand and remember what one reads

Oral reading comprehension—the ability to understand and remember what one reads aloud

Silent reading comprehension—the ability to understand and remember what one reads silently

Writing

Penmanship—the ability to form and write the letters of the alphabet correctly

Written expression—the ability to clearly express oneself through written language

Style—the use of cursive or manuscript as one's means of written expression

Arithmetic

Arithmetic concepts—the ability to count and use simple numbers to represent quantity

Arithmetic processes—the ability to add, subtract, multiply, and divide

Arithmetic reasoning—the ability to apply basic arithmetic processes

Arithmetic applications—the ability to apply basic arithmetic processes to word problems

Arithmetic computation—the ability to use basic math facts in solving arithmetic problems

Spelling

Written spelling—the ability to spell in written form
Visual spelling—the ability to spell in oral form

ACHIEVEMENT TESTS

Specific tests are available to cover certain achievement areas. Most achievement tests cover several areas, but be aware that the subtest titles may not include the variety of skills that need to be covered under a certain skill area. If the subtest indicates "Arithmetic," be sure that many skill areas are covered and not just one, for example, computation, since the score reported may be incorrectly assumed to be a measure of the child's total math skills.

The following information indicates the areas and possible tests that could be used to measure a particular skill. For a more detailed summary of the specific test indicated under each skill area, refer to the alphabetized list at the end of the chapter.

Reading Tests

DECODING: PHONIC SKILLS, SIGHT WORD VOCABULARY, ORAL PARAGRAPH READING

Durrell Analysis of Reading Difficulty—Grades 1–6
Gates-MacGinitie Silent Reading Tests—Grades 1–12
Gates-McKillop Reading Diagnostic Tests—Grades 1–6
Wide Range Achievement Tests—Revised—Ages 5–adult
Peabody Individual Achievement Tests—Grades K–12
Woodcock Reading Mastery Tests—Grades K–12
Spache Diagnostic Reading Scales—Grades 1–8 and 9–12 (students with reading deficiencies)
Brigance Diagnostic Inventory of Basic Skills—Grades K–6
Gray Oral Reading Test—Grades 1–College
Gilmore Oral Reading Test—Grades 1–8
Wechsler Individual Achievement Test—Ages 5–18
Kauffman Individual Achievement Test—Ages 5–18

COMPREHENSION: ORAL READING, SILENT READING, LISTENING

Durrell Listening-Reading Series—Grades 1–9

Durrell Analysis of Reading Difficulty—Grades 1–6

Gates-MacGinitie Silent Reading Tests—Grades 1–12

Gates-McKillop Reading Diagnostic Tests—Grades 1–6

Wide Range Achievement Tests—Revised—Ages 5–adult

Peabody Individual Achievement Tests—Grades K–12

Woodcock Reading Mastery Tests—Grades K–12

Spache Diagnostic Reading Scales—Grades 1–8 and 9–12 (students with reading deficiencies)

Brigance Diagnostic Inventory of Basic Skills—Grades K–6

Gray Oral Reading Test—Grades 1–College

Gilmore Oral Reading Test—Grades 1–8

Wechsler Individual Achievement Test—Ages 5–18

Kauffman Individual Achievement Test—Ages 5–18

Writing Tests

PENMANSHIP

Slingerland Screening Tests for Identifying Children with Specific Language Disability—Ages 6–12

Malcomesius Specific Language Disability Test—Grades 6–8

Durrell Analysis of Reading Difficulty—Grades 1–6

WRITTEN EXPRESSION

Myklebust Picture Story Language Test—Ages 7–17

Test of Written Language (TOWL)—Grades 1–6

Spelling Tests

WRITTEN: PHONIC WORDS, IRREGULAR WORDS

Wide Range Achievement Test—Revised—Ages 5–adult

Brigance Diagnostic Inventory of Basic Skills—Grades K–6

Larsen Hammill Test of Written Spelling—Ages 5–15

Diagnostic Word Patterns—Grades 2–College

Wechsler Individual Achievement Test—Ages 5–18

Kauffman Individual Achievement Test—Ages 5–18

VISUAL: RECOGNITION OF SIGHT WORDS

Peabody Individual Achievement Test—Ages 5–adult

Wechsler Individual Achievement Test—Ages 5–18

Kauffman Individual Achievement Test—Ages 5–18

Arithmetic Tests

CONCEPTS

> **Peabody Individual Achievement Test**—Ages 5–adult
> **Key Math Diagnostic Arithmetic Tests**—Preschool–Grade 6
> **Brigance Diagnostic Inventory of Basic Skills**—Grades K–6
> **Wechsler Individual Achievement Test**—Ages 5–18
> **Kauffman Individual Achievement Test**—Ages 5–18

COMPUTATION: ADDITION, SUBTRACTION, MULTIPLICATION, DIVISION

> **Wide Range Achievement Test**—Ages 5–adult
> **Brigance Diagnostic Inventory of Basic Skills**—Grades K–6
> **Key Math Diagnostic Arithmetic Test**—Preschool–Grade 6
> **Wechsler Individual Achievement Test**—Ages 5–18
> **Kauffman Individual Achievement Test**—Ages 5–18

WORD PROBLEMS: ORAL AND WRITTEN

> **Peabody Individual Achievement Test**—Ages 5–adult
> **Brigance Diagnostic Inventory of Basic Skills**—Grades K–6
> **Key Math Arithmetic Test**—Preschool–Grade 6
> **Wechsler Individual Achievement Test**—Ages 5–18
> **Kauffman Individual Achievement Test**—Ages 5–18

More Widely Used Tests

The special educator must now choose tests that will offer a well-rounded picture of a child's achievement abilities and deficiencies. There are many tests available on the market today, and the choice is up to the educator. However, some tests are more widely used and may include the following:

> **Brigance Diagnostic Inventory of Basic Skills**—Grades K–6. This test is used to assess basic readiness and academic skills.
> **Diagnostic Word Patterns**—Grades 2–College. This test is used to provide a quick assessment of basic sound-symbol associations in spelling and reading.
> **Durrell Analysis of Reading Difficulty**—Grades 1–6. This test is used to assess various aspects of the reading process and to identify weaknesses in reading.
> **Durrell Listening-Reading Series**—Grades 1–9. These are a series of group tests of listening and reading ability that permit a comparison of these two language areas.
> **Gates-McKillop Reading Diagnostic Tests**—Grades 1–6. This test is used to assess a variety of skills related to reading.

Gilmore Oral Reading Test—Grades1–8. This test is used to assess oral reading accuracy and comprehension skills.

Gray Oral Reading Test—Grades 1–college. This test is used to measure growth in oral reading and to aid in the diagnosis of oral reading problems.

Kauffman Individual Achievement Test—Ages 5–18. This is an individually administered test which covers a wide range of reading, spelling, and mathematical skill areas.

Key Math Diagnostic Arithmetic Test—Preschool–Grade 6. This is an individually administered comprehensive math test that measures fourteen arithmetic subskills.

Larsen-Hammill Test of Written Spelling—Ages 5–15. This test provides a valid measure of written spelling.

Malcomesius Specific Language Disability Test—Grades 6–8. This is a diagnostic tool that helps to identify students with specific language disabilities.

Myklebust Picture Story Language Test—Ages 7–17. This test assesses various written language skills.

Peabody Individual Achievement Test—Revised—Ages 5–adult. This is an individually administered achievement battery that measures mathematics, visual spelling, reading recognition, reading comprehension, spelling, and general knowledge.

Spache Diagnostic Reading Scales—Grades 1–8 and 9–12. This test is used to assess reading skills and supplementary phonic skills for students with deficient reading ability.

Wide Range Achievement Tests—Revised—Ages 5–adult. This test is used to assess skills in decoding, mathematical computation, and written spelling.

Woodcock Reading Mastery Tests—Grades K–12. This test is an individually administered test used to measure a child's skills in identification of words, word attack, word comprehension, and passage comprehension.

Woodcock Johnson Psychoeducational Battery—Preschool through adult. This is a measure of a child's overall achievement and cognitive ability levels.

Wechsler Individual Achievement Test—Ages 5–18. This is an individually administered test which covers a wide range of reading, spelling, and mathematical skill areas.

Section 6

How to Effectively Evaluate a Student's Perceptual Strengths and Weaknesses

THE LEARNING PROCESS

The perceptual evaluation is theoretically based upon the concept of the learning process (the process by which information is received and the manner in which it is processed). In very simple terms, the learning process can be described in the following way:

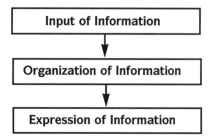

Information is received in some manner, and is filtered through a series of psychological processes. As information progresses along this "assembly line," it is given meaning and organized in some fashion and then expressed through a variety of responses. When we evaluate a child's perceptual abilities, we are looking to see if there is a deficit in some area of the learning process that may be slowing down the processing of information there by interfering in the child's ability to receive, organize, memorize, or express information. Severe deficits in the learning process can have adverse affects upon a child's academic performance.

To understand how learning takes place, we must first understand the specific parts that make up the learning process. There are six modalities or channels (avenues through which information is received):

- ◆ **Auditory modality**—The delivery of information through sound
- ◆ **Visual modality**—the delivery of information through sight
- ◆ **Tactile modality**—the delivery of information through touching
- ◆ **Kinesthetic modality**—the delivery of information through movement
- ◆ **Gustatory modality**—the delivery of information through taste
- ◆ **Olfactory modality**—the delivery of information through smell

Information is delivered to the senses through one or several of the foregoing channels. Once it is received, the information goes through a series of processes that attempt to give meaning to the material received. There are several processes that comprise the learning process:

♦ **Reception**—the initial receiving of information
♦ **Perception**—the initial organization of information
♦ **Association or organization**—relating new information to other information and giving meaning to the information received
♦ **Memory**—the storage or retrieval process which facilitates the associational process to give meaning to information or help in relating new concepts to other information that might have already been learned
♦ **Expression**—the output of information through vocal, motoric, or written responses

When placed in a chart form the learning process may look like the this:

PROCESSES

Modalities or Channels	Reception (initial receiving of information)	Perception (initial organizing of information)	Association (relating new information to other information)	Memory (short term, sequential and long term)	Expression (vocal, written or motoric)
Auditory	Auditory reception	Auditory perception	Auditory association	Auditory memory	Auditory vocal/motoric
Visual	Visual reception	Visual perception	Visual association	Visual memory	Visual vocal/motoric
Tactile	Tactile reception	Tactile perception	Tactile association	Tactile memory	Tactile vocal/motoric
Kinesthetic	Kinesthetic reception	Kinesthetic perception	Kinesthetic association	Kinesthetic memory	Kinesthetic vocal/motoric
Gustatory	Gustatory reception	Gustatory perception	Gustatory. association	Gustatory memory	Gustatory vocal/motoric
Olfactory	Olfactory reception	Olfactory perception	Olfactory association	Olfactory memory	Olfactory vocal/motoric

It is more likely that skills would be taught using all six modalities in the primary grades, nursery school to grade 1. By grade 2 most teachers will teach through approximately four of the modalities with a greater emphasis on visual and auditory input. By the upper elementary grades this can shift to skill development through the use of only two modalities, visual and auditory. This pretty much remains the source of informational input in most classrooms until possiby college, when information is usually presented through only one modality, auditory (only lectures). Children should be taught using *multisensory approaches* (the input of information through a variety of receptive mechanisms, e.g., sight, hearing, and touching) whenever possible.

Objectives of Perceptual Evaluation

Now that we have some understanding of how the learning process functions, we can explore the objectives of the perceptual evaluation. The objectives are as follows:

1. To help determine the child's stronger and weaker modality for learning. Some children are visual learners, some are auditory, and some learn best through any form of input. However, if a child is a strong visual learner in a class where the teacher relies on auditory lectures, then it is possible that the child's ability to process information may be hampered. The evaluation may give us this information, which is very useful when making practical recommendations to teachers about how to best input information to assist the child's ability to learn.
2. To help determine a child's stronger and weaker process areas. A child having problems in memory and expression will fall behind the rest of the class very quickly. The longer these processing difficulties continue, the greater the chance for **secondary emotional problems** (emotional problems resulting from continued frustration with the ability to learn) to develop.
3. To develop a learning profile which can help the classroom teacher understand the best way to present information to the child and therefore increase the chances of success.
4. Along with other information and test results, to help determine if the child's learning process deficits are suitable for a regular class or so severe that he or she may require a more **restrictive educational setting** (an educational setting or situation best suited to the present needs of the student other than a full-time regular class placement, e.g., resource room, self-contained class, and special school).

Whatever perceptual battery the special educator chooses, it should be one that covers enough skill areas to make an adequate diagnosis of process and modality strengths and weaknesses. Areas that need to be measured in choosing a series of tests include the following:

Perceptual Areas

Visual Perceptual Areas

Visual coordination—the ability to follow and track objects with coordinated eye movements

Visual discrimination—the ability to differentiate visually the forms and symbols in one's environment

Visual association—the ability to organize and associate visually presented material in a meaningful way

Visual long-term memory—the ability to retain and recall general and specific long-term visual information

Visual short-term memory—the ability to retain and recall general and specific short-term auditory information

Visual sequential memory—the ability to recall in correct sequence and detail prior auditory information

Visual-vocal expression—the ability to reproduce vocally prior visually presented material or experiences

Visual-motoric expression (visual-motor integration)—the ability to reproduce motorically prior visually presented material or experiences

AUDITORY PERCEPTUAL AREAS

Auditory discrimination—the ability to differentiate auditorially the sounds in one's environment

Auditory association—the ability to organize and associate auditorially presented material in a meaningful way

Auditory long-term memory—the ability to retain and recall general and specific long-term auditory information

Auditory short-term memory—the ability to retain and recall general and specific short-term auditory information

Auditory sequential memory—the ability to recall in correct sequence and detail prior auditory information

Auditory-vocal expression—the ability to reproduce vocally prior auditorially presented material or experiences

Auditory-motoric expression—the ability to reproduce motorically prior auditorially presented material or experiences

As has been indicated, a major objective of a perceptual evaluation is to identify those areas that may have a direct impact on a child's ability to process information adequately and possibly interfere in his or her academic achievement. There are many symptoms that may indicate problems in a certain perceptual area. Some of these are observable, while others are obtained through intakes and testing. What follows is a list of symptoms that may reflect perceptual disabilities in a variety of areas.

Diagnostic Symptoms for Perceptual Disabilities

VISUAL-MOTOR CHANNEL DISABILITY

- Exhibits poor motor coordination
- Exhibits awkwardness motorically; frequently trips, stumbles, bumps into things, has trouble skipping, jumping
- Has short attention span, little perseverance
- Behaves in a restless manner
- Exhibits poor handwriting, artwork, drawing
- Reverses "b," "d," "p," "q," "u," "n" when writing beyond a chronological age of seven or eight

- Frequently inverts numbers ("17" for "71"), reversals as well
- Can give correct answers when teacher reads test aloud but cannot put answers down on paper
- Performs poorly in group achievement tests
- Appears brighter than test scores indicate
- Perceives perception of time and space poorly
- Gets lost easily

AUDITORY-VOCAL CHANNEL DISABILITY

- Appears less intelligent than IQ tests indicate
- Does many more things than one would expect: puts puzzles together, fixes broken objects, and so on
- Appears to have a speech problem
- May emphasize wrong syllables in words
- May sequence sounds oddly
- May use "small words" incorrectly
- Appears not to listen or comprehend
- Watches teacher's or adult faces intently trying to grasp words
- Offers little in group discussions; appears shy
- Answers in one-word answers
- Follows in one-word answers
- Follows directions better after being shown rather than told.
- Cannot learn rote-memory tasks such as alphabet and/or number combinations, addresses, and phone numbers

RECEPTIVE PROCESS DISABILITY

Visual
- Does not enjoy books, pictures
- Fails to understand what is read
- Cannot give a simple explanation of contents of a picture
- Cannot categorize pictures

Auditory
- Fails to comprehend what is heard
- Exhibits poor receptive vocabulary
- Fails to identify sounds correctly
- Fails to carry out directions

AUDITORY ASSOCIATION DISABILITY

- Does not enjoy being read to
- Has difficulty comprehending questions

- Raises hand to answer question but gives inappropriate response
- Is slow to respond; takes a long time to answer
- Has difficulty with abstract concepts presented auditorially
- Exhibits poor concept formation in verbal responses
- Relies heavily on picture clues

VISUAL ASSOCIATION DISABILITY

- Cannot tell a story from pictures; can only label objects in the pictures
- Does not understand what is read
- Fails to handle primary workbook tasks
- Needs auditory cues and clues

MANUAL EXPRESSIVE DISABILITY

- Exhibits poor handwriting and drawing skills
- Communicates infrequently with gestures
- Has difficulty "acting out" ideas, feelings
- Appears clumsy and uncoordinated
- Performs poorly at game playing; cannot imitate other children in games

VERBAL EXPRESSIVE DISABILITY

- Mispronounces common words
- Uses incorrect word endings, plurals
- Omits correct verbal endings
- Makes grammatical or syntactical errors that do not reflect those of parents
- Has difficulty in sound blending

MEMORY DISABILITIES

Auditory Memory

- Does not know address and/or phone number
- Cannot remember instructions
- Cannot memorize nursery rhymes, poems
- Does not know alphabet
- Cannot count
- Fails to learn multiplication, addition, or subtraction facts

Visual Memory

- Frequently misspells words, even after extensive practice
- Misspells own name frequently
- Cannot write alphabet, numbers, computation facts
- Identifies words one day and fails to the next

There are a variety of evaluative measures frequently used by special educators. These tests vary from *single-process tests* (tests used to measure a single perceptual process, e.g., visual-motor integration) to *multiprocess tests* (tests that contain a variety of subtests used to measure many perceptual areas). Following is a review of some available perceptual tests.

Single-Process Tests

Beery-Buktenica Developmental Test of Visual-Motor Integration—Ages 2–15. This test is used to assess visual perception and fine motor coordination

Bender Visual-Motor Gestalt Test—Ages 5–adult. This test is used to measure visual-motor perceptual maturity. The age range for this particular measure depends upon the scoring system used—Koppitz (ages 5–11), Watkins (ages 5–15), or the Pascal and Suttell Scoring System (ages 15–50).

Goldman-Fristoe-Woodcock Test of Auditory Discrimination—Ages 4–adult. This test is used to measure speech sound discrimination under ideal listening conditions as well as controlled background noise.

Lindamood Auditory Conceptualization Test—Preschool–adult. This test is a measure of auditory discrimination.

Motor Free Perceptual Test—Ages 4–9. This test is used solely for the measure of a child's visual perceptual processing ability.

Wepman Auditory Discrimination Test—Ages 5–8. This test is used strictly for the evaluation of a child's level of discrimination of auditory stimuli.

Multiprocess Tests

Detroit Tests of Learning Aptitude—(DTLA—3)—Ages 3–19. This test contains a variety of perceptual information including reasoning ability, verbal ability, time and spatial relationships, auditory and visual attention, and motor ability.

Illinois Tests of Psycholinguistic Abilities—Ages 2–10. This test is used to assess visual-motor and auditory-vocal skills.

Woodcock Johnson Psychoeducational Battery—Preschool through adult. This is a measure of a child's overall achievement and cognitive ability levels.

Malcomesius Specific Language Disability Test—Grades 6–8. This test measures auditory, visual, and kinesthetic skills related to reading, writing, and spelling.

Slingerland Screening Tests for Identifying Children with Specific Language Disability—Ages 6–12. This test measures visual, auditory, and kinesthetic skills related to reading and spelling.

Section 7

How to Write a Comprehensive Psychoeducational Report

The special education teacher may be called upon to evaluate a child and write a comprehensive report based on the findings. This report may be given to the parent, sent to an outside doctor or agency, or presented to the CSE. In any case, the report needs to be as professional, comprehensive, and practical as possible. Citing many general recommendations is useless. Writing a report that contains loads of jargon that no one other than the writer understands is also useless. Completing an eighteen-page report in an attempt to be comprehensive will only result in losing your reader by the fifth page.

There are some practical guidelines to consider when writing a educational report.

1. Try to write the report in the third person, for example, "According to the examiner...," or "It was felt that...," or "There seems to be...." Never write "I think..." or "If it were up to me...."
2. Single-space your report to condense the length.
3. Separate your recommendation section into three parts—one for the school, one for the teacher, and one for the parents.
4. Try to write the report in the past tense as often as possible.
5. Separate sections by skipping two lines for purposes of clarity.
6. Underline paragraph headings so that they stand out and are easy to locate.
7. Write reports using complete sentences. Relying on phrases will make it read like a telegram.

ORGANIZING A PSYCHOEDUCATIONAL REPORT

Psychoeducational reports can take many forms, and the final version is usually left to the examiner. However, certain information must be included. What follows is a outline that would meet all the criteria for a comprehensive report.

Identifying Data

The first section is called "Identifying Data" and contains all the necessary basic information about the child:

Name	Parent Name(s)
Address	Teacher
Phone	Referred by
Date of Birth	Date(s) of Testing
Grade	Date of Report
School	Examiner

CHRONOLOGICAL AGE AT TIME OF TESTING While most of this information is usually found in the school records, having it all in one place saves time. Make sure that the date(s) of testing and the date of the report are always included for comparisons. Some evaluations are finished several months before the report is typed, and the scores can be misleading if the reader assumes that they represent the child's present levels on the date of the report when they may really be reflective of ability levels in prior months. Try to have the two dates within one month of each other.

Reason for Referral

The second section is called "Reason for Referral" and explains to the reader the specific reasons why an evaluation is taking place. It should not be more than two to three sentences, but should be comprehensive enough to clarify the purpose. Following are some examples of this section:

> Miguel was referred by his teacher for evaluation as a result of inconsistent academic performance and poor social skills.
>
> Mary was referred by her parents for evaluation in order to determine if a learning disability was interfering in her ability to learn.
>
> Benjamin is being tested as part of the triennial evaluation.

This section should not contain a great deal of parent or teacher information. That is part of another section which offers a more detailed explanation of the child.

Background History

The next section is called "Background History" and contains a very thorough description of the child's family history, developmental history, academic history, and social history. (Refer to the parent intake form to see the type of information requested.)

Behavioral Observations

The fourth section is called "Behavioral Observations" and includes a description of the child's behavior during the testing sessions. (Refer to the section entitled

"What to Look for in a Student's Behavior During Testing" for the information that might be contained in this section.) This can be a very important section, since it may reinforce what is seen in the class or be very different in which case the structure of the testing environment should be explored for clues to learning style.

Tests and Procedures Administered

The next section is called "Tests and Procedures Administered" and includes a simple list of the individual tests included in the test battery and any procedures used to enhance the report, for example, classroom observation, review of records, and parent intake.

Test Results

The sixth section, "Test Results," is a crucial section in that it analyzes the results of each test and looks at the child's individual performance on each measure. There are several approaches to this section, but the two most widely used approaches are the *test-by-test analysis* and the *content area–by–content area analysis*. The approach chosen is a personal choice and preference of the examiner.

A test-by-test approach analyzes the child's performance on each test separately. It analyzes the results of the different subtests and provides indications of strengths and weaknesses, manner of approach, and indications of whether or not the scores on the specific test should be considered valid.

A content area–by–content area approach takes all the reading subtests, math subtests, spelling subtests, and writing subtests from each evaluation measure and analyzes the results separately by content area.

Conclusions

The next section is probably the essence of the report and is called the "Conclusion" section. In this section the examiner indicates in very simple terms to the reader the trends in the child's testing results that may indicate academic strengths and weaknesses, modality strengths and weaknesses, process strengths and weaknesses, and overall diagnosis and level of severity of the problems areas indicated.

Recommendations

The last section of the report is probably the most valuable section for the reader— "Recommendations." It should contain practical recommendations that will bring some hope and direction for the identified problem areas. Try to separate the following sections:

"RECOMMENDATIONS TO THE SCHOOL" This section might contain suggestions like further testing from other professionals on staff, vision or hearing tests by the school nurse, recommendation for a review by the CSE, remedial reading assistance, or an English as a second language evaluation.

"RECOMMENDATIONS TO THE TEACHER" This section should contain useful information for the teacher, including an indication of the conditions under which the child learns best. The teacher is probably mainly interested in "What do I do" to help the child learn. Keep in mind that even before you begin the evaluation process, you should ask the teacher what he or she has already tried in an attempt to alleviate the problems. This should be done so that your recommendations do not include suggestions already attempted by the teacher. Doing this will avoid having your recommendations being viewed as "Nothing I haven't already tried before."

"RECOMMENDATIONS TO THE PARENT" This section should be very practical, direct, and diplomatic. The suggestions should also be inclusive enough to answer the questions "Why" and "How" so that parents do not have to interpret them.

Finally, each section should contain suggestions in priority order. Try to number each recommendation separately for purposes of clarity.

Examples of two reports, one on an elementary-aged student and the other on a secondary-aged student, can be found in the appendix to this book.

The Special Educator's Role in the Special Education Process

Section 8

Basic Educational Law for Special Educators

There is little doubt among professionals in the field that special education teachers should have a good working knowledge of the laws that govern disabled children. These laws are always changing, and it is crucial that teachers be as up to date on them as possible. As a special education teacher you will come in contact with parents, administrators, and sometimes even students who are very knowledgeable about the law and their rights. Without a thorough understanding of the law, you may find yourself in a very uncomfortable position or may give advice that may be contrary to the rights of the students.

While it is not necessary to be a "lawyer," there are basic concepts that should be learned and maintained. You should also be aware that your state may have a somewhat different interpretation of the laws concerning the rights of disabled children. However, there are basic concepts common to all interpretations. While regulations from the commissioners of education of each state may be complex, with numerous pages of "legalese," one need only obtain the section of the state law pertaining to the education of disabled students to become familiar with state regulations.

The areas that are most relevant for special education teachers involve parents' rights, due process, and responsibilities of the special education teacher in the special education process. While this review in no way covers all the legal requirements or aspects of your state law, it would be to your advantage to request a copy of all the laws on special education from your State Department of Education. These agencies are usually located in the state capital and can provide you with many materials on all aspects of special education, both state and federal.

A working knowledge of basic special educational law should start with common terminology that you may need to know.

BASIC TERMINOLOGY

Adaptive behavior—the manner and effectiveness with which a child or adult deals with the social demands of his surrounding environment.

Adaptive physical education—a specially designed physical education program for disabled children who cannot, as a result of their disability, benefit from the normal school program. This program is an individually designed program of games, sports, and developmental activities that are suited to the needs, interests, capabilities, and limitations of each disabled child.

Aging out—the date on which the disabled child will no longer be eligible for tuition-free educational services.

Annual review—an annual review of a disabled child's classification and educational program by the Committee on Special Education (CSE). The purpose of this review, which includes the parent and sometimes the student, is to determine the continuation, modification, or termination of classification; placement or individual educational plan (IEP) needs; and related services for the upcoming year.

Approved private school—a private school which has met state and federal guidelines for providing appropriate services to disabled children and as a result appears on a state-approved list from which public schools may enter into contract for services.

Change in placement (with reference to a disabled child)—any change of educational setting from or to a public school, local special school, or state-approved school.

Change in program (with reference to a disabled child)—any change in a component of the child's IEP.

CPSE (Committee on Preschool Special Education)—the multidisciplinary team that oversees the identification, monitoring, review, and status of disabled preschool children under the age of five.

CSE (Committee on Special Education)—the multidisciplinary team that oversees the identification, monitoring, review, and status of all disabled children residing within the school district.

Impartial hearing officer—an independent individual assigned by the district's board of education or commissioner of education to hear an appeal and render a decision. These individuals can in no way be connected to the school district, may have to be certified (depending upon state regulations), are trained, and usually must update their skills.

Independent evaluation—a full and comprehensive individual evaluation conducted by an outside professional or agency not involved in the education of the child.

Individual psychological evaluation—a full and comprehensive evaluation by a state certified school psychologist (if the child is evaluated within the school district) or a licensed psychologist for the purpose of educational planning.

Occupational therapy—the evaluation and provision of services for disabled children to develop or maintain adaptive skills designed to achieve maximal physical and mental functioning of the individual in his or her daily life tasks.

Paraprofessional—a teacher assistant or aide in a special education setting.

Physical therapy—treatment by a specialist under the supervision of a physician to students with motor disabilities.

Preschool program—a special education program for disabled children who are not of public school age.

Pupils with a disability—any school age child (any child who has not attained the age of 21 prior to September 1) who, because of mental, physical, or emotional reasons has been identified as having a disability and is entitled to special education services.

Related services—auxiliary services provided to disabled children including speech pathology, audiology, psychological services, physical therapy, occupational therapy, counseling services, and art therapy.

Resource room program—part-time supplementary instruction on an individual or small-group basis outside the regular classroom for disabled children.

Special class—a class consisting of children with the same disability or different disabilities who have been grouped together as a result of similar educational needs and levels for the purpose of being provided with special educational services.

Surrogate parent—any person appointed to act on the parent's or guardian's behalf when a child's parents are not known or are unavailable or when he child is the ward of the state.

Transitional support services—temporary special education services, according to a child's IEP provided to students who are no longer classified as disabled and may be transferring to a regular program or to disabled children who may be moving to a program or service in a less restrictive environment.

Triennial review—a full and comprehensive reexamination of a disabled child held every three years. This reexamination may include educational, psychological, medical, or any evaluation deemed necessary by the CSE to determine the child's continuing eligibility for special education.

The next aspect that you need to know about concerns the Committee on Special Education. You may at some point be asked to present information to the committee concerning a child you may have evaluated, observed, or taught.

UNDERSTANDING COMMITTEES ON SPECIAL EDUCATION

According to federal law P.L. 94-142, every public school district is required to have a Committee on Special Education. If the population of special education students reaches a certain level, then more than one CSE may be formed. Committees on Special Education are responsible for the identification of disabled children within the district and for recommending appropriate education at public expense for students identified as having a disability.

This committee is usually made up of mandated members and assigned members whom the board of education deems necessary. Most states require that certain professionals and individuals be core members. These usually include an administrator or director of pupil personnel services or director of special education, school psychologist, a medical doctor (does not need to be in attendance at every meeting but should be present anytime medical issues are involved, e.g., health-related classifications and issues involving medication), and a parent of a disabled child residing within the district. Other professionals may be appointed such as a guidance counselor, social worker, nurse teacher, and so on. The child's teacher is usually required to attend the meeting but at the secondary level; where a child may have numerous teachers, the guidance counselor usually represents all the teachers' views and comments after consultation with the child's teachers.

Responsibilities of the Committee on Special Education

Some of the responsibilities of the Committee on Special Education are as follows:

1. Following appropriate procedures and taking appropriate action on any child referred as having a suspected disability.

2. Determining the suitable classification for a child with a suspected disability. The classifications from which the CSE chooses are defined as follows:

   Autistic—a disorder characterized by a difficulty in the child's ability to respond to people, events, and objects. Responses to sensations of light, sound, and feeling may be exaggerated and delayed speech and language skills may be associated features. The onset of this condition is usually observed before two and one-half years of age.

   Blind—a child whose vision requires special Braille equipment and reading materials. The condition is so severe that the child does not have what is considered functional sight.

   Deaf—a child whose loss of hearing so severe, usually above an 80-decibel loss, that it hinders effective use of the sense of hearing. This disability usually necessitates the use of specialized services or equipment in order for the child to communicate.

   Emotionally Disabled—a child whose severity of behavior disorders over a long period of time have made adequate performance in school impossible. The disturbances may interfere in developing meaningful relationships, result in physical symptoms or irrational fears, and limit the individual's overall production.

   Hard of Hearing—a child whose hearing loss may or may not be permanent and has some sense of hearing with or without an aid. However, this student still requires specialized instruction and special education assistance.

   Learning Disabled—a child with a disability in receiving, organizing, or expressing information. These children are of average intelligence but have difficulty listening, thinking, speaking, reading, writing, or doing arithmetic, and this results in a significant discrepancy between ability and school achievement. This is not the result of emotional, mental, physical, environmental, or cultural factors.

Mentally Disabled—a child with a developmental delay that causes learning to occur at a slower pace. These children also exhibit a significantly lower level of intelligence and marked impairment in social competency skills. This category includes educable mentally disabled—IQ usually between 55 and approximately 80—and trainable mentally disabled—IQ below 55.

Multiply Handicapped—a category set aside for children who are disabled in more than one category, such as deafness and blindness.

Orthopedically Impaired—a child who is physically disabled and whose educational performance is directly affected by this condition. Such conditions as cerebral palsy and amputation fall into this category.

Other Health Impaired—a child who has limited strength, vitality, or alertness to chronic or acute health problems. Conditions which fall into this area include heart conditions, asthma, Tourette's syndrome, attention deficit hyperactive disorder, diabetes, and so on.

Partially Sighted—a child who has some functional sight, usually 20/70 or better with best correction. This student may be able to learn to read regular print with glasses or to read special books that are printed with large type.

Speech Impaired—a child with a communication disorder. These children are unable to produce speech sounds correctly, have difficulty in understanding or using words or sentences, or exhibit stuttering or some other voice impairment.

3. Reviewing, at least annually, the status of each disabled child residing within the district.

4. Evaluating the adequacy of programs, services and facilities for the disabled children in the district.

5. Reviewing and evaluating all relevant information that may appear on each disabled student.

6. Maintaining ongoing communication in writing to parents with regard to planning, modifying, changing, reviewing, placing, or evaluating the program, classification, or educational plan for a disabled child.

7. Advising the Board of Education as to the status and recommendations for all disabled children in the district.

8. Determining the least restrictive educational setting for any child having been classified as having a disability.

Most Committees on Special Education try to remain as informal as possible to reduce the anxiety of the situation. This is a crucial issue, since a parent may enter a room with numerous professionals and feel overwhelmed or intimidated. The parent member usually serves as a liaison and advocate for the parent(s), establishing contact prior to the meeting to reduce anxiety and alleviate any concerns that the parent(s) may have. School personnel should also be in contact with the parent(s) prior to the meeting to go over the process, their rights, and what may take place at the meeting. At no time should anyone in contact with the parent(s) prior to the meeting give them false hope, make promises, or second guess the CSE. What needs to be communicated are procedural issues and options and the awareness that it is the CSE that will make the recommendation, not one individual. Further, the parent(s) must be made aware of their rights, and you should make sure they understand their right to due process if they do not agree with the CSE recommendation. Making sure parents understand their rights before the meeting may reduce the possibility of conflict.

The process of identifying and finding an appropriate educational placement for a disabled child should be a joint process between the district and the family. When both work in the best interests of the child, the process can be very positive and rewarding. However, there can be times when the district and the family disagree. When this occurs, the parents or the school has the right to due process. This procedure protects the rights of both the school and the family and allows for another avenue for resolution.

The Concept of Procedural Due Process

The procedure of due process as it applies to special education describes the legal procedures and requirements developed to protect the rights of children, parents, and school districts. In respect to children suspected of having a disability, due process guarantees a free and appropriate public education in the least restrictive educational setting. For parents, due process protects their rights to have input into the educational program and placement of their child, and to have options in cases of disagreement with the recommendations of the school district. For school districts, due process offers recourse in cases of parent resistance with a request for evaluation, challenges to an independent evaluation sought by parents at public expense, or unwillingness of parents to consent to the CSE recommendation. The components of due process include the following procedural safeguards:

APPROPRIATE WRITTEN NOTICE Notice to parents is required in the following situations:

1. Actions proposed by the CSE to evaluate the existence of a suspected disability
2. Meetings by the CSE to discuss the results of the evaluation to determine a suspected disability
3. Meetings to discuss the planning of an individual educational plan
4. Proposed actions to review an individual educational plan
5. Proposed actions to reevaluate the child's classification or placement
6. Aging out notification for disabled children no longer eligible for tuition-free educational services

WRITTEN CONSENT FROM PARENTS Written consent is required in four specific situations. They are

1. Consent for an initial evaluation on a child not previously classified as having a disability
2. Consent allowing for the provisions recommended by the CSE in regard to classification and special education placement
3. Notification prior to providing services for the first time for a disabled child in a twelve-month program
4. Notification prior to the disabled child's aging out of public education

CONFIDENTIALITY OF RECORDS A parent's confidentiality of records is protected under due process. Confidentiality ensures that only educational institutions or agencies that have legitimate interest in the child's education will be permitted to see the records. However, written consent from parents is required for the release of any information on their child other than the following:

1. Staff members or school officials within the school district in which the child is a resident who must have a legitimate interest in the child's education.
2. Release of information to other school districts in which the disabled child may enroll. In this case the parents are notified of the transfer of information, may request copies of the information sent, and may contest through a hearing the content of the transferred information.

SURROGATE PARENTS In most cases the child with a suspected disability is represented by his or her parents at CSE meetings. However, if the parents are unknown or unavailable, or the child is a ward of the state, the CSE must determine if there is a need for the assignment of a surrogate parent to represent the child. When this happens, the Board of Education chooses a surrogate from a list of eligible individuals.

IMPARTIAL HEARINGS An impartial hearing is a procedure used to resolve disagreements between parents and the school district. This procedure of due process can be utilized when

1. A parent disagrees with a CSE recommendation.
2. A parent disagrees with a Board of Education determination.
3. The CSE fails to evaluate and recommend a program within thirty days of the signed consent by the parents.
4. The CSE fails to implement its recommendations within the thirty-day requirement period.
5. There is failure on the part of the school district to administer a triennial evaluation.
6. Failure on the part of the school district to hold an annual review on a disabled child.
7. Parent(s) are unwilling to give consent for an evaluation.

8. Parents are unwilling to consent to the recommendations of the CSE concerning the classification or special education placement of a disabled child.

APPEALS TO THE COMMISSIONER OF EDUCATION This option provides another level of resolution for parents and school districts when an impartial hearing cannot resolve the disagreement. This is a legal process, and the procedures are usually outlined in state manuals on the Commissioner's regulations.

WHAT THE SPECIAL EDUCATOR NEEDS TO KNOW IF ASKED TO PRESENT AT THE CSE

The responsibilities of the special education teacher on the CSE depend upon their role in the district. Your responsibilities when making a presentation will vary, but proper preparation is crucial. Keep in mind the following aspects depending upon your involvement with the case:

The Special Educator as Educational Evaluator

If your role on the committee has resulted from your educational and perceptual evaluation of the child, then you need to keep the following in mind:

1. Prior to the meeting, you should meet with the parents and go over your results. Follow the procedures outlined in Part 3.
2. Make sure that you have your report complete and typed at least one week to ten days prior to the CSE meeting. In some districts, the CSE requires that the entire packet be forwarded a week in advance.
3. Prior to the meeting, outline the important points of the report that you wish to make. Do not go through the report at the CSE meeting looking for the issues that you feel need to be discussed. Preparation will make you look more professional.
4. Make sure you report strengths as well as weaknesses.
5. Even though everyone should have copies of your report in front of them, the length of the report may make it impossible for them to filter out the crucial sections in the time allotted for the meeting. Therefore, you may want to develop a one-page summary sheet that clearly outlines what you will be presenting. This would be handed out as you begin your presentation.
6. Remember that this is not a parent conference to review the entire report. You should have done that earlier, so keep it brief and highlight the important issues. There are several individuals who may need to report results or speak, and the CSE may have several meetings that day.
7. If you feel that the nature of the case may require more time than that normally set aside by the CSE for a review, then call the chairperson and make a

request for a longer meeting time. It is very uncomfortable when crucial meetings have to be ended because of time constraints.

8. Be prepared to answer questions about your findings or some aspect of the report by either a parent, committee member, lawyer (sometimes brought by the parent), and others. Even though this may not happen, you should be ready to answer without being defensive or anxious. Carefully review your report to be prepared for questions regarding your findings.

The Special Educator as Classroom Teacher of the Child

There may be times when you will be asked as the child's classroom teacher to attend a CSE meeting for a review of classification, placement, annual review, change in an IEP, or a special meeting requested by the parent. When this occurs, keep the following in mind:

1. The first thing you need to do when you receive a request for your participation at a CSE meeting is to find out the reason for the meeting. The material required may vary, but your preparation prior to the meeting is crucial. If the meeting was called by the parents, you may want to have them in for a conference to discuss their concerns.

2. Once you know why the meeting will be held, organize yourself so that you will have information in front of you. For example, you will need

    a. The child's present academic levels in reading, math, spelling, and writing. These may be available as a result of recent individual or group achievement tests, informal evaluations that you may have administered, observation (although try to be more objective), class tests, and so on. Determine grade levels if possible, and where the child falls in comparison to others in the class.

    b. The child's present pattern of classroom behavior. Write this up in behavioral terms (factual, observable, and descriptive notes of behavior that do not include analysis or judgment).

    c. The child's present levels of social interaction and social skills.

    d. The child's interest areas and areas of strength.

    e. The child's present schedule.

    f. Samples of the child's work.

    g. Outline of parent conferences, phone conversations, or meetings and the purpose and outcome of each. These notes should be kept on an ongoing basis.

    h. Your opinion as to whether the child is benefiting from his or her present placement.

    i. Any physical limitations noted and their implication on the learning process.

    j.   Your opinion on the child's self-esteem.

    k.   Any pertinent comments made by the child that may have an impact on his or her present situation.

3. You should be well prepared to answer any questions with the foregoing information at hand. When it is your turn to present, do it in an organized manner. You may want to provide the participants with an outline of what you will be covering.

4. Try not to be defensive even if the reason for the meeting is the parents' concern over the child's placement in your class or the work load. Try to listen carefully to what the parent is really asking for; it may not be as big a problem as you may think. Try to be solution oriented, even if the parent is blame oriented.

The Special Educator as a Member of the CSE

There are times when the special education teacher will be asked to sit on the CSE to review a case even though the teacher does not have or know the child or has not evaluated him or her. The participation of the special education teacher in this situation is for their expertise in reviewing academic and perceptual material that may be presented. This material may come from other evaluators within the district or from an outside agency or professional. If your role involves this aspect, then keep the following in mind:

1. Try to get a copy of the reports prior to the meeting. In some districts, this is the procedure. If not, request it so that you can review the findings and make notes.

2. Your role here is to review and analyze the test results and offer concrete and practical suggestions to the CSE in the following ways:

    a.   Indications of areas of strength and weakness: level of severity of the problem—mild, moderate, or severe.

    b.   Educational implications in determining least restrictive placement.

    c.   Whether or not the recommendations coincide with the test result findings. For example, in some cases outside agencies or professionals will recommend resource room even though the child's scores do not reflect a disability.

    d.   Whether or not the new findings support or disagree with past scores. For this you should do some research into the child's historical academic patterns by reviewing any prior reports, achievement test scores, report card grades, and so on.

    e.   Whether or not the findings require modifications and selecting those modifications, such as a revised test format or flexible scheduling.

3. Be prepared. Do not wait until the last minute. It will look more professional if you come with notes, questions, and suggestions.

Section 9

Suggested Materials for CSE Presentations

A school may be required to gather materials for the CSE for several reasons:

1. An initial review on a new student who may have a suspected disability
2. An annual review meeting where the child's present disability and placement are reviewed
3. A triennial evaluation
4. A request for a special CSE meeting such as a change in an existing individual educational plan (IEP)

Once the review is requested, the school should prepare a packet of information for a presentation at the meeting. While state requirements may differ, a complete and well-organized packet should be sufficient for any situation.

To accomplish this task, one person may be designated as the coordinator of the case, and it would be his or her responsibility to ensure that all required material is placed in the packet. Once this is accomplished, the packet is then sent to the chairperson of the CSE prior to the meeting.

A well-organized presentation packet could include the following information:

Cover Sheet

This form gives the CSE office all the necessary identifying data on a child with a potential disability. It can also serve as a work sheet for the CSE chairperson during the meeting. An example of how this form may look is provided.

COVER SHEET

Goals Submitted and Attached to Packet: _____yes _____no

Student ID No.:_____

Goals Changed (re-review):_____yes_____no

Student Birthdate:_____

CSE Date:_____ (FOR CSE USE ONLY)

Committee: _____

_____

Also Present (for CSE use only):_____

_____

Case Presented by:_____

_____

Student Name:_____

Parent's Name(s): _____

Status: Married_____Single_____Divorced_____Widowed_____

Address: _____

_____

All correspondence and information should be sent to:

Mother_____ Father_____ Both_____ Legal Guardian_____

Current School:_____

Current Teacher (Elementary Level Only):_____

Current Grade:_____

Current Contact Teacher If Previously Classified (middle school and high school only):

_____

Guidance Counselor: _____

Dominant Language—Student:_____

Dominant Language—Home:_____

Ethnicity:_____

Reason for the Meeting (Check one):

Initial Review _____ Review of Present Classification_____

Declassification_____ Review of Placement _____ Pendency _____

Annual Review_____ Triennial Review _____

Date Entered Program (for a review case only):_____

Diploma Type:_____

Other:_____

EVALUATION INFORMATION
(test names and score type)

IQ Test Information

Test_____

VIQ_____% Rank_____

PIQ_____% Rank_____

FSIQ_____% Rank_____

Psychoeducational Test Information

Area Measured (e.g., Reading)

Test Name_____ Percentile_____ Test Date_____

Test Name_____ Percentile_____ Test Date_____

Test Name_____ Percentile_____ Test Date_____

Examiner: Psychological_____

Educational_____

Speech/Language_____

Student Name:_____SE Date: _____

Student ID: _____Student Birthdate: _____

School:_____

FOR CSE USE ONLY

Recommended:

1. Classification_____   Sec. Con._____
2. Placement_____   Staff Ratio _____
3. Related Service_____   Times/Wk _____
   Related Service_____   Times/Wk_____
   Related Service_____   Times/Wk_____
4. Adaptive Devices_____
5. Mainstreamed Classes_____

   _____

6. Test Modifications_____

   _____

   _____

7. Transportation: yes_____ no_____ Triennial Date _____
8. Special Transportation Needs_____

9. Foreign Language Exempt yes_____ no_____ NA_____
10. Service Start Date for Placement_____
    For Related Service_____
11. Related Service Provider(s)_____
12. Recommended Teacher or Contact Teacher

13. Least Restrictive Statement

CSE Packet Checklist

This checklist is a good tool to use to ensure that the school or task coordinator has included all the necessary materials required by the CSE for a particular type of review. An example of this form is included for your use.

CSE PACKET CHECKLIST

Name of Student_____

School_____ Grade_____

Type of Meeting: Initial _____ Special_____ Annual Review_____

Initial Referral

Required Forms

____A. Initial Referral to CSE from School Staff

____B. Initial Referral to CSE from Parent/Guardian

____C. Parent Consent for Evaluation

Evaluation

____Social History

____Medical Report

____Classroom Observation

____Psychological

____Educational

____Speech/Language

____Vocational (Secondary Level Only)

____Other (e.g., Occupational Therapist, Physical Therapist, ESL, Reading)

Specify_____, _____, _____

Guidance Materials

____Child's Schedule

____Transcript of Past Grades

____Latest Report Card

____Teachers' Reports

____Educational

Other

____Discipline Information

____PPT-Related Documents (e.g., minutes)

____Standardized Achievement Test Scores

____Report Cards

____Needs (Levels of Development: Social, Physical, Academic,   Management)

____Recommended Goals and Objectives (Draft)

____Attendance Records

____Other

Special Meeting

Name of Current Contact Teacher_____

____Special Meeting Referral Form

____Current Teacher(s) Report

____Recommended Goals and Objectives

____New Evaluations If Completed

____Other Documents: Specify_____

_____

Annual Review

____Prep Sheet

____Current IEP

____Evaluations Completed: Specify_____

_____

____Needs (e.g., Social, Physical)

____Recommended Goals, Objectives

____Other Documents: Specify_____

_____

Triennial Evaluation Documents

____Parent Notice of Triennial Evaluation Form

____Psychological

____Educational

____Speech/Language

_____Medical Report

_____Social History Update

_____Transcript of Grades

_____Child's Schedule

_____Recent Report Cards

_____Teacher Reports

_____Other: Specify_____

_____

Recommended CSE Participants:_____

Case Manager:_____Date:_____

INITIAL REFERRAL FORMS

There are several forms that may have to be used when referring a case for a CSE review. These forms are used for initial reviews, special meetings, and triennial evaluations.

Initial Referral to the CSE from School Staff

This form is used to alert the CSE that a case concerning a child with a suspected disability may be coming up for a review depending upon the outcome of evaluations. This occurs when the school suspects a disability. This form is forwarded with or without a signed parent consent for evaluation. If it is not sent with the signed evaluation, the CSE chairperson will send one out to the parent requesting it be signed and returned. Again local policy may differ, and many schools try to have the parent sign this consent when they meet with them to discuss the initial reasons for the referral.

REFERRAL TO THE CSE FROM SCHOOL STAFF

From _____
      Name/Title

School_____Date_____

The following student is being referred to the CSE for suspicion of a disability.

Student Name_____Grade_____

Parent/Guardian Name_____

Address_____

City_____State_____Zip_____

Telephone (   ) _____ Birthdate_____

Current Program Placement_____

Teacher (Elementary)_____

Guidance Counselor (Secondary)_____

Is there an attendance problem? yes____no____

Language spoken at home?_____

Did student repeat a grade? yes___no___ If yes, when?_____

Is an interpreter needed? yes___no___ Deaf_____

Test Scores Within Last Year (e.g., Standardized Achievement, Regents Competency)

Test	Percentile Score	Comment
_____	_____	_____
_____	_____	_____
_____	_____	_____
_____	_____	_____
_____	_____	_____
_____	_____	_____

Prior Parent Contact:_____

_____

Reasons for Referral

Describe the specific reason and/or situations that indicate that a referral to the CSE is needed. Also, indicate attempts to resolve problems within the current educational program.

Specific Reasons for Referral

_____

_____

Attempts to Resolve

_____

_____

Principal's signature_____ Date_____

Date forwarded to CSE_____

Chairperson_____

Initial Referral to the CSE from Parent/Guardian

This initial referral may be initiated by any school staff member—teacher, counselor, administrator, psychologist—or by a parent. However, if a parent requests an initial review by the CSE, a different form may be used.

INITIAL REFERRAL TO CSE FROM PARENT/GUARDIAN

Date_____

To:_____

     Principal or CSE Chairperson

I am writing to refer my child_____, age_____, to the Committee on Special Education. I am asking you to conduct an individual evaluation to determine whether a handicapping condition exists that would make my child eligible for Special Education Services.

I am concerned about my child's educational difficulties in the following areas:

Please contact me as soon as possible to discuss my referral.

Sincerely,

Parent/Guardian_____Phone_____

Address_____

City_____State_____Zip_____

Child's Birthdate_____ School_____ Grade_____

Date received by CSE_____

Parent Consent for Evaluation

State laws and/or district policies usually mandate that parent(s) must sign a consent form allowing the school to administer an evaluation of their child. As previously mentioned, the school usually obtains this form through the mail or at the initial meeting with the parent to discuss the reasons for the referral or through the mail. Either way, this consent is required before any evaluation can take place. An example of such a form is provided for you.

PARENT CONSENT FOR EVALUATION

To the Parent/Guardian of:_____

Birthdate_____

School_____Grade_____

We would like to inform you that your child_____ has been referred for individual testing because of the suspicion of a disability. Testing results will help us in determining your child's educational needs and in planning the most appropriate program. The evaluation procedures and/or tests may include the following:

Intelligence:_____

Communication/Language/Speech:_____

Physical:_____

Behavior/Emotional:_____

Academic:_____

Vocational:_____

Other:_____

Before we can begin testing, it is necessary that the School District CSE have your written permission to evaluate your child. You have had the opportunity to discuss the need for this testing and the possibilities for special educational services with the school principal/designee.

The evaluation(s) will be conducted by the multidisciplinary team who will share the results of said evaluation with you at a building level meeting. Both this meeting and a CSE meeting will be held within 30 school days of receipt of this notice.

I grant permission for the evaluation(s) mentioned above:_____

I do not grant permission for the evaluation(s) mentioned above:_____

Date_____ Parent's Signature_____

Date_____ Administrator/Designee_____

EVALUATIONS

Psychological Evaluation

A full psychological evaluation including all identifying data, reason for referral, background and developmental history, prior testing results, observations, tests administered, test results (including a breakdown of scaled scores), conclusions, and recommendations is required. This evaluation must be conducted within one year of the CSE meeting. It may also be helpful to include any prior evaluations done over the years.

Educational Evaluation

A psychoeducational evaluation including identifying data, reason for referral, academic history, prior testing results, observations, tests administered, test results, conclusions, and recommendations is required. This report should identify achievement strengths and weaknesses and perceptual strengths and weaknesses.

Speech-Language Evaluation

A speech-language evaluation including identifying data, reason for referral, observations, tests administered, test results, conclusions, and recommendations should be included if applicable. A description of the severity of the language deficit should also be included and if possible the prognosis.

Reading Teacher's Report

If indicated, a full reading evaluation including identifying data, reason for referral, observations, prior standardized reading test percentiles, tests administered, test results, conclusions, and recommendations should be included. A description of the severity of the deficit that outlines the specific areas in need of remediation should also be included.

Vocational Evaluation

A copy of the child's differential aptitude test (middle and high school only) results or other measures of vocational aptitude should be included if applicable.

Outside Reports

From time to time, parents will have a variety of reports from outside agencies, for example, medical, neurological, psychological, audiological, and visual training. These reports should be included only when they are relevant to the possible disability. If outside reports are to be used in lieu of the district's own evaluations, they should be fairly recent, for example, within the past six months to one year.

Required Assessments Related to the Suspected Disability

These measures may include the following areas: communication skills, motor abilities, hearing, vision, gross and fine motor abilities, physical therapist's evaluation, occupational therapist's evaluation, and adaptive physical education evaluation (e.g., Brunicks Oserenski).

ACADEMIC DATA

Standardized Achievement Test Data

This information should reflect standardized test score results including percentiles as far back as possible. This is included to allow the members to see patterns, strengths, weaknesses, and so on in the child's group scores.

Report Cards

> **Elementary level**—copies of all report cards including teacher comments (grades K–6)
>
> **Secondary level**—copies that should reflect quarter grades, final grades, absences, and so on, beginning from grade 7

Classroom Teacher's Reports

This report should include a behavioral description of the child's academic, social, intellectual, behavioral, and physical status. Observations should be worded in behavioral terms, and any informal testing results should be included.

Attendance and Disciplinary Reports

A listing of all disciplinary reports, including reason for referral and disposition, should be included for both elementary and secondary level. An accurate attendance record should also be included.

Student Class Schedule

A copy of the child's present class schedule should be included that clearly outlines the level of classes enrolled (e.g. modified, regents) and teacher's names.

Classroom Observation Sheet

This form must be completed by the special education teacher, psychologist, administrator, social worker, or guidance counselor. This form must be included in the CSE packet for an initial referral.

DEVELOPMENTAL DATA

Social and Developmental History Form

This form should be filled out in full with the parent present if possible. It is important that it include answers to all the information requested so that the Committee members have a thorough understanding of the child's history.

SOCIAL AND DEVELOPMENTAL HISTORY FORM

Date_____

Name_____

Sex _____

School_____ Grade_____ Birthdate_____

Address_____

_____

Telephone_____

Natural Parents_____ or Child Resides with_____ (check one)

Father's Name_____ Age_____

Education_____

Occupation_____ Business Phone_____

Mother's Name_____Age_____

Education_____

Occupation_____ Business Phone_____

Guardians or Other Individual's Names with Whom Child Resides:

Name_____

Relationship_____ Employment_____

Business Phone_____

Relationship_____ Employment_____

Business Phone_____

Siblings

Names	Ages	School
_____	_____	_____
_____	_____	_____
_____	_____	_____
_____	_____	_____
_____	_____	_____

Others in Home

Names	Ages	Relationship
_____	_____	_____
_____	_____	_____
_____	_____	_____
_____	_____	_____
_____	_____	_____
_____	_____	_____

Name:_____ School_____

Presenting Problem (as perceived by respondent)

Developmental History

Include birth and infancy periods—prenatal, birth, and postnatal facts; include any unusual aspects in attainment of developmental milestones—critical stages, traumatic experiences, falls or injuries, hospital stays, previous testing, medical conditions, medication, etc.; include any medical facts that might have an implication in the outcome of this case:

Family History

Name:_____ School_____

116

Social History

Include indications of child's conduct in social skills, involvement in groups or organizations, relationship to peers, hobbies, interests, etc.

School Adjustment (age and grade entrance to school, attendance, retention, change of schools, previous psychological evaluations, or prior reviews by CSE in another district)

Behavioral Patterns

(eating, sleeping, relationship with adults)

Other Residences

(hospitals, schools, with relatives, foster homes, etc.)

Recommendations

Individual filling out form_____

Title_____

Medical Health Record

This form is usually filled out by the nurse/teacher, then forwarded to the psychologist, and attached to the CSE packet. It contains all the child's pertinent medical history and should include results from a medical examination within the past year.

MEDICAL REPORT FOR COMMITTEE
ON SPECIAL EDUCATION

To be completed by the nurse/teacher and included in the CSE Packet.

Date_____

Student's Name_____ Grade_____

Address_____

City_____ State_____ Zip_____

Date of last medical examination_____

Name and address of physician_____

_____

Medical findings (attach copy if pertinent)_____

_____

Last vision exam_____

Results_____

Last hearing exam_____

Results_____

Speech_____

Additional information that might have implications in determining the outcome of this case:

© 1994 by The Center for Applied Research in Education

OTHER REQUIRED INFORMATION AND PROCEDURES

Written Consent for Evaluation

A copy of this signed form should be included in the packet so that the committee has a record of this consent and has an indication of the thirty-day time limit requirement.

Draft of Recommended Objectives and Goals

Appropriate members of the pupil personnel team (PPT) should develop a draft of initial goals and objectives. These goals and objectives will be used in the development of the IEP at the time of the CSE meeting. These goals and objectives may be modified at the time of the meeting. The form, specific goals and objectives from which to choose, and other factors may differ from district to district.

Some districts may develop this form at the time of the meeting and may not require a prior draft. However, it is recommended that if this is the case, prepare yourself anyway with your own recommended goals and objectives so that you can contribute to the IEP at the time of the meeting.

Statement of Least Restrictive Environment

If a PPT is recommending additional services under a classifying condition, please state the reasons why additional services or less restrictive environment would be necessary. This statement is also very important if the PPT feels that the child's needs may be better served in an out-of-district placement. While the final decision for placement is up to the CSE, the school still needs to substantiate its recommendation.

Parent Given Rights Booklet Prior to CSE Meeting

A parent must be given a copy of the state booklet on parent's rights prior to the CSE meeting. This will give the parent(s) the opportunity to become familiar with the procedure and allow them time to develop any questions that they might have.

Agreement to Withdraw CSE Referral

There may be times when the parent and school agree that the evaluation and findings do not seem to substantiate the suspected disability that was originally considered. When this occurs the school and parent must meet and discuss other methods that will be used to remediate the problem(s). At the time of the meeting, an *Agreement to Withdraw the CSE Referral* form must be filled out and forwarded to the principal and then to the CSE chairperson. This will officially withdraw the original referral and stop the CSE process.

There are usually time requirements and constraints with this procedure so check with your district and state policies.

AGREEMENT TO WITHDRAW CSE REFERRAL

Initial Conference

Student Name_____

Date of Agreement_____

Date of Birth_____Date of Referral_____

Current Program_____

Name of Referring Party_____

Position of Referring Party_____

Persons Present at Conference

The following method (s) will be used to attempt to resolve _____ identified learning difficulties: (attach additional sheets, as needed)

If necessary, a follow-up conference to review the student's progress will be held on _____

We agree to the above conditions. The referral is hereby withdrawn.

Referring Party Signature_____

Date_____

Parent/Guardian Signature_____ Date_____

CC: Student's Cumulative Educational Record

Parent/Guardian

Referring Party

Learning Profile—For CSE Packet

LEARNING PROFILE—FOR CSE PACKET

Name_____Grade_____

School_____ Birthdate_____

Address_____

City_____ State_____ Zip_____

Phone_____ Date _____

1. Self-concept

2. Peer Relationships

3. Adult Relationships

4. Intellectual Characteristics

5. Academic Characteristics

6. Modality Strengths and Weaknesses

7. Environmental Factors

8. Classroom Structure

9. Prior Evaluations

10. Attention to Task

11. Motivation

12. Response to Pressure

13. Response to Difficulty

14. Organizational Ability

15. Special Skills, Talents, Interests

16. Home Environment

17. Medical or Physical Problems

The CSE referral process and materials are a major factor in the process of identifying a student with a disability. These materials become part of the child's official record and contain crucial information that could benefit educators who work with the child.

Section 10

Understanding Individual Educational Plans

The individual educational plan is a legally binding contract of services provided by a school district for children classified as having a disability. Only children who are classified by the CSE receive an IEP. While certain information is required by each state to be included in this document, there is no specific form that a school district must follow. As a result you have as many different-looking IEPs as there are school districts.

There are basically seven general sections to any IEP:

1. General identifying data
2. Current placement data
3. Recommendations by the CSE
4. Goals and objectives
5. Mastery levels
6. Evaluation procedures
7. Testing and classroom modifications

Each section will be dealt with individually but all are tied together to form one individual educational plan.

GENERAL IDENTIFYING DATA

Under this section the school district provides information on a variety of different areas pertaining to a child's background. The information for this section is taken from the background history form. This section may include

Name
Address
Phone
Birthdate
Parent's Names
Dominant Language of Child
Dominant Language Spoken at Home
Date Child Entered Program (this is filled in only for previously classified students and basically informs the reader about when the child first started receiving special education services)

CURRENT PLACEMENT DATA

This section contains all the necessary information pertaining to the current educational placement of the child. This information is usually taken from evaluation reports, prior IEPs (if child has already been classified), school records, and so on. It includes

Classification—this is filled in if the child had been presently classified.

Grade—present grade.

Current Placement—regular class for an initial review by the CSE or present special education setting if child has already been classified.

Class Size Ratio—only filled in for previously classified students.

Length of Program—ten- or twelve-month program

School—present school.

Teacher—child's present teacher or guidance counselor if a secondary level student.

Diploma—this will either be a local diploma or an IEP diploma—can be given to classified students who may not meet the school requirements for graduation but have accomplished all the objectives on their IEP.

Transportation—this is filled in if the child is presently receiving special transportation arrangements.

Physical Education—present class type (e.g., regular, adaptive).

Annual Review Date—usually April, May, or June of the school year.

Triennial Review Date—usually three years from the date of the last full evaluation.

Intelligence Test Results—must be within one year of review by CSE and indicates Verbal, Performance, or Full-Scale IQ.

RECOMMENDATIONS BY THE CSE

Under this section the recommendations of the CSE meeting are recorded indicating the proposed plan of placement and services until the annual review or any CSE meeting called to reevaluate the IEP. This can normally be done by the school or parent if a change or addition to an IEP is requested. As a rule, no changes to this document can take place without a full meeting of the CSE. This is a very important section of the IEP since it indicates to the reader the plan for special educational services for the coming year. Information contained in this section might include the following:

Classification—the child must fit the criteria for one of the state-defined classification categories, and the disability must significantly impede his or her ability to learn.

Grade—projected grade for the coming year.

Placement—this depends upon the child's least restrictive educational setting.

Class Size Ratio—an indication of the maximum student population allowed, the number of teachers required, and the number of assistant teachers or aides required. This is discussed at length in Section 12.

Length of Program—some special education programs maintain a ten-month calendar. Programs for more seriously disabled students may be twelve months long.

School—projected school for the coming year.

Teacher—identifies the child's contact teacher for the coming year. When a child has several special education teachers as in a departmentalized special education high school program, one teacher is assigned as the contact teacher. On the elementary and secondary levels, it can also be the resource room teacher, if the child is assigned there, or the child's self-contained special education teacher if this more restrictive program is used.

Program Initiation Date—indicates when the special education services will begin.

Transportation Needs—indicates whether or not the child has special transportation needs as with a severely physically handicapped child who may require door-to-door service with a special bus to allow easy access and departure.

Physical Education—indicates whether the child is being recommended for regular physical education or adaptive physical education means a specially designed program of developmental activities, games, sports, and rhythms suited to the interests, capacities, and limitations of pupils with disabilities who may not safely or successfully engage in unrestricted participation in the activities of the regular physical education program.

Related Services—indicates other services that the child will be receiving that support the academic special education process. Also noted in this section would be the number of sessions per week, minutes per session, maximum group size, start date, and end date. Related services may include

In-school individual counseling

In-school group counseling

Resource room

Speech-language therapy

Occupational therapy

Physical therapy

Art therapy

Adaptive physical education

Mainstreamed Courses—a listing must be included on the IEP if the child's disability allows for any mainstreamed class in which the student will participate.

Special Classes—indicates the types of special education classes the child will have in the coming year (e.g., math, social studies, health)

Testing Information—reviews the academic test results, including the tests administered, date administered, percentile, and or age or grade equivalents.

Comments—indicates any questions, reminders, reviews, parents concerns, identified areas of strengths and weakness, and progress to date.

GOALS AND OBJECTIVES

There are usually two separate parts to this section. The first deals with general social, physical, academic, and management goals (SPAM goals) that relate to the environment and specific conditions under which the child will be learning or learns best.

Examples of these are as follows:

Social Development—means the degree and quality of the pupil's relationships with peers and adults, feelings about self, and social adjustment to school and community environments.

Physical Development—means the degree or quality of the pupil's motor and sensory development, health, vitality, and physical skills or limitations that pertain to the learning process.

Academic Characteristics—means the levels of knowledge and development in subject and skill areas, including activities of daily living, level of intellectual functioning, adaptive behavior, expected rate of progress in acquiring skills, and information and learning style.

Management Needs—means the nature and degree to which environmental modifications and human material resources are required to enable the pupil to benefit from instruction.

The second part of this section deals with the specific academic goals and objectives that will be remediated. The basis for this area comes from the evaluation and the diagnosis of strengths and weaknesses. Also included in this section may be specific content area goals, for example, science, social studies, math, and English, if the child is in a special education setting for these subjects.

Examples of these types of goals and objectives follow.

MASTERY LEVELS

When determining an objective, mastery levels need to be considered. A **mastery level** is a predetermined level of competency indicating a clear understanding of a particular skill. This is the teacher's way of validating a child's movement to the next objective.

Setting the mastery levels too low will increase the possibilities of luck or chance influencing success, while setting them too high may set the child up for constant frustration and failure because of careless mistakes or minute errors. Mastery levels can be indicated according the following standards:

Ratio-based mastery level—John will be able to...eight out of every ten attempts

Percentage-based mastery level—Mary will be able to...75 percent of the time

Time-based mastery level—Ben will be able to...12 responses within a ten-minute period

There may be times when one general statement of mastery level can apply to all the objectives, for example, "All objectives will be completed with 80 percent accuracy."

EVALUATIVE MEASURES

Some IEPs may include measures or techniques that will be used to evaluate the success levels for each objective. These techniques or measures are used to qualify the mastery levels applied to each objective and indicate whether or not the child has accomplished the objective and is competent enough to move to the next objective. There are many available:

- Student assignments and projects
- Informal conferences between student and teacher
- Student self-evaluation
- Textbook tests and quizzes
- Standardized tests
- Review of quarterly report cards
- Discussions with classroom teachers
- Parent-teacher conferences
- Record of attendance
- Stanford Diagnostic Test
- Teacher-made tests
- Teacher evaluation
- Homework assignments
- Criterion-referenced tests

ALTERNATE TESTING MODIFICATIONS

Children classified by the CSE are entitled to alternate testing and classroom modifications as long as there is substantiated evidence for such a need in the testing or background of the child. There are no limits as to the number of modifications, but include them in the IEP only if they will enable the child to be more successful in school.

Examples of these modifications include

- Flexible scheduling in testing
- Testing in a flexible setting
- A revised test format
- Extended time for testing
- Revised test direction
- The opportunity to record answers in any manner
- The use of a calculator for testing
- The use of a tape recorder for testing
- The use of a typewriter or word processor
- The use of a Braille writer
- Questions or test may be read
- Not penalized for spelling errors on tests
- The use of a typewriter/computer/word processor for written work to compensate for handwriting/spelling deficits
- Enlarged print
- Enlarged answer sheets

What Special Education Teachers Need to Know About Testing Modifications

Alternate testing techniques are modifications that take into account the individual needs of a child having a disability and as a result modify testing procedures or formats. These modifications attempt to provide these students with equal opportunity to participate in testing situations.

These techniques, which must appear on the student's IEP, provide the opportunity to demonstrate a disabled student's mastery of skills without being unfairly restricted by the presence of that disability.

STUDENT ELIGIBILITY FOR USE OF TESTING TECHNIQUES

Only students who have been identified as having a disability by the Committee on Special Education normally receive alternate testing techniques. However, there are three other possible avenues that can be taken to provide alternate testing techniques without being classified.

1. The law usually allows the school principal the authority to approve testing modifications that do not alter the intended purpose of a test for a student who may have a disability not severe enough to warrant identification by the CSE. An example of this may be a student who has attention deficit disorder (ADD) and as a result may have some mild problems but they do not constitute a severe discrepancy in his or her functioning.
2. For certain tests (e.g., college entrance SATs), two pieces of documentation from outside professionals (not working in the same agency) indicating the need for alternate testing techniques (e.g., untimed tests) may allow the student these privileges even thought they have not been identified by the CSE.
3. Students receiving transitional services (these services are provided to students having been declassified by the CSE) are entitled to receive services and/or modifications up to one year after declassification.

CRITERIA FOR ALTERNATE TESTING TECHNIQUES

Alternate testing techniques are determined by the CSE for students identified as having a disability. The Committee takes into account several variables when making this determination:

1. The individual needs of the child as determined by evaluation, observation, background history, and other pertinent information presented at the CSE meeting
2. The necessity for modification in light of the student's past academic and test performance without modifications
3. The student's potential benefit from the modification

The CSE tries to keep in mind that all students could benefit from alternate testing techniques, and as a result a recommendation based just on potential to enhance performance may be inappropriate. The need for modifications must be substantiated in the evaluation results.

ALTERNATE TESTING TECHNIQUES THAT MODIFY MANNER OF PRESENTATION

Alternate testing techniques that modify a student's manner of presentation constitute the largest category of modifications that may appear on a student's IEP. These are separated into several categories and each contains several options.

Flexible Scheduling

This modification is usually provided for students who may have problems in the rate by which they process information, for example, physical disabilities such as motor or visual impairments. Examples of modifications that fall under this category are the following:

◆ Administration of untimed tests
◆ Administration of a test in several sessions during the course of the day
◆ Administration of a test in several sessions over several days

Flexible Setting

This modification allows disabled students to take a test in another setting other than a regular classroom. This may become necessary in cases where a child has health impairments and may be unable to leave home or the hospital or where a child's disability interferes with his or her remaining on task. In other cases a disabled student may require special lighting or acoustics or a specially equipped room. Examples include the following:

◆ Individual administration of a test in a separate location
◆ Small-group administration of a test in a separate location
◆ Provisions for special lighting

- Provisions for special acoustics
- Provisions for adaptive or special furniture
- Administration of test in a location with minimal distractions

Revised Test Format

This modification is utilized by students whose disability may interfere with their ability to take a test using the standard test format, for example, students with visual or perceptual disabilities who may not be able to read regular size print. Examples include the following:

- Use of a large-print edition
- Increased spacing between items
- Reduction in the number of items per page
- Use of a Braille edition
- Increased size of answer bubbles on test answer forms
- Rearrangement of multiple-choice items with answer bubble right next to each choice

Revised Test Directions

This modification allows students with certain disabilities a greater chance of understanding directions and thereby successfully completing a test.

- Ability to have directions read to child
- Ability to reread the directions for each page of questions
- Ability to simplify the language in the directions
- Ability to provide additional examples

Use of Aids

Some disabled students require the use of aids in order to interpret test items, for example, hearing impaired children. These may include the following:

- Auditory amplification devices
- Visual magnification devices
- Auditory tape of questions
- Masks or markers to maintain the student's place on a page
- Having questions read to the student
- Having questions signed to the student

ALTERNATE TESTING TECHNIQUES THAT MODIFY MANNER OF RESPONSE

Use of Aids

These modifications allow disabled students to record their answers to examination questions in something other than the conventional manner. These techniques may include the following:

- Use of a tape recorder
- Use of a typewriter
- Use of a communication device
- Use of a word processor
- Use of an amanuensis (secretary)

Revised Format

Some disabled students may be unable to record their responses to test questions on conventional answer forms and as a result require a change in the test format. These may include the following:

- The ability to record answers directly in the test booklet
- The ability to increase the spacing between questions or problems
- The ability to increase the size of the answer blocks
- The ability to provide cues (stop sign, arrows) directly on the answer form

ALTERNATE TESTING TECHNIQUES THAT MODIFY PROCESS USED TO DERIVE RESPONSE

Use of Aids

Some students may possess the innate ability to process mathematical information, but may have a disability that prohibits them from using paper and pencil to solve computations. Other disabled students may not be able to memorize arithmetic facts but can solve difficult word problems. When these problems occur with disabled students, the following modifications can be used:

- Use of a calculator
- Use of an abacus
- Use of arithmetic tables

SPECIAL EDUCATION TEACHER'S ROLE
AND RESPONSIBILITIES FOR IMPLEMENTATION
OF ALTERNATE TESTING TECHNIQUES

The special education teacher provides a crucial role in the implementation of alternate testing techniques. This is accomplished in the following ways:

1. A special education evaluator provides a clear understanding of a child's strength and weakness areas, learning style, and the effects of the child's disability upon academic performance. With this information in hand, the special education teacher can analyze the need for specific modifications that can be substantiated by the results of the evaluation.

2. A special education teacher in a self-contained special education classroom comes in direct contact with the student in classroom instruction. This experience provides a strong basis for recommending specific changes or additions to the modifications on a student's IEP.

3. The special education teacher on the CSE provides background experience that can assist the committee in recommending appropriate test modifications that may become part of a initial referral IEP, initiate changes in an IEP during an annual review, or modify alternate testing techniques as the result of a report from an outside agency.

4. The special education teacher can also assist the parent of a special education student in understanding alternate testing techniques and available options.

5. The special education teacher may serve as a consultant to teachers, parents, and administrators and offer advice on testing modifications to students.

6. The special education teacher may monitor the implementation of assigned modifications for a particular student to ensure that the student's rights are being followed.

Section 12

Least Restrictive Educational Placements

The concept of **least restrictive education (LRE)** applies to the placement of disabled students in the most advantageous educational placement suitable for their needs. Contrary to the belief of many teachers and parents, LRE does not mean that every disabled student should be placed in a regular classroom. The concept should be fully understood by special education teachers so they can relieve the anxiety of teachers, parents and students when it comes to appropriate educational placement.

The placement of disabled students is the responsibility of the Committee on Special Education with the input of staff and consent of parents. The CSE must analyze all the available information and determine the best "starting placement" for the child that will ensure success and provide the child with the highest level of stimulation and experience for his or her specific disability and profile of strengths and weaknesses.

To accomplish this task, the CSE has a variety of placements from which to choose. These placements range in levels of restriction, including class size, student teacher ratio, length of program, and degree of mainstreaming.

In the normal course of events, it is hoped that children are placed in a more restrictive environment only if it is to their educational advantage. However, they should be moved to a less restrictive setting as soon as they are capable of being educated in that environment.

The placements listed next follow a path from least restrictive to most restrictive.

1. **Regular Class Placement**—This placement is the least restrictive placement for all nondisabled children. However, this placement alone without some type of special education supportive services is not suitable for a disabled child and is usually not considered suitable by the CSE.

2. **Regular Class Placement with Consulting Teacher Assistance**—A consultant teacher model is used when supportive special education services are required but the CSE feels that the child will be better served while remaining in the classroom rather than be pulled out for services. Since the child remains within the class, even though he or she is receiving services, this placement is considered the next LRE setting.

3. **Regular Class Placement with Some Supportive Services**—This placement may be used with mildly disabled students who require supportive services but can remain in the regular class for the majority of the day. The services that may be applied to this level include adaptive physical education, speech

and language therapy, in school individual or group counseling, physical therapy, and occupational therapy.

4. **Regular Class Placement with Specialist Assistance**—These services (services subcontracted by the district and provided by outside agencies) are usually provided for students when the disability is such that the district wishes to maintain the child in the district but there are not a sufficient number of students with that disability to warrant hiring a teacher. An example of this may be a hard-of-hearing child who can maintain a regular class placement as long as supportive itinerant services by a teacher specializing in hearing impairments are provided.

5. **Regular Class Placement with Resource Room Assistance**—This placement is usually provided for students who need supportive services but can successfully remain within the regular classroom for the majority of the day. This type of program is a "pull-out" program and the services are usually provided in a separate room. The teacher ratio with this type of service is usually 5:1, and the amount of time spent within the resource room cannot exceed 50 percent of the child's day.

6. **Special Class Placement with Mainstreaming**—This placement is for students who need a more restrictive setting for learning, or for behavioral or intellectual reasons, cannot be successful in a full-time regular class or with a "pull-out" supportive service but can be successfully mainstreamed for a part of the school day. The nature of the mainstream is determined by the special education teacher.

7. **Full-Time Special Class in a Regular School**—This placement is viewed as the LRE setting for students whose disability does not permit successful participation in any type of regular class setting, even for part of the day. These are students who usually require a very structured, closely monitored program on a daily basis but not so restrictive as to warrant an out-of-district placement. These students can handle the rules and structure of a regular school building, but not the freedom or style of a less restrictive setting within the school.

8. **Special Day School Outside the School District**—This type of restrictive educational setting is desirable for students whose disability is so severe that they may require a more totally therapeutic environment and closer monitoring by specially trained special education teachers or staff members. The child is transported by district expense to the placement setting—many state policies try to discourage travel time on the bus to more than one hour.

   These types of programs may have student-teacher ratios of 6:1:1, 6:1:2, 9:1:1, 9:1:2, 12:1:1, or 15:1:1, depending upon the severity of the child's disability. The more severe the disability, the lower the number of the student-teacher ratio. These programs can run ten or twelve months, again depending upon the severity of the disability and the individual needs of the child.

9. **Residential School**—Residential placements are considered the next most restrictive placement. Not only does the disabled student receive his or her

education within this setting but usually resides there for the school term. The nature and length of home visits depend upon several factors that are usually determined by the residential school staff after evaluation and observation. For some students home visits may not take place at all, while others may go home every weekend.

Some students are placed in residential placements by the court. In this case, the child's local school district is only responsible to provide the costs of the educational portion, including related services if needed.

10. **Homebound Instruction**—This very restrictive setting is usually provided for students who are in the process of transition between programs and have yet to be placed. It should never be used as a long-term placement because of the social restriction and limitations.

    This option is also used when a child is restricted to his or her house because of an illness, injury, and so on, and this option remains the only realistic educational service until the child recovers. Homebound instruction requires an adult at home when the teacher arrives or can be held at a community center, library, or some other site deemed appropriate by the CSE.

11. **Hospital or Institution**—The most restrictive setting used is a hospital or institutional setting. While this is the most restrictive setting, it may be the LRE setting for certain students, for example, attempted suicide by an adolescent, pervasive clinical depression, or severe or profound retardation.

In conclusion, the least restrictive educational setting is not something that is etched in concrete. It is something that is normally looked at every year during the annual review, and changes are made in either direction if the situation requires such a change.

Section 13

The Special Educator's Role in the Annual Review Process

Another important role for the special education teacher is demonstrated in the annual review process. This review is a legal responsibility of the district and must be provided to all classified students who reside within the school district. The review involves a yearly evaluation by the CSE of the student's classification and educational program. Included in these two general areas are a review of related services provided, the need to add or remove test modifications, parents' concerns or requests, academic progress, transportation needs, and goals and objectives for the upcoming school year.

As with a regular CSE meeting, there are several people who may attend this meeting (this may vary from district to district), including the director of special education services or assignee, school psychologist, parent member, parent(s) of the child, guidance counselor (secondary level), assigned teacher (at the secondary level this may be the classroom teacher in a self-contained class), resource room teacher if this is the only service provided, or one of the child's special education teachers in a special education departmentalized program), classroom teacher (elementary level), speech and language therapist (if the child classification requires attendance), the child (if the professionals feel that the child could benefit from the discussion or may be able to shed light on a concern or recommendation being considered), and any other individual deemed necessary.

The role of the special education teacher is a very important one since a great deal of the information provided will come from this area. Consequently, many of the recommendations, changes, or additions may result from what the special education teacher reports to the CSE during the annual review. Therefore, this meeting should be taken very seriously since it will determine the child's educational direction and objectives for the coming year. As a result you should be prepared and familiar with the following materials:

- Any pre- and poststandarized test scores indicating the child's academic progress for the year
- A copy of the child's report card clearly outlining grades and attendance for the year
- Suggested goals and objectives for the coming year
- An evaluation indicating whether or not the child benefited from the modifications allowed on his or her IEP, and the reasons why they may or may not have been beneficial

- If applicable, recommendations for additional test modifications
- If applicable, recommendations for additional related services and the reasons why
- If applicable, recommendations for reduction of related services and the reasons why
- Samples of the child's work over the course of the year
- A review of the child's overall social progress for the year

This information should be sufficient to present a professional judgment of the child's progress and needs for the coming year.

Section 14

The Special Educator's Role in Triennial Evaluations

One of the responsibilities for the special education teacher may be involvement in the **triennial evaluation** (a complete and updated evaluation required every three years for all children classified as having a disability by the Committee on Special Education). This is a very important phase of the special education process because it reviews the factors that accounted for the child's classification and placement.

There are several phases to the triennial evaluation that may involve many staff members from a variety of disciplines. The objectives for the special education teacher in the triennial evaluation include the following:

1. To retest the child's achievement skill areas.
2. To retest the child's perceptual skill areas.
3. To analyze the results and compare the similarities in patterns to past evaluation results.
4. To write a detailed and comprehensive updated report of the findings which will be shared with the Committee on Special Education as well as the staff and parents.
5. To participate in the annual review meeting (a required yearly meeting for all classified students at which time the child's classification and educational placement are reviewed) and discuss the results to help the Committee on Special Education make a decision on continuation of classification and services or **declassification** (an option considered by the CSE when the classified child no longer requires special education services to maintain success in mainstream classes).
6. To share the results with parents.
7. To help interpret and analyze achievement and perceptual test results that may be submitted from outside agencies or professionals pertinent to the triennial evaluation of a specific child. This can occur if the parent chooses an independent evaluation.

It should be noted that a new release for testing involving a triennial evaluation is not required by law. The school may proceed with this process without a new release but must inform the parents that the process will be taking place. An example of that communication to parents might look like this:

PARENT NOTICE LETTER OF TRIENNIAL EVALUATION

Date _____

To Parents/Guardian of:_____

Dear Parents,

Please be advised that the Committee on Special Education has arranged for a comprehensive reevaluation of your child which, according to state regulations, is required every three years.

The school psychologist will be available to review all the results with you when the reevaluation is completed. If you have any questions, please don't hesitate to call the school psychologist or me.

A Statement of Parents' Rights is enclosed for your information.

Sincerely,

The reevaluations to be done are

_____

_____

_____

An example of a Statement of Parent's rights appears below:

Statement of Parent's Rights

Dear Parent(s):

It is important that you be aware of, and understand, that you have the following rights in accordance with Section _____ of the Regulations of the Commissioner of Education:

1. To inspect all school files, records, and reports pertaining to your child. Such reports shall be available for duplication at reasonable cost.

2. To obtain an independent educational evaluation at public expense if you disagree with the evaluation obtained by the school district. However, the school district may initiate a hearing to show that its evaluation is appropriate. Such services may be obtained at

_____

_____

3. To obtain free or low-cost legal services at no cost to the school district. Such services may be obtained at

_____

_____

4. To appeal the recommendations of the Committee on Special Education and request, in writing, an impartial formal hearing to determine the appropriateness of the proposed placement to change the program.

The impartial formal hearing will be conducted in accordance with the following rules:

- The board of education or trustees shall appoint an impartial hearing officer to conduct the hearing. The hearing officer shall be authorized to administer oaths and to issue subpoenas in connection with the administrative proceedings before him or her.

- A written or electronic verbatim record of the proceedings before the hearing officer shall be maintained and made available to the parties.

- At all stages of the proceeding, where required, interpreters of the deaf, or interpreters fluent in the dominant language of pupil's home, shall be provided at district expense.

- The impartial hearing officer shall preside at the hearing and shall provide all parties an opportunity to present evidence and testimony.

- The parties to the proceeding may be represented by legal counsel or individuals with special knowledge or training with respect to the problems of children with disabilities, and may be accompanied by other persons of their choice.

- Unless a surrogate parent shall have previously been assigned, the impartial hearing officer shall determine whether the interests of the parent are opposed to or inconsistent with those of the child, or whether for any other reason the interests of the child would best be protected by assignment of surrogate parent, and, where he so determines, the impartial hearing officer shall designate a surrogate parent to protect the interests of such child.

- The hearing shall be closed to the public unless the parent requests an open hearing.

- The parents, school authorities, and their respective counsel or representative shall have an opportunity to present evidence and to confront and question all witnesses at that hearing. Each party shall have the right to prohibit the introduction of any evidence the substance of which has not been disclosed to such party at least five days before the hearing.

- The parents shall have the right to determine whether the child shall attend the hearing.

- The impartial hearing officer shall render a decision, and mail a copy of the decision to the parents and to the board of education, not later than 45 calendar days after the receipt by the board of education of a request for a hearing or after the initiation of such hearing by the board. The decision of the impartial hearing officer shall be based solely upon the record of the proceeding before the impartial hearing officer, and shall set forth the reasons and the factual basis for the determination. The decision shall also include a statement of such a decision by the commissioner in accordance with Subdivision ___ of the hearing officer, the board of education shall mail a copy of such decision, after deleting any personally identifiable information, to the Office of Children with Handicapping Conditions, State Education Department, for the use of the State advisory panel.

- A review of the decision of a hearing officer rendered in accordance with Subdivision___ of this section may be obtained by an appeal to the commissioner. The written decision of the commissioner, a copy of which will be mailed to the parent and board of education, shall be final.

The triennial review is required to be completed no later than three years from the previous date of testing. Therefore, it is important to maintain an updated list each year of all students that will be up for a triennial evaluation that year. Begin early enough so that you meet the deadlines in the law and avoid any problems. Lateness could create some concern from administrators as well as parents.

While the special education teacher is updating the child's achievement and perceptual levels, other professionals may be involved in the triennial evaluation as well. This may include the psychologist, speech and language therapist, nurse teacher, social worker, guidance counselor, classroom teacher(s), and parents. The entire triennial packet is outlined in the following form:

TRIENNIAL REVIEW FORM—REQUIRED MATERIALS

To:

Referring School_____

From:_____

Date:_____

Re:_____

Grade_____

Check Off

Evaluations

_____New Psychological Evaluation(s)

_____New Psychoeducational Evaluation(s)

_____New Speech/Language Evaluation(s)—If Applicable

_____Outside Reports—If Applicable

Academic Data

_____Most Recent Report Card

_____Classroom Teachers' Reports

Developmental Data

_____New Social and Developmental History Form

Other Required Information and Procedures

_____Parent Letter of Triennial Review Sent

_____Medical Update

Classroom Management Techniques for Special Education Teachers

Section 15

Classroom Management of Different Personality Styles

This section is designed to offer you some practical information concerning a variety of children you may find in your classroom. It is also hoped that this information will help you identify and better understand those children who may have personality problems.

This information does not intend to replace therapeutic treatment. For that, you should use all the resources available, such as guidance counselors, nurses, doctors, school psychologists, and outside agencies, for consultation.

Regardless of the resources used, however, the brunt of coping with children's personality problems falls on the teacher. A teacher with an intelligent, constructive, and immediate attitude and actions can be a tremendous help to children.

You may also want to keep in mind that there are many overlapping characteristics in the "types" of personalities mentioned. Also, every child does not evidence all the symptoms listed. You should look for a pattern of behavior but always keep in mind that there is something to like about every child. This section deals with the Aggressive Child, the Withdrawn Child, the Underachieving Child, the Frightened Child, and the Slow Learner.

THE AGGRESSIVE CHILD

Symptoms

- Looks for trouble
- Wants his or her own way
- Is always on the defensive
- Blames others for inappropriate behavior
- Is quarrelsome
- Disrupts class and the routine procedures
- Destroys property
- Is resentful, defiant, rude, sullen, or insolent
- Defies authority
- May bully other children

Possible Reasons for Behavior

- Domineering, overstrict parent
- Weak overindulgent parents who give into the child's every whim
- Fear of expressing feelings to his or her parents—takes it out on other children
- Lack of parents' affection
- Unhappiness in his or her relations with others
- Masking intense feelings of vulnerability or inadequacy

Teaching/Management Suggestions

- Direct child's energy to keep him or her busy.
- Give child large-muscle activities to do.
- Give child leadership responsibilities.
- Place child on a daily progress report so that positive changes are seen immediately.
- Reprimand child in private.
- Attempt to reach or make friends with child.
- Meet with child more often privately on a one-to-one basis.
- Give simple but definite standards of conduct.
- Hold conferences with parents and student.
- Let child work with modeling clay to release frustrations.
- Recommend individual or group in-school counseling.
- Shape positive behavior with success-oriented tasks.
- Try to reward or compliment child when he or she least expects it.

Things to Keep in Mind

- Improvement will usually be slow, especially if symptoms have been historic.
- Parents may not recognize or may deny the problem.
- There will be relapses even with improvement.
- Arguing will not solve the problem.
- Review your own feelings and actions toward the child.
- Be sure the child's actions are not just "normal" misbehaving.

THE WITHDRAWN CHILD

Symptoms

- Talks in a very soft voice
- Sits quietly most of the time

- Has difficulty in carrying on a conversation
- Withdraws and hangs back
- Has few if any friends
- Has difficulty making decisions
- May be fearful of adults
- Tires without apparent reason
- Avoids contact with people

Possible Reasons for Behavior

- Family may be the same way
- Fear of failure; child may come from an overly critical home and does not want try anything new
- Parents may be perfectionists
- Low-energy levels resulting from depression
- Extremely overprotected
- Learned helplessness

Teaching/Management Suggestions

- Praise, notice, and talk with the child.
- Find occasions for errands—first with no oral message and later with very simple messages.
- Always call on child when volunteering.
- Have a smile ready for child any time you catch his or her eye.
- Use puppets and have child talk for the puppet.
- Encourage child's interest in collecting things such as baseball cards or coins.
- Assign routine tasks with automatic rotation such as leading the pledge or taking the lunch count.
- Try to involve the child in a group with other shy children in the school.
- Consult with parents and professionals if a pattern exists.

Things to Keep in Mind

- The child will need to know exactly what to do in each situation.
- Pushing the child into the limelight may make the situation worse.
- Make sure other students don't always do things for the child or always come to the rescue.
- Recognize that courage follows success.
- Improvement will be slow and growth may be gradual.
- Determine if child may have some health problem or hidden physical abnormality.

THE UNDERACHIEVING CHILD

Symptoms

- Avoids effort—dawdles over writing assignments
- Does messy, incomplete work
- Waits for help and does not try to solve problems
- Tends to be listless and careless
- Seldom volunteers
- Gives many excuses for failure to complete work
- Is slow in starting a task or assignment—can't find pencil or paper; is slow in doing or finishing anything
- Daydreams
- Fails to concentrate on work

Possible Reasons for Behavior

- Frustration—work is too difficult
- Inappropriate parental expectations
- Too many failures and too few successes
- Little praise and much criticism
- Lack of challenging school work
- Health or physical deficiencies
- Cover-up for lack of ability
- Lack of adequate sleep

Teaching/Management Suggestions

- Praise child for each effort.
- Study child's home life; talk to parents.
- Help develop a skill or hobby at which child might succeed
- Overlook minor failures.
- Study results of diagnostic tests for clues.
- Adjust work to child's ability level.
- Time child's assignments and try to have student beat his or her record
- See that child starts work more promptly by helping him or her through transitions.
- Use shorter but more frequent assignments.

Things to Keep in Mind

- Underachievement is not normal—it is a symptom.
- A child who appears lazy has some sort of problem.

- Praise for good work promotes activity.
- Apparent signs of laziness may disappear in later stages of development.
- Underachievement is not necessarily an indication of intelligence.
- A capable student's work should meet certain standards before acceptance.

THE FRIGHTENED CHILD

Symptoms

- Panics easily or gets frustrated
- Shows anxiety
- Withdraws
- May tremble at the slightest provocation
- May be moody
- May be overly afraid of being hurt
- Rarely takes chances
- May be extremely emotional
- Fears criticism
- Requires constant reassurance

Possible Reasons for Behavior

- Parents who also have fears and openly express them
- Death or injury to someone close to them
- Overly protective parents
- A history of unfortunate or traumatic experiences
- Constant and harsh punishments
- Slow physical development
- Bullying playmates

Teacher/Management Suggestions

- Try a variety of creative activities to release child's fears.
- Have child write an article on "Things That Make Me Afraid"
- Reassure child whenever he or she shows fear.
- Suggest to the parents that they seek outside consultation if the pattern is historical.
- Give child work at which he or she can succeed.
- Build up child's confidence by using a variety of success-oriented tasks.
- Praise child for his or her accomplishments.
- Explain that others also have fears.

- Check child's health record.
- Organize a group of other children with the same condition.

Things to Keep in Mind

- Fears may be imaginary.
- The teacher's own reactions are important since they affect the child.
- Fears melt with affection.
- Fears diminish with maturity.
- It is natural for most people to fear some things.

THE SLOW-LEARNING CHILD

Symptoms

- May have a short attention span
- May not be able to generalize
- May feel insecure
- Consistently achieves below grade level
- Has a low intellectual ability
- Withdraws and does not participate
- Seldom volunteers in class
- Has trouble getting started
- Has trouble finishing assignments

Possible Reasons for Behavior

- Familial pattern of slow learners
- Lack of environmental stimulation
- Possible learning disabilities especially if greater potential is indicated in spite of a low intellectual quotient
- Frequent illness causing gaps in critical stages of learning
- Rejection by parents or playmates
- Low nutrition
- Severe emotionality interfering in cognitive functioning

Teaching/Management Suggestions

- Provide many learning materials at child's level of ability.
- Ask for an intellectual or academic evaluation using individual tests.
- Give child many opportunities for success and a feeling of achievement.
- Try to get child interested in hobbies or extracurricular activities.

- Provide a place to work where distractions are at a minimum.
- Investigate child's physical and health condition.
- Praise child whenever possible and build up his or her good qualities.
- Have child work with a peer tutor.
- Make the parents aware of child's limitations so that they do not add to the problem with inappropriate demands.

Things to Keep in Mind

- Requiring more than he or she can do will cause frustration.
- Improvement in academic achievement will always be slow.
- Parents often reject the idea that their child is a true slow learner.
- Expect child to achieve only up to his or her ability.
- Be careful child doesn't get "lost in the crowd."

Try to keep in mind that the learning disabled and the slow learner may exhibit many of the same behaviors. However, there are specific differences between these two groups:

- True slow learners present intellectual patterns within the low-average range, usually between 80 and 89. The pattern is also consistent with past evaluations and does not indicate any further potential as reflected by the scatter of the scores. Children with learning disabilities, on the other hand, may also score within the low-average range. However, their patterns indicate a greater potential, probably well within the average to above-average range.
- True slow learners will never perform on grade level in all areas. The underlying assumption with learning disabled children is that they will attain grade level performance with support and modifications.
- Learning disabled children show a marked discrepancy between intellectual potential and academic achievement. Slow learners will have academic percentiles very close to their intellectual ability.

Section 16

Working with the Learning Disabled Child in the Classroom—Instructional Techniques

Most classroom teachers encounter children who have been diagnosed as learning disabled, but these teachers may not have the resources or individuals at hand who can offer practical suggestions and techniques.

There is no doubt that given the right preparation, material, and techniques, most teachers would be happy to become involved with such students. However, without proper training, many teachers may feel inadequate and may not want to do anything that might aggravate the situation.

The teacher should be aware that not all techniques will work with all students and should try as many of them as possible. The following techniques should create a better learning environment for learning disabled children.

MAKING ADJUSTMENTS IN THE TYPE, DIFFICULTY, AMOUNT, AND SEQUENCE
OF MATERIALS REQUIRED FOR LD STUDENTS

1. Give shorter but more frequent assignments.
2. Shorten the length of the assignments to ensure a sense of success.
3. Copy chapters of textbooks so that the child can use a highlighter pen to underline important facts.
4. Make sure that the child's desk is free from all unnecessary materials.
5. Correct the student's work as soon as possible to allow for immediate gratification and feedback.
6. Allow the student several alternatives in both obtaining and reporting information—tapes, interviews, and so on.
7. Break assignments down to smaller units. Allow the children to do five problems, or five sentences, at a time, so that they can feel success, receive immediate feedback if they are doing the assignment incorrectly, and direct their energy to more manageable tasks.
8. Hold frequent, even short, conferences with the child to allow for questions, sources of confusion, sense of connection, and avoidance of isolation that often occurs if the work is too difficult.

ADJUSTING SPACE, WORK TIME, AND GROUPING FOR THE LD CHILD

1. Permit the child to work in a quiet corner or a study carrel when requested or necessary. This should not be all the time since isolation may have negative consequences. This technique depends on the *specific learning style* of the child who may be less distracted by working under these conditions.
2. At first, the teacher may want to place the child closer to her or him for more immediate feedback.
3. Try to separate the child from students who may be distracting.
4. Alternate quiet and active time to maintain levels of interest and motivation.
5. Make up a work contract with specific times and assignments so that the child has a structured idea of his or her responsibilities.
6. Keep work periods short and gradually lengthen them as the student begins to cope.
7. Try to match the student with a peer helper to help with understanding assignments, reading important directions, drilling him or her orally, summarizing important textbook passages, and working on long-range assignments.

CONSIDER ADJUSTING PRESENTATION AND EVALUATION MODES FOR THE LD STUDENT Some LD students learn better by seeing (visual learners), some by listening (auditory learners), some by feeling (tactile learners), and some by a combination of approaches. Adjustments should be made by the teacher to determine the best functional system of learning for the LD child. This will vary from child to child and is usually included in the child's evaluation.

If the child is primarily an *auditory learner*, offer adjustments in the mode of presentation by using the following techniques:

1. Give verbal as well as written directions to assignments.
2. Place assignment directions on tape so that students can replay them when they need.
3. Give students oral rather than written tests.
4. Have students drill on important information using tape recorder, reciting information into the recorder and playing it back.
5. Have students drill aloud to themselves or to other students.
6. Have children close their eyes to try and hear words or information.

If the child is primarily a *visual learner*, offer adjustments in the mode of presentation by doing the following:

1. Have students use flash cards printed in bold bright colors.
2. Let students close their eyes and try to visualize words or information in their heads, see things in their minds.
3. Provide visual clues on chalkboard for all verbal directions.

4. Encourage students to write down notes and memos to themselves concerning important words, concepts, and ideas.

If the child is primarily a *tactile learner*, offer adjustments in the mode of presentation by trying the following techniques:

1. Provide many opportunities for the students to touch objects, such as feeling geometric shapes that have four sides.
2. Have the student recognize a numeral or letter drawn on his/her back, arm, or palm.
3. Encourage students to indentify the differences between various types of surfaces, such as rough or smooth, metal or plastic, and so on.
4. Ask students to match pairs of items by touching their shape, size, and/or texture.

Section 17

Working with the Emotionally Disturbed Child in the Classroom

DEFINING EMOTIONAL DISTURBANCE A student can be defined as having an emotional disability if he or she exhibits certain behavior patterns to a marked extent and over a prolonged period of time. Such patterns may include

- An inability to learn on a consistent basis which cannot be explained by intellectual capability, hearing and vision status, and physical health anomalies
- An inability or unwillingness to develop or maintain satisfactory interpersonal relationships with peers, teachers, parents, or other adults
- Extreme overreactions to minimally stressful situations over a prolonged period of time
- A general pervasive mood of sadness or depression
- A tendency to develop somatic complaints, pains, or excessive fears associated with home, school, or social situations

Some common characteristics of emotional disorders that may be observed by the teacher over a period of time include

- Academic underachievement
- Social isolation or withdrawal
- Excessive latenesses
- Excessive absences
- Frequent trips to the nurse
- Negativism
- Open defiance to authority or rules
- Highly distractible
- Poor social relationships
- Feelings of hopelessness
- Verbal aggression
- Confrontational behavior
- Inappropriate classroom behaviors

155

- Impulsive behavior
- Rigid behavior patterns
- Anxious and worried, excessive fears and phobias
- Easily frustrated even when confronted with a simple task
- Resistant to change

Since the behavior of emotionally disabled children can vary from withdrawal, in the case of depression, to aggressive tendencies, in the case of a conduct disorder, teachers need to be aware of techniques which can be utilized in a variety of situations. However, certain behaviors should be targeted as priorities when dealing with emotionally disabled children in the classroom. These target behaviors include

- Attendance and tardiness
- Challenges to authority
- Inappropriate verbalizations and outbursts
- Incomplete classwork
- Difficulty remaining seated
- Social relationships
- Following directions and paying attention

While many or all of these behaviors may be exhibited by the emotionally disabled child, the teacher should try to focus on one target pattern at a time. Patience, fairness, willingness to confront inappropriate behaviors, a sense of conviction in maintaining boundaries, and a sense of fair play in establishing consequences are all aspects required by the teacher in these situations.

DEALING WITH ATTENDANCE AND TARDINESS PROBLEMS

- Reward the child for being on time. This reward can be extra free time, a token (if a token economy is being used), a note home, a verbal compliment, and so on.
- Work with the parent on rewarding on-time behavior.
- Plan a special activity in the morning.
- Use a chart to visually project a pattern of punctuality and lateness for the child. This reduces the child's level of denial and may make him or her more aware of his or her behavior.
- Encourage and assist the child to start a club in his or her area of greatest interest and make participation contingent upon his or her positive pattern of attendance.
- Use a point system for on-time attendance. These points may be later turned in for class privileges.

- Set up a buddy system if the child walks to school to encourage on-time behavior.
- Set up a nightly contract for the child listing all the things he or she needs to do to make the morning easier to manage. Have the parent sign it and reward the child when he or she brings it in.

DEALING WITH CHALLENGES TO AUTHORITY, INAPPROPRIATE VERBALIZATIONS, AND OUTBURSTS

- Arrange a time-out area in the classroom. The time spent in the area is not as significant as you being able to begin the consequence and end it. Therefore, make the time-out period something you can control.
- Structure a time when the child is allowed to speak to you freely without an audience around. In this way, the child will have an opportunity to speak his or her concerns rather than act them out. It will also allow you to deflect any confrontations to that specific time.
- Approach the child as often as possible and ask if there is anything bothering them that they would like to speak about. Offering this opportunity, even if they refuse, may reduce their need for "spotlight" behaviors in front of the class.
- Offer an emotional vocabulary so that the child is more able to label feelings. Tension is expressed either verbally or behaviorally. Providing the student with the proper labels may reduce frustration.
- Move the child away from those students who might set him or her off.
- Preempt the child's behavior by waiting outside before class and telling him or her in private what you expect during class. Also make the child aware of the rewards and consequences of his or her appropriate as well as inappropriate actions.
- Offer other options and indicate that any inappropriateness is the child's decision by making the child realize that personal behavior is his or her responsibility and that avoiding inappropriate behavior is also in his or her control.
- Establish clear classroom rules stating rewards and consequences.
- Praise student for complying with rules and carrying out directions without verbal resistance.

DEALING WITH INCOMPLETE CLASSWORK

- Work out a contract with the child where he or she can determine the rewards for completion.
- Give shorter but more frequent assignments.
- Do not force the child to write if handwriting is beyond correction. Compensate with a word processor or typewriter.

◆ Correct assignments as soon as possible and hand them back for immediate gratification.

◆ Reward students for handing in neat, completed, and timely assignments.

◆ Help the student become organized by keeping very little in his or her desk, using a bound book for writing rather than a looseleaf folder where pages can fall out and add to disorganization, using large folders for the child to keep work in, and so on.

◆ Have students mark their own work.

◆ Be very specific about what you mean by "neat," "organized," and so on. Abstract labels have different meanings for different people. For clarity say, "Please be neat, and by neat I mean...."

DEALING WITH THE CHILD'S DIFFICULTY IN REMAINING SEATED

◆ Try to determine a pattern when the child gets up out of his or her seat. Once this is determined you can arrange to have the child run an errand, come up to your desk, and so on. In this way you are channeling the tension and remaining in control.

◆ Use an external control like an egg timer so that the child has an anchor to control his or her behavior.

◆ Praise other students or hand out rewards for remaining in their seats and following the rules.

◆ Give the child a written copy of the rules that will result in reward or positive feedback. Also give the child a list of the behaviors that will lead to consequences.

◆ Close proximity to the child will assist in developing positive in-seat behavior. Seat the child close to your desk or stand near the child during a lesson.

HELPING THE CHILD DEVELOP SOCIAL RELATIONSHIPS

◆ Role play with another student during private time so that the child can get feedback from a peer.

◆ Provide the child with a "tool box" of responses and options for typical social situations.

◆ Speak with the school psychologist about including the child in a group.

◆ Arrange for a peer to guide the child through social situations. The child may be more willing to model peer behavior.

◆ Start the child in a small-group activity with only one child. Slowly increase the size of the group as the child becomes more comfortable.

◆ Arrange for goal-oriented projects where students must work together to accomplish a task. At first, limit this to the student and one other child.

◆ Have the child and responsible peer organize team activities or group projects. Some children rise to the occasion when placed in a leadership role.

- Praise the student as often as realistic when not exhibiting aggressive or inappropriate social behavior.

HELPING THE CHILD FOLLOW DIRECTIONS AND STAY ON TASK

- Use a cue before giving the child directions or important information.
- Give one direction at a time and make it as simple as possible.
- Have the child chart his or her own patterns of behavior in relation to attention and direction.
- Physical proximity may assist the child in focusing on your directions.
- Praise the student for following directions or paying attention. However, be aware that if some emotionally disabled students have a hard time accepting praise, especially in front of a group, accomplish this in private.
- Provide optional work areas that may have less distraction.
- Randomly question the child and encourage participation to increase his or her interest in the lesson.
- Make sure the materials being presented are compatible with the child's learning levels. In this way you can avoid frustration, which is also a cause of inattention.
- Use a variety of visual and auditory techniques, such as overhead projector, tape recorder, or computer, to enhance the lesson and stimulate attention.

Section 18

Working with the Mildly Mentally Disabled Child in the Classroom

DEFINING A MENTAL DISABILITY

A student can be defined as having a mental disability if he or she exhibits certain learning, social, and behavior patterns to a marked extent and over a prolonged period of time. Such patterns may include
A consistently subaverage intellectual level

- Impaired adaptive functioning in such areas as social skills, communication, and daily living skills
- A consistently slow rate of learning with the result that their level of development resembles that of a younger child
- Delays in most areas of development

Some common characteristics of a mild mental disability that may be observed by the teacher over a period of time include the following:

- Academic underachievement
- Difficulty with abstract concepts
- Difficulty generalizing learned concepts to new situations
- Social isolation or withdrawal
- Poor social relationships
- Anxiety and worry, excessive fears and phobias
- Tendency to frustration even when confronted with a simple task
- Resistance to change
- Short attention span

While many or all of these characteristics may be exhibited by the mentally disabled child, the teacher should try to focus on one area at a time. Patience, fairness, nurturance, humor, and a sense of conviction in maintaining boundaries are all aspects required by the teacher in these situations.

However, students who are mildly mentally disabled learn in the same way as normal students. A number of adaptations and a variety of techniques need to be utilized. Consequently, certain behaviors should be targeted as priorities when dealing with these children in the classroom. These target areas include the following:

♦ Functional academics
♦ General work habits
♦ Career awareness

HELPING THE CHILD ATTAIN FUNCTIONAL ACADEMICS

General

♦ Design practice activities in any basic skill that may relate to the child's daily life problems.
♦ Provide materials that are commensurate with the child's skill levels.
♦ Present activities that will reinforce independent work. If the activity is too hard, the child may become too dependent on teacher supervision.

Reading

♦ Provide activities that focus on reading for information and leisure.
♦ Provide activities that require the child to become more aware of his or her surrounding environment. For example, have the child list the names of all food stores in the community to increase his or her familiarity with the surrounding environment.
♦ Have the child collect food labels and compare the differences.
♦ Allow them to look up the names of the children's families in the phone book. Use the smaller local guide for this activity.
♦ Develop activities that help children to become familiar with menus, bus and train timetables, movie and television schedules, or job advertisements.

Handwriting/Spelling

♦ Have the child make a list of things to do for the day.
♦ Have the child run a messenger service in the classroom so that he or she can write the messages and deliver them from one student to another.
♦ Provide activities for older children that incorporate daily writing skills necessary for independence such as social security forms, driver's license application, bank account applications, and so on.

Math

♦ Provide opportunities for the child to buy something at the school store.
♦ Have the child make up a budget on how he or she plans to use his or her allowance.

- Encourage the child to cook in school or at home to increase familiarity with measurements.
- Have the child record the daily temperature.
- Involve the child in measuring the height of classmates.
- Have older children apply for a loan or credit card.
- Show the child how to use a daily planning book.
- Provide activities that teach the child how to comparison shop.
- Provide a make-believe amount of money and a toy catalog and have the child purchase items and fill out the forms.

HELPING THE CHILD IMPROVE GENERAL WORK HABITS This particular area is composed of many skill areas that are necessary to allow the child success in the regular classroom. They include

Work Completion

- Make reward activities contingent upon successful completion of work.
- Have the child maintain a performance chart on the number of tasks completed each day.
- Evaluate the length and level of an assignment to make sure it is within the ability level of the child.
- Give shorter but more frequent assignments.
- Build a foundation of success by providing a series of successful assignments. In this way the child can gain a sense of confidence.

Attendance and Punctuality

- Communicate to the child the importance of being on time to class.
- Let the child know your expectations in clear terms concerning attendance and punctuality.
- Have the child maintain a record of attendance and on-time behavior.
- Develop a make believe time clock that the child has to punch in when entering the classroom.
- Encourage punctuality by scheduling a favorite activity in the morning
- Have the child sign a contract establishing the consequences and rewards of on time behavior.

Working with Others

- Provide the child with small-group activities that are geared to his or her ability levels.
- Utilize peer tutors for the child so that relationships can be established.
- Have the child participate in many group activities that require sorting, pasting, addressing, folding simple assembly, and so on.

- Provide the child with some simple job that requires the other students to go to him or her. For example, place the child in charge of attendance and have him or her check off the children when they report in.
- Help the child start a hobby and then start a hobby club involving other students.
- Have the child be part of a team that takes care of the class pets or some other class activity. Calling it a team will make the child feel more connected.
- Speak with the school psychologist and see if he or she can run a group in your classroom.

HELPING THE CHILD WITH CAREER AWARENESS   Career awareness is a skill that can be part of the classroom curriculum in many ways. Many of the skills mentioned in this chapter will enhance the child's career skills. Some specific activities that will enhance a child's awareness and experiences of various career opportunites and utilize the various school activities of writing, math, and spelling may include the following:

1. Help children develop a career and vocational vocabulary list. Encourage them to seek out words that pertain to career education such as part-time, full-time, social security, credit, harzardous, and so on.

2. Have them become familiar with the pages of the phone book that advertise companies and products. Let them call or write for information.

3. Have them become familiar with various career forms that they may encounter such as job applications, W-2 forms, Social Security applications, and so on.

4. Let them do some comparison shopping using the advertisements included in the newspapers. Encourage them to come up with reasons for the differences in pricing.

5. Allow children to set up their own businesses once a wee. You may want to have a business day where the other classmates would be able to purchase items with vouchers or make believe money that they earned by doing things in the classroom.

6. Have contests to see who can list the most business related signs that can be found in the community such as *Sale, 10% Discount, Mark Down,* and so on.

7. Have children make copies of or borrow a menu from a local restaurant and see if they can come up with all the ingredients necessary to make certain meals on the menu. This will help them become familiar with food processing.

Part

What Special Education Teachers Need to Know About...

165

Section 19

What Special Educators Need to Know About Attention Deficit Hyperactive Disorder

The disorder known as Attention Deficit Hyperactive Disorder was previously referred to by a variety of names, including hyperactivity, hyperkinetic reaction to childhood, hyperkinetic syndrome, minimal brain dysfunction, hyperactive child syndrome, and others. The present disorder, abbreviated ADHD, has two subtypes, attention deficit hyperactive disorder and undifferentiated attention deficit disorder.

At the present time, attention deficit hyperactive disorder affects approximately 3–5 percent of the elementary-aged population, or approximately 2 million children. It is far more common in boys (80–90 percent) than in girls. This disorder also accounts for the largest category of psychological referrals to clinics and other health-related facilities.

DIAGNOSTIC CRITERIA FOR ADHD

A child with this disorder will display for his or her mental and chronological age (M.A. and C.A., respectively) signs of developmentally inappropriate *inattention, impulsivity,* and *hyperactivity.*

These signs are usually reported by teachers and parents and tend to worsen in situations requiring self-application, such as in a classroom setting. The following list of symptoms and conditions apply for children between the ages of eight and ten, the peak age range for a referral of this type. In much younger children, the severity and quantity of symptoms increases. The opposite applies to older children.

INATTENTION—AT LEAST THREE OF THE FOLLOWING

1. The child often fails to finish things he or she starts.
2. The child often doesn't seem to listen.
3. The child is easily distracted.
4. The child has difficulty concentrating on schoolwork or other tasks requiring sustained attention.
5. The child has difficulty sticking to a play activity.

IMPULSIVITY—AT LEAST THREE OF THE FOLLOWING

1. The child often acts before thinking.
2. The child shifts excessively from one activity to another.
3. The child has difficulty organizing work.
4. The child needs a lot of supervision.
5. The child frequently calls out in class.
6. The child has difficulty awaiting turn in games or group situations.

HYPERACTIVITY—AT LEAST TWO OF THE FOLLOWING

1. The child runs about or climbs on things excessively.
2. The child has difficulty sitting still or fidgets excessively.
3. The child has difficulty staying seated.
4. The child moves about excessively during sleep.
5. The child is always "on the go" or acts as if "driven by a motor."

ADDITIONAL CRITERIA

1. Onset before the age of seven
2. Duration of at least six months
3. Not due to schizophrenia, affective disorders (disturbance of mood), or profound retardation

Teachers should be aware that many children with this disorder may experience severe academic problems, social difficulties, and problems adjusting to authority requests. This is not to say that all children with this disorder will exhibit such problems. However, if they should, action should be taken to avoid the appearance of secondary problems.

Since these children have a greater chance of encountering difficulties, treatment should be instituted as quickly as possible. Available treatment plans and consultation with a professional should alleviate the confusion about which plan may be more appropriate for the child.

TREATMENT PLANS FOR CHILDREN WITH ADHD

Help for children with Attention Deficit Hyperactive Disorder must be individualized. It may concern a variety of treatments, including psychotherapy, medication, parental counseling, school management classroom modifications, special education programs, and so on.

Pharmacological Intervention

The most common treatment plan for children with this disorder includes pharmacological intervention (medication). The types of medication used may vary with age and severity, but the most common include psychostimulants like Ritalin®, Cylert®, and Dexedrine®. Such stimulants tend to heighten the child's awareness of the surrounding world and allow for greater selectiveness of behavior. Approximately 50 percent of children with this disorder will exhibit a decrease in inappropriate symptoms. Approximately 10 percent of these children respond so positively to this intervention that their behavior reaches the normative range. Other reports indicate improvements in attention span, classroom behavior, and ability to think more clearly during academic tasks. Keep in mind that such medication does not "cure" this disorder; it merely alleviates the primary symptoms.

Other studies have indicated adverse side effects such as reduction of weight, nausea, and loss of appetite. Usually, such symptoms can be relieved by regulating the dosage. Since there are many issues to consider, parents should be sure they feel comfortable with this intervention.

One concern often raised by parents involves the issue of drug dependency. There is no research or evidence that indicates stimulant drugs in children with ADHD results in drug abuse. In general, the effects of medication can be more easily monitored and regulated when given in the context of a therapeutic environment.

Psychotherapy

Another treatment alternative for children with Attention Deficit Hyperactive Disorder involves psychotherapy. This process will help the child increase self-esteem and vent feelings and conflicts that may give rise to other symptoms, gain some control over impulsive actions, and assist parents with their approach to behavior management. Some therapies may utilize a form of treatment called *behavior modification*. This is a process whereby children, assisted by parents and teachers, learn to modify unacceptable behavior through the use of a variety of management techniques, including incentive systems, daily report cards, time-outs, selective attention, and so on. Some treatment plans include a combination of both medication and psychotherapy.

Diet

Another approach used by some parents in treating children with this disorder involves the use of a special diet. Some researchers have hypothesized that hyperactivity is a result of hypersensitivity to artificial colors, artificial flavorings, the preservatives BHA and BHT, and naturally occurring substances called salicylates. They have suggested that elimination of such substances from the child's diet will result in remission of their problems. However, there is a vast body of research that disputes the claims suggested by this, the Feingold theory. Dietary treatment of ADHD continues to raise a great deal of controversy and further research is needed in this area.

TEACHER'S CHECKLIST

Accurate and early diagnosis is crucial for the child with Attention Deficit Disorder and will facilitate a treatment plan and reduce the chances of secondary problems. Review the following checklist if you think a child in your room may have Attention Deficit Disorder.

1. Compare the child's behavior with the list of symptoms presented under inattention, impulsivity, and hyperactivity.
2. See if the observed behaviors also appear in the classroom as well as other school areas.
3. If they do, ask the school psychologist to observe the child.
4. If the school psychologist agrees that a possibility of ADHD exists, have him or her notify the parent so that the family's doctor can examine the child. A neurological examination may be suggested to determine the presence of the disorder. Medication may or may not be suggested.
5. If the disorder is diagnosed, meet with the parent(s) and psychologist to plan a management program at home and in school.
6. If the disorder is serious and affects the child's ability to learn, the child may need to be reviewed by your district's Committee on Special Education so that a suitable program can be determined.
7. A full psychological and academic evaluation would also assist in determining a proper course of action.

In conclusion, early diagnosis and active treatment will greatly enhance the child's opportunity for a meaningful and improved life both at home and in school.

Section 20

What Special Educators Need to Know About Dyslexia

Dyslexia is a very specific and severe learning disability. All learning disabled children are not dyslexic, but all dyslexic children are learning disabled. It is important for parents to understand this learning problem fully so that diagnosis can occur as early as possible. It is also important that parents understand dyslexia in order to alleviate the undue fear and anxiety that may accompany the situation in which their child is experiencing learning problems.

As we know, problems with learning can occur for a variety of reasons including, for example, stress, emotional problems, social disturbances, and learning disabilities. The cause of dyslexia is unknown. Problems in neurological development, inherited factors, brain damage, environmental deprivation, severe emotional problems, and illness have all been explored as possibilities.

What we do know is that dyslexia is an inability to read in spite of normal eyesight, hearing, and intelligence. This severe problem can also be manifested in math (dyscalculia), writing (dysgraphia), and spelling (dysorthographia). For reasons unexplained, the greater percentage of dyslexics are boys.

HISTORY OF DYSLEXIA

Dyslexia has been identified in many famous individuals, including Thomas Edison, Nelson Rockefeller, Albert Einstein, Nils Bohr (physicist), General George Patton, Woodrow Wilson, and possibly Leonardo da Vinci. Dyslexia has been recognized as a problem only in the last forty to fifty years. In 1896 W. A. Morgan in England described a case of congenital "word blindness." He explained that children could see with their eyes but then acted as if they were blind to words on the printed page.

Dr. Samuel Orton, an American neurologist, thought the inability to read was a laterality problem. He considered dyslexia as a confusion between the two hemispheres of the brain. The short-circuits might be caused by the lack of hemispheric dominance in the brain or a competition of the two sides possibly producing mixed-up words and letters.

If an individual fails to develop consistent dominance of one side in preference to the other, reversal tendencies will result, and reading will be seriously affected.

171

STATISTICS

Dyslexia occurs more frequently among boys than girls. The ratio is 4 to 1. Twenty-three million is a low estimate of the number of people with some degree of dyslexia in the United States today. The odds against all dyslexics increase as they grow older. If remedies are administered in the first and second grade, the chances for some success are around 80 percent. By fourth grade the success rate drops to 42 percent. By seventh grade chances for correction diminishes to 5–10 percent.

The results of dyslexia are devastating. As feelings of inadequacy increase, emotional disturbance, frustration, and behavioral problems may increase. Inattention, distractibility, somatic complaints, and avoidance symptoms with schoolwork are some of the manifestations of this condition.

CHARACTERISTICS FOR EARLY DETECTION

Primary

1. The child has poor ability to associate sounds with corresponding symbols.
2. The child ignores details of words and has difficulty retaining the words in his or her mind.
3. Word guessing is frequent. The child won't look at the word but will seek pictorial clues.
4. The child has confused spatial orientation. He or she reverses words, letters, and numbers. Mirror reading and writing are frequently encountered.
5. The child has poor auditory discrimination.
6. The child exhibits confusion of left and right (referred to as mixed dominance).
7. The child frequently loses his or her place on a page and frequently skips lines.
8. The child has difficulty in working with jigsaw puzzles, holding a pencil, and walking a chalk line.
9. Newly learned words are forgotten from day to day. Reading rhythm is usually poor and labored.

Secondary

1. There is no mental disability, and intelligence is measured as average to superior.
2. The child exhibits general confusion in orientation, confusing days, time, distance, size, and right and left directions.
3. The child displays poor motor coordination, a swaying gait and awkwardness when playing games.

4. There are speech delays and the child has difficulty in pronunciation.
5. The child feels inadequate and has low self-esteem.
6. Special tutoring with conventional reading methods doesn't work.
7. The child displays general irritability, aggressiveness, avoidance reactions, defensiveness, withdrawal, and general behavioral problems.

WHAT SHOULD YOU DO IF YOU SUSPECT THAT A CHILD HAS DYSLEXIA?

This is one of those cases where it is better to be safe than sorry. The earlier the diagnosis, the greater the chance for success and the less chance for serious secondary problems to occur. If you suspect that a child may be experiencing dyslexia, contact your school psychologist or resource room teacher immediately and request that the student be tested by both the psychologist and the learning disabilities specialist. Ask for a psychoeducational evaluation. This type of evaluation should identify the possibility of a dyslexic problem.

TESTS TO INCLUDE IN THE PSYCHOEDUCATIONAL EVALUATION

It is very important that all the tests administered be individual, not group, tests. Some tests to look for are the following:

INTELLIGENCE TESTS

- Wechsler Preschool and Primary Scale of Intelligence (WPPSI)
- Wechsler Intelligence Scale for Children—III (WISC—III)
- Wechsler Adult Intelligence Scale—Revised (WAIS—R)
- Stanford-Binet

TESTS USED TO IDENTIFY LEARNING DISABILITIES

- Bender Gestalt Visual Motor Test
- Woodcock Johnson Achievement and Cognitive Battery
- Peabody Individual Achievement Test
- Slingerland Specific Language Disability Test
- Benton Visual Retention Test
- Wepman Auditory Discrimination Test
- Illinois Tests of Psycholinguistic Abilities
- Detroit Tests of Learning Aptitude—Revised
- Key Math Test

ORGANIZATIONS TO CONTACT TO GET MORE
INFORMATION

Of the many organizations that deal with this issue, two that are highly regarded are the Orton Dyslexic Society and the Association for Children with Learning Disabilities. Both organizations have chapters in most states and are listed in the phone book.

READING TUTORS

Beware! In the case of dyslexia, a reading tutor may not be trained to deal with this condition and may further aggravate the situation. There are people in special education who are professionally trained to handle children with dyslexia. If the school cannot offer names, contact the Orton Society or the Association for Children with Learning Disabilities. They should be able to help.

Section 21

What Special Educators Need to Know About Adolescent Depression

Everyone becomes depressed from time to time for different reasons. Family problems, economic concerns, failing grades, changing jobs, illness, and social difficulties are some examples of everyday situations that may result in feelings of depression. Whatever the cause, most of us will experience depression as a temporary state and one that does not greatly interfere with our ability to function.

For many teenagers, however, depression is more than a passing mood or a period of temporary discomfort. The symptoms exhibited may be indications of a very serious illness requiring immediate professional intervention. Unfortunately, it is sometimes not easy to distinguish between the two. In many cases, parents, friends, and even teachers have not responded to the seriousness of such an illness in a teenager due to a lack of education. In some of these situations the consequences have been serious.

Many parents assume that all teenagers experience mood swings on a monthly, weekly, or even a daily basis. In some cases, this is true. What distinguishes normal depression usually observed in this developmental period from clinical depression, is the severity, intensity, and duration of the symptoms. Clinical depressions usually last for more than two weeks and tend to create interference in the ability of the teenager to function with his or her ordinary daily activities.

There does not seem to be any single cause of depression in teenagers. Rather, many factors may contribute to the feelings of hopelessness and despondency experienced by males and females. Some factors include chemical or hormonal abnormalities, heredity, personality characteristics such as low self-esteem, and environmental factors involving loss of a loved one, social rejection, divorce, economic hardship, long-term drug involvement, and so on.

The major concern for professionals is the fact that depression is a common factor related to suicide. There are a number of statistics that point up the seriousness of this situation:

- One out of ten teenagers will attempt to kill themselves.
- Suicide is the second leading cause of death among the young.
- There has been a 300 percent increase in teenage suicides over the past twenty years.
- Sixty-five hundred teenagers will succeed in committing suicide this year.

175

◆ There are one thousand suicide attempts a day by teenagers.

Parents of teenagers who have attempted or succeeded at suicide often look back in amazement at their lack of awareness of the seriousness of the situation. Some parents may dismiss the moods or feelings as "growing pains," while others may acknowledge them but not follow through on treatment. In either case, education concerning depression and suicide involving causes, symptoms, and intervention is a must for any parent of a teenager.

BEHAVIORAL INDICATIONS

The following symptoms, events, or clues may be indications of potential suicide:

1. Child exhibits sudden changes in behavior—withdrawal, apathy, too much sleep or too little sleep, dramatic drop in academic grades or performance.
2. Child has sustained recent losses—divorce, separation from family members, loss of self-esteem, loss of a relationship (boyfriend, girlfriend), loss of status (exclusion from peer group, not making grades).
3. Child appears moody or irritable—excessive fighting or abusive behavior, changes in behavior lasting more than two weeks, overnight feelings of happiness after long bouts of depression (frequently exhibited by teenagers who have decided to kill themselves and are now feeling the calm or peace of mind that follows the decision to die).
4. Child begins to give away personal possessions.
5. Child is preoccupied with dying, that is, begins asking questions about dying and life after death, reading poetry with morbid themes, making statements like, "Everyone would be better off without me," or more direct, "I feel like killing myself." Parents should also be aware of the criteria that could determine the lethality of the suicidal threat.

CRITERIA TO CONSIDER

DESIRE TO BE RESCUED Teenagers who plan suicide attempts in areas with little or no chance of interruption have the greatest chance of success. When a teenager reports this to someone, the risk should be considered very serious. Many suicide attempts are made with the knowledge, because of routine, of someone coming home and, it is hoped, ensuring a rescue. However, many deaths have occurred when such a plan has failed, as for example, when a parent stops by a neighbor's house on the way home.

THE TIME OF THE ATTEMPT The chance of a suicide attempt increases dramatically whenever a teenager expresses the time he or she would "do it." According to statistics, most teenagers will attempt suicide in their homes between midafternoon and midnight.

UNDER THE INFLUENCE OF ALCOHOL OR DRUGS Whenever a teenager is under the influence of drugs and/or alcohol and is talking about suicide, the suicide risk is very high. Such factors greatly reduce controls and add to the teenager's impulsivity.

PREVIOUS ATTEMPTS Any teenager who has made previous attempts at suicide is at very high risk.

A SUICIDAL NOTE OR PLAN Teenagers who write a note to parents, friends, or others indicating the possibility and manner of hurting themselves will have a greater likelihood of attempting suicide.

ILLNESS OR LONGSTANDING EMOTIONAL PROBLEMS When a chronic illness or long-term emotional stress is present, the teenager is more at risk for suicide.

LACK OF SUPPORT SYSTEMS The chances for suicide are greatest when teenagers have few peer support systems and/or little parental involvement or support.

AVAILABILITY OF OPTIONS Teenagers who threaten to hurt themselves a certain way, and have the availability of that method are at a higher risk, for example, a plan to use a parent's gun.

If a parent recognizes that a teenager may have suicidal tendencies, refer the parent to the following guidelines suggested by The State Education Department of New York or your own state until professional help can be secured.

Step 1: Be an active listener. A person in mental crisis needs someone who will listen to what he or she is saying. Every effort should be made to understand the problems behind the statements and the many levels that may be represented by a statement.

Step 2: Evaluate the intensity or severity of the emotional disturbance. Determine the frequency, intensity, and duration of the depressed symptoms. It is possible that the youngster may be extremely upset but not suicidal. (Again, use the clues and criteria for risk explained earlier.)

Step 3: Determine the child's available resources. The teenager may have inner resources, including various mechanisms for rationalization and intellectualization, which can be strengthened and supported. Other resources such as ministers, relatives, and friends can be contacted for additional support.

Step 4: Ask directly if the child has entertained thoughts of suicide. Do not be afraid to bring this issue to the surface right from the start. Many people make the mistake of feeling uncomfortable or fear alienating the child. While the teenager may not openly mention suicide during the crisis period, experience shows that harm is rarely done by inquiring directly about suicide at an appropriate time. As a matter of fact, the teenager frequently is glad to have the opportunity to open up and discuss it.

Step 5: Do not be misled by the teenager's comments that he or she is no longer feeling depressed. Often the youth will feel initial relief after talking about suicide, but the same thinking may recur later.

Step 6: Be affirmative, but supportive. Taking a strong, stable position is essential in the life of a depressed teenager. Act with conviction so that the child gets the feeling that you know what you are doing, and that everything will be done to assist the teenager.

Step 7: Never undervalue any complaint or feeling that the teenager expresses. In some cases, the child may minimize his or her difficulty, but beneath an apparent calm may be profoundly distressed feelings.

Step 8: Act quickly. Do something tangible by giving the teenager something definite to hang onto, such as arranging to see a professional or other resource (minister). Nothing is more frustrating to a teenager than to feel as though he or she has gained nothing from the discussion.

Contacting professional help is crucial. Many local agencies, hospitals, and crisis centers are listed in the phone book. If parents do not want to wait, try the emergency room at a local hospital. There is usually a psychiatrist on duty, and he or she will help you evaluate the situation.

Section 22

What Special Educators Need to Know About Medication

There may be times when the special education teacher will be exposed to a student whose condition requires the use of medication. While it is not important to possess a deep knowledge of medications, it is important to understand the nature of the medication, the reason for its use, and possible side effects that may exhibit themselves during the school day. When a child is on medication, it is also helpful to the medical doctor to receive observational reports on the child's reaction to the medication during the school day. The side effects mentioned in the discussions that follow do not include all possible conditions to the medication. The more common ones that might be observed in the classroom will be noted. With this in mind, here are the common medications used to treat certain conditions that the teacher will encounter.

ATTENTION DEFICIT HYPERACTIVE DISORDER

Psychostimulants are medications that have been referred to as paradoxical because they act in the reverse. The main purpose of these medications is to increase wakefulness, attention to task, and alertness by either releasing the neurotransmitter norepinephrine in the cases of Ritalin®, Cylert®, and Dexedrine® or brain stimulation as in the case of Pondimin®. These characteristics are usually not present in the behavior of ADHD children who appear to exhibit restlessness, impulsivity, distractibility, and inattention.

RITALIN®
Generic name: Methylphenidate
Ritalin® is a mild stimulant that acts upon the central nervous system and is widely prescribed in cases of ADHD. This medication is usually part of a total treatment plan which may also include individual counseling, family counseling, educational intervention, and social behavior modification.

The more common possible side effects may include loss of appetite, nervousness, difficulties sleeping, abdominal pains, and weight loss. Ritalin® is usually taken 30–45 minutes before meals and also comes in a sustained- or time-release tablet.

Caution is noted in the prescription of this medication when there is a history of Tourette's syndrome in the family and the individual is already experiencing a tic disorder or when there may be a possibility of glaucoma.

CYLERT®
Generic name: Pemoline

Cylert® is a medication that is used to treat children with ADHD. It is usually taken once a day in the morning, and some common side effects may include drowsiness, dizziness, insomnia, headaches, irritability, tics, nausea, yellowing of skin and eyes, and weight loss.

Children who are on Cylert® for extended periods of time need to be carefully monitored because the drug can stunt growth and may affect the kidneys and liver.

DEXEDRINE®
Generic name: Dextroamphetamine

This medication is available in liquid as well as tablet form and sustained-release tablets. It is usually prescribed as part of the treatment plan for children with ADHD, narcolepsy, and obesity. Possible side effects included are irritability, excessive restlessness, difficulties sleeping, agitation, and dry mouth; the drug may also aggravate any tendency that an individual may have toward tics.

This medication is usually taken in the morning because it may cause insomnia. Close monitoring should be undertaken because of the possibility of the medication affecting the child's growth. Unlike Cylert®, which is rarely prescribed under the age of six, Dexedrine® is prescribed for children as young as three years of age.

Other psychostimulants include Pondimin®.

PSYCHOSIS

Antipsychotic medications work by blocking one of the chemical messengers of the central nervous system: dopamine. These drugs are sometimes referred to as *neuroleptic drugs* because they block the dopamine receptors in the brain and restore the imbalance of nerve transmissions associated with psychotic behaviors.

Neuroleptic drugs should be considered very powerful and as a result pose potential risks. Careful monitoring is required, and withdrawal symptoms such as headaches, nausea, dizziness, and increased heart rate may occur if abruptly stopped. It should also be noted that alcohol consumption during the time the individual is on these medications may enhance the effects of the drug and increase the risk of depression.

HALDOL®
Generic name: Haloperidol

Haldol® is frequently prescribed to treat the psychotic behaviors associated with schizophrenia. It is also prescribed for children with oppositional behavior or combative behavior patterns, hyperactivity, and tic disorders. This medication may also result in *tardive dyskinesia*, a condition marked by involuntary muscle spasms and twitches in the face and body.

Some common side effects that may be observed in the classroom include coughing, anxiety, blurred vision, chewing movements, dry mouth, dizziness, drowsiness, lack of muscular coordination, physical rigidity and stupor, and protruding tongue. Withdrawal symptoms may include muscle spasms and twitches.

MELLARIL®
Generic name: Thioridazine

Mellaril® is commonly used to treat psychotic disorders, depression, and anxiety in adults. It is also used to treat behavior problems in children and panic disorders in the elderly. As with Thorazine®, tardive dyskinesia may be a side effect.

Some common side effects that may be observed in the classroom include hypokinesis, an abnormal lack of movement, muscle rigidity, blurred vision, chewing movements, dry mouth, eye spasms, fixed gaze, and swelling in the throat.

NAVANE®
Generic name: Thiothixene

Navane® like most neuroleptics work by lowering levels of dopamine in the brain. Excessive levels of dopamine are associated with severe sense of distorted reality typical of psychotic disorders.

Some common side effects that may be observed in the classroom are coughing, anxiety, blurred vision, chewing movements, dry mouth, dizziness, drowsiness, lightheadedness, puffed cheeks, seizures, sensitivity to light, and restlessness.

Navane® has been known to mask symptoms of brain tumors and intestinal obstructions. Consequently, close monitoring is important.

PROLIXIN®
Generic name: Fluphenazine

Prolixin® is a neuroleptic medication that is used to reduce the symptoms associated with psychotic disorders such as schizophrenia. Prolixin® may also cause tardive dyskinesia and should never be taken with alcohol.

Common side effects observed in the classroom may include muscle rigidity, blurred vision, chewing movements, complete loss of movement, dizziness, drowsiness, fixed gaze, muscle spasms, puckering of mouth, twitching, and yellowing of the skin and eyes.

STELAZINE®
Generic name: Trifluoperazine

Stelazine® is a medication that is used to reduce the symptoms associated with psychotic disorders like schizophrenia. While not the medication of choice, Stelazine® is sometimes used to treat anxiety that does not respond to ordinary tranquilizers. As with most neuroleptics, Stelazine® may cause tardive dyskinesia and should not be taken with alcohol.

Some common side effects that may be observed in the classroom include coughing, anxiety, blurred vision, chewing movements, dry mouth, dizziness, drowsiness, lack of muscular coordination, physical rigidity, and stupor and protruding tongue.

Stelazine is usually not prescribed if the individual has liver problems, is already taking central nervous system depressants or is suffering from blood conditions.

THORAZINE®
Generic name: Chlorpromazine
Thorazine® is a medication that is used to reduce the symptoms associated with psychotic disorders like schizophrenia. During treatment with Thorazine®, patients may experience tardive dyskinesia. This may be a chronic condition, but it is usually more common with the elderly.

Some possible side effects of Thorazine may include chewing movements, difficulty breathing, drooling, difficulty swallowing, eye problems observed as a fixed gaze, and twitching in the body.

TRILAFON®
Generic name: Perphenazine
Trilafon® is used to reduce severe anxiety associated with psychotic disorders and to reduce the symptoms of hallucinations and delusions. Common side effects include drowsiness, tardive dyskinesia, and dry mouth.

Other antipsychotic medications are

- ◆ Serentil®
- ◆ Loxitane®
- ◆ Orap®
- ◆ Moban®
- ◆ Compazine®
- ◆ Clozaril®

TOURETTE'S SYNDROME

Tourette's syndrome is a disorder characterized by motor and vocal ticking which may be exhibited in the form of grunting, coughs, barks, touching, knee jerking, drastic head movements, head banging, squatting, and so on. A variety of medications are used to reduce the symptoms which can be so severe at times that they may be mistaken for seizures. With many Tourette's patients, one medication may be given for the ticking and one for the symptoms of obsessive compulsive disorder (OCD) while still other medications may be given to reduce the side effects of those already administered. The more common medications used to treat this disorder are the following:

ORAP®
Generic name:Pimozide
Orap® is an oral medication that is usually prescribed with Haldol®, a primary choice medication. Orap® reduces the intensity of physical and verbal tics, jerk-

ing motions, twitches, and verbally bizarre outbursts. This medication should be used only when the tics are so severe that their onset hampers the individual's ability to function.

Some side effects that may be observed in the classroom include increase in appetite, blurred vision, trembling of hands, drooling, dizziness, changes in handwriting, loss of movement, swelling around the eyes, and excessive thirst.

CATAPRES®

Generic name: Clonidine

Catapres® is usually prescribed for high blood pressure but has been used with Tourette's syndrome. The more common side effects include dry mouth, skin reactions, dizziness, and drowsiness.

HALDOL®

Generic name: Haloperidol

Haldol® is a widely used medication that suppresses the symptoms associated with Tourette's syndrome. As previously mentioned, Haldol® is also used to reduce the symptoms associated with psychotic behavior as well as for children with severe behavior problems and hyperactivity.

DEPRESSION

Antidepressants, sometimes referred to as tricyclic drugs, affect the symptoms associated with depression by adjusting the levels of neurotransmiters in the brain such as dopamine, serotonin, and epinephrine. These medications are usually prescribed when the treatment of the condition is considered long term. Doctors do not usually like to use such powerful tricyclic antidepressants for short-term or transitory depression.

These medications tend to elevate the individual's mood, improve sleep patterns, increase energy levels and physical activity, and restore perception to a more positive level.

In the case of some antidepressants, once the doctor feels comfortable with the levels of medication attained, he or she may prescribe a single dose at night, a practice called *nightloading*.

ELAVIL®

Generic name: Amitriptyline hydrochloride

Other brand name: Endep

Elavil® is a medication that is prescribed for the relief of severe mental depression. Some possible side effects that may be observed in the classroom include abnormal movements, speech difficulties, dry mouth, lightheadedness, fatigue, fainting, hallucinations, insomnia, loss of coordination, tingling sensation, and pins and needles.

TOFRANIL®
Generic name: Imipramine
Other brand name: Janimine

Tofranil® is a commonly used tricyclic antidepressant. It is also used to treat *enuresis*, or bedwetting, on a short-term basis. It is a powerful medication that needs to be monitored closely. It is usually not prescribed for individuals who are already on monoamine oxidase (MAO) inhibitors such as Nardil® and Parnate®.

Some common side effects may include sensitivity to light, abdominal cramps, frequent urination, agitation, sore throat, fatigue, loss of appetite, nausea insomnia, and inflammation of the mouth. It is not usually administered to children under the age of six.

NORPRAMIN®
Generic name: Desipramine

Norpramin® is a medication that is prescribed for the relief of symptoms associated with severe mental depression such as inability to fall asleep, inability to concentrate, loss of appetite, feelings of despondency, low energy levels, and feelings of helplessness.

Some common side effects may include black tongue; red, black, or blue spots on the tongue; sensitivity to light; abdominal cramps; frequent urination; agitation; sore throat; fatigue; loss of appetite; nausea; insomnia; and inflammation of the mouth.

PAMELOR®
Generic name: Nortriptyline

Pamelor® is prescribed to relieve the symptoms associated with severe mental depression. However, this medication seems to be more successful with *endogenous depression*, depression resulting from physical causes within the body.

This medication is never prescribed if the individual is already taking a MAO inhibitor such as Nardil®, Parnate®, or Marplan® because high fevers, convulsions, and death have occurred with this combination of medications.

Some common side effects may include black tongue; red, black, or blue spots on the tongue; sensitivity to light; abdominal cramps; frequent urination; agitation; sore throat; fatigue; loss of appetite; perspiration; ringing in the ears; nausea; insomnia; and inflammation of the mouth.

PROZAC®
Generic name: Fluoxetine

Prozac® is a very popular medication that is prescribed for the treatment of long-term depression that has impaired the individual's ability to function on a daily basis. Prozac should never be taken with any MAO inhibitor because of serious complications.

Some possible side effects may include convulsions, dilation of pupils, dimness of vision, ear pain, eye pain, hostility, irrational ideas, and vague feelings of body discomfort.

Other tricyclic antidepressants are

- Sinequan®
- Desyrel®
- Parnate®
- Surmontil®
- Ludiomil®
- Eutonyl®
- Limbitrol®

- Adapin®
- Wellbutrin®
- Vivactil®
- Asendin®
- Marplan®
- Elderyl®

ANXIETY OR PANIC DISORDERS

Antianxiety agents are medications that work by diminishing the activity of certain parts of the brain, called the limbic system. The symptoms associated with anxiety may include tension, agitation, irritability, panic attacks, and feelings of dying or going crazy. Physical symptoms include excessive sweating, heart palpitations, chills, fainting, racing pulse, and flushes. Anxiety may be a disorder by itself or a component of other psychiatric disorders.

VALIUM®
Generic name: Diazepam
Perhaps one of the more widely used antianxiety medications, Valium® is used in the short-term treatment of the symptoms associated with anxiety. This medication is also prescribed in the treatment of acute alcohol withdrawal, as a muscle relaxant, and to treat along with other medications certain convulsive disorders. Valium® belongs to a class of agents known as benzodiazepines.

Concerns about possible dependence need to be considered, and close monitoring is suggested. Serious withdrawal symptoms may occur if the medication is stopped abruptly. Side effects include loss of muscle coordination, lightheadedness, and nausea.

LIBRIUM®
Generic name: Chlordiazepoxide
Other brand name: Libretabs
Librium® is used in the short-term treatment of the symptoms associated with anxiety. This medication is also prescribed in the treatment of acute alcohol withdrawal and anxiety or apprehension before surgery. As with Valium®, concerns about possible dependence need to be considered, and close monitoring is suggested. Serious withdrawal symptoms may occur if the medication is stopped abruptly.

Side effects include confusion, drowsiness, and unsteadiness. Symptoms due to abrupt withdrawal may include convulsions, tremors, vomiting, muscle cramps, and sweating.

XANAX®

Generic name: Alprazolam

Xanax® is a tranquilizer prescribed for the short-term treatment of symptoms associated with anxiety as well as panic disorders. This medication is also used to treat anxiety associated with depression. Xanax is considered a short-acting drug in that it acts quickly and, unlike Valium®, leaves the body relatively quickly. Regardless of the nature and course of action, Xanax® has a high dependency factor and should be closely monitored.

Side effects include dizziness, fainting, poor coordination, abnormal involuntary movement, agitation, confusion, dry mouth, and tremors.

ATIVAN®

Generic name: Lozazepam

Like Xanax®, Ativan® belongs to a group of drugs called benzodiazepines, is considered short acting, and leaves and enters the body rapidly. It is usually prescribed for short-term treatment, about four months, and produces the fewest cumulative effects of all the medications in this group. It is commonly prescribed with other antidepressive or antipsychotic medications in the treatment of other psychiatric disorders.

When being discontinued, use should taper off slowly since rapid stoppage may result in irritability, insomnia, convulsions, depressed mood, and tremors.

Other antianxiety agents are

◆ Buspar®   ◆ Catapres®
◆ Inderal®   ◆ Tranxene®
◆ Centrax®   ◆ Paxipam®
◆ Serax®

While medication can be a positive influence, it should be noted that monitoring by a trained professional is crucial. Parents should never administer an extra dosage or reduce the amount given to the child without consultation. If a child in your class is taking medication, you must inform the nurse, who will put that information on file in case of an emergency or bad reaction to the medication.

Section 23

What Special Educators Need to Know About Common Psychological Disorders

Special educators may in the course of their experience encounter a wide variety of special education conditions. Many of these conditions may be caused by intellectual, social, emotional, academic, environmental, or medical factors. It is important that you have at least a basic understanding of the more common conditions that may be presented by certain students. Your knowledge of these conditions can assist parents, doctors, and other students in the class, as well as the actual student involved. Understanding the nature of certain disorders can only enhance your total understanding of the child and all the factors that play a role in the child's educational development.

This section will deal with the more common psychological disorders that you may encounter in your role as a special education teacher. A description of each disorder, etiology, symptoms associated with the disorder, educational implications, possible treatment options, and other factors specific to the disorder will be considered.

The most commonly used source for psychological disorders used by professionals today is the *DSM—III-R (Diagnostic and Statistical Manual of Mental Disorders—III-Revised)*. This publication has changed several times in its scope, understanding, and format from its inception as *DSM—I* in 1952. You may want to purchase this manual as a reference source.

DEVELOPMENTAL DISORDERS

Mental Retardation

Description. A group of disorders characterized by severe delayed development in the acquisition of cognitive, language, motor, or social skills. The general characteristics of this diagnostic category are

1. Consistent and significant subaverage intellectual performance
2. Significant deficits in the development of adaptive functioning
3. Onset prior to the age of eighteen

Etiology. There are several possible contributing factors to this disorder, including heredity, prenatal damage (prior to birth, for example, maternal alcohol consumption and chromosomal changes, perinatal problems (at the time of birth, for example, malnutrition), and postnatal problems (occurring

187

after birth, for example, infections, trauma, and environmental or sensory deprivation during critical stages of development).

Types. There are several subtypes that are classified by educational or psychological terminology. They are

Educational Category	DSM-III-R Classification	IQ Range	DSM-Code
Educable mentally disabled	Mild	55-77.5 approx.	317.00
Trainable mentally disabled	Moderate	35-55 approx.	318.00
Severely mentally disabled	Severe	25-35 approx.	318.10
Profoundly mentally disabled	Profound	below 25	318.20

Educational Implications. The more severe the category, the greater the possibility of associated features being present, such as seizures and visual, auditory, or cardiovascular problems. Other educational implications involve poor social skills, severe academic deficits, and possible behavioral manifestations such as impulsivity, low frustration tolerance, aggressiveness, low self-esteem, and in some cases self-injurious behavior.

Possible Least Restrictive Educational Setting. Least restrictive educational settings for this type of student usually range anywhere from self-contained in a regular school with mainstreaming options for educable students to institutionalization for profoundly disabled individuals.

DSM—III-R Diagnostic Code. 317, 318, 318.10, 318.20, 319.

PERVASIVE DEVELOPMENTAL DISORDERS

Autistic Disorder

Description. A very serious developmental disorder characterized by severe impairment in the development of verbal and nonverbal communication skills, marked impairment in reciprocal social interaction (a lack of responsiveness to, or interest in people), and an almost nonexistent imaginative activity. Also known as infantile autism or Kanner's syndrome.

Etiology. The condition is usually reported by most parents before the child reaches the age of three. The condition is, in almost all cases, lifelong. This condition is thought to result from a wide range of prenatal, perinatal, and postnatal conditions (e.g., maternal rubella and anoxia during birth) that affect brain function.

Sex Ratio. The condition is more common in males, approximately 3 or 4:1.

Educational Implications. Poor social skills and impaired cognitive functioning and language. The onset of puberty may increase oppositional or aggressive behavior. Other complications are seizures and low intellectual development.

Possible Least Restrictive Educational Setting. Most children with this condition require the most restrictive educational setting possible. The student-teacher ratios are usually 6:1:2 or smaller because of the close supervision required. Those who are not capable of maintaining this type of setting may have to be institutionalized. In rare cases the individual may improve to the point of completing formal education or advanced degrees.

DSM—III-R Diagnostic Code. 299.00.

SPECIFIC DEVELOPMENTAL DISORDERS

Developmental Arithmetic Disorder

Description. A serious marked disability in the development of arithmetic skills. This condition, often called dyscalculia, cannot be explained by mental disability, inadequate teaching, or primary visual or auditory defects and may be consistent throughout school.

Age of Onset. Usually becomes apparent between ages six (first grade) and ten years (fifth grade).

Educational Implications. Seriously impaired mathematical ability which may require modifications like extended time, use of a calculator, flexible setting for tests, and revised test format. Other implications may involve poor self-esteem, social self-consciousness, and avoidance, which may increase secondary problems.

Possible Least Restrictive Educational Setting. Children with this disorder may receive assistance through special educational services like resource room or a consultant teacher, and are usually able to maintain placement within a normal class setting.

DSM—-R Diagnostic Code. 315.10.

Developmental Expressive Writing Disorder

Description. A disorder characterized by a serious impairment in the ability to develop expressive writing skills that significantly interfere in the child's academic achievement. This condition is not the result of a mental disability, inadequate educational experiences, visual or hearing defects, or neurological dysfunction.

Age of Onset. Considering the nature of the disorder and the levels of impairment, the age of onset can range from age seven (second grade) for the more severe types to age ten or eleven (fifth grade) for the less severely impaired.

Symptoms. The symptoms associated with this disorder include an inability to compose appropriate written text coupled with serious and consistent spelling errors, grammatical or punctuation errors, and very poor organization of thought and text.

Educational Implications. Teachers should be aware that these children may exhibit a series of symptoms, including avoidance, procrastination, denial, and possibly disruptive behaviors when written assignments are involved as a means of covering up the seriousness of the disorder.

Possible Least Restrictive Educational Setting. Children with this disorder may receive assistance through special educational services like resource room or a consultant teacher, and are usually able to maintain placement within a normal class setting.

DSM—III-R Diagnostic Code. 315.80.

Developmental Reading Disorder

Description. A disorder whose more common features include a marked impairment in the development of the child's decoding and comprehension skills that significantly interfere in the child's academic performance. As with most developmental disorders, this condition is not the result of mental disability, inadequate educational experiences, visual or hearing defects, or neurological dysfunction. It is commonly referred to as "dyslexia."

Age of Onset. This disorder is usually observed in children as young as age six (first grade). Diagnosis of such a serious impairment in the later grades may result from the child's ability to compensate with high intellectual ability or poor educational diagnostics.

Symptoms. Typical symptoms of this disorder include a slow, halting reading pace, frequent omissions, loss of place on a page, skipping lines unknowingly while reading, distortions, substitutions of words, and a serious inability to recall what has been read.

Educational Implications. Teachers should be aware that early diagnosis of this disorder is crucial to avoid serious secondary symptoms of poor self-esteem, behavior disorders, and educational failure. Teachers should focus on the possible symptoms exhibited by children with this disorder so that they can assist in early identification of this high-risk child. Teachers should also be aware of the various reading techniques used to assist children with this disorder. (A more thorough description of this disorder appears in Section 22, entitled What Special Education Teachers Need to Know About Medication.)

Possible Least Restrictive Educational Setting. Children with this disorder may receive assistance through special educational services like the resource room or a consultant teacher, and are usually able to maintain placement within a normal class setting.

DSM—III-R Diagnostic Code. 315.00.

Developmental Expressive Language Disorder

Description. A disorder characterized by a serious impairment in the child's ability to develop expressive language. This condition is not the result of a mental disability, inadequate educational experiences, visual or hearing defects, or neurological dysfunction.

Symptoms. Some common symptoms associated with this disorder may include limited use of vocabulary, shortened sentences, slow rate of language development, simplified sentence structure, and omissions of parts of sentences.

Age of Onset. The more serious forms of this disorder are usually diagnosed by age three, while less severe forms may not be noticed until much later in development.

Educational Implications. Teachers should be aware that from 3–10 percent of school-aged children suffer from this disorder. In many cases this greatly hampers a child's social interaction skills as well as academic performance.

Possible Least Restrictive Educational Setting. Children with this disorder may receive assistance through special educational services like the resource room or consultant teacher or services from a speech therapist, and are usually able to maintain placement within a normal class setting.

DSM—III-R Diagnostic Code. 315.31.

Developmental Articulation Disorder

Description. A disorder in which children have consistent problems using developmentally expected speech sounds, including but not limited to misarticulations, substitutions, and omissions, often sounding very similar to a more infantile form of speech. This condition is not the result of a mental disability; neurological, intellectual, or hearing disorders; or oral speech mechanism defects.

Educational Implications. The prognosis for complete recovery with this disorder is very positive, especially when speech therapy is part of the treatment plan. In some milder cases, the condition may run its course by age eight without intervention.

Age of Onset. In the more severe cases, children with this disorder are usually diagnosed by age three or later if the symptoms are milder.

Possible Least Restrictive Educational Setting. Children with this disorder may receive assistance through special educational services like resource room, a consultant teacher, or a speech therapist and are usually able to maintain placement within a normal class setting.

DSM—III-R Diagnostic Code. 315.39.

Developmental Receptive Language Disorder

Description. A disorder characterized by a serious impairment in the child's ability to develop language comprehension. This condition is not the result of mental retardation, inadequate educational experiences, visual or hearing defects, or neurological dysfunction.

Symptoms. Common symptoms associated with this disorder include an inability to understand simple sentences, particular types of words or statements, auditory sound discrimination, auditory memory, auditory association, retrieval, and sequencing.

Age of Onset. The more severe cases of this disorder appear around age two and typically before the age of four.

Educational Implications. Teachers should be aware that children with this disorder may have a difficult time communicating with gestures and actively participating in activities that require imaginary play.

Possible Least Restrictive Educational Setting. Children with this disorder may receive assistance through special educational services like resource room or consultant teacher or speech therapist and are usually able to maintain placement within a normal class setting.

DSM—III-R Diagnostic Code. 315.31.

DISRUPTIVE BEHAVIOR DISORDERS

Attention Deficit Hyperactive Disorder

Description. A disorder in which children exhibit behaviors of inattention, hyperactivity, and impulsiveness that are significantly inappropriate for their age levels. These behaviors may be severe and have an adverse effect on the child's academic achievement. (A more detailed discussion of this condition will be found later in this section.)

Etiology. The condition is six–nine times more common in males than in females, and several conditions may contribute to the development of the disorder. These include neurologic factors and central nervous system dysfunction, while other factors may be environment, abuse, and neglect.

Symptoms. The symptoms for this disorder should be present for a minimum of six months and may include some of the following:

◆ Constant fidgeting
◆ Difficulty maintaining himself or herself in a seat
◆ Excessive talking at inappropriate times
◆ Inability to listen
◆ Careless
◆ Disorganized
◆ Difficulty sustaining a focus on tasks or play activities
◆ Easy distractibility
◆ Difficulty following instructions

Educational Implications. Teachers should be aware of the academic as well as the social difficulties experienced by students with this disorder. Social rejection, which is common, may contribute to low self-esteem, low frustration tolerance, and possibly aggressive or compulsive behavior patterns.

Possible Least Restrictive Educational Setting. Children with mild forms of this disorder may be able to maintain a normal class placement with the intervention of medication and/or behavior management techniques. More serious cases may require more restrictive settings, especially for those children with associated oppositional or conduct problems. In such cases, special schools or residential settings may be the least restrictive setting.

DSM—III-R Diagnostic Code. 314.01.

Conduct Disorder

Description. A condition characterized by a persistent pattern of behavior that intrudes on and violates the basic rights of others without concern or fear of implications. This pattern is not selective and is exhibited in the home, at school, with peers, and elsewhere in the child's community. Other behaviors present with this condition may include vandalism, stealing, physical aggression, cruelty to animals, and fire setting.

Sex Ratio. Empirical studies seem to indicate that 9 percent of the males and 2 percent of all females suffer from this disorder.

Etiology. The age of onset is usually before puberty for males and after puberty for females. The causes of this disorder are varied and may include parental rejection, harsh discipline, early institutional residence, inconsistent parenting figures as experienced in foster care, and so on.

Categories.

Type	Description	DSM-III-R Code
Solitary aggressive type	Aggressive behavior towards peers and adults	312.00
Group type	Conduct problems mainly with peers as a group	312.20
Undifferentiated type	For those not classified in either above group	312.90

Educational Implications. Children with this condition may be physically confrontational to teachers and peers, have poor attendance, have high levels of suspension and thereby miss a great deal of academic work, and exhibit other forms of antisocial behavior.

Possible Least Restrictive Educational Setting. Children with this condition may be educated in a special class within a regular school if the condition is mild. However, the majority of students with this disorder are educated in a more restrictive program housed within special schools, residential schools, or institutions if the antisocial behavior is extreme.

DSM—III-R Diagnostic Code. 312.00.

Oppositional Defiant Disorder

Description. This disorder is usually characterized by patterns of negativistic, hostile, and defiant behaviors with peers as well as adults. This disorder is considered less serious than a conduct disorder because of the absence of serious behaviors which violate the basic rights of others. Children with this disorder usually exhibit argumentative behaviors toward adults, which may include swearing and frequent episodes of intense anger and annoyance. These symptoms are usually considered to be more serious and intense than those exhibited by other children of the same age.

Age of Onset. The behaviors associated with oppositional defiant disorder usually appear around age eight and usually not later than early adolescence.

Educational Implications. Teachers who have children with this disorder in their classes may observe low frustration tolerance, frequent temper outbursts, low sense of confidence, an unwillingness to take responsibility for their actions, consistent blaming of others for their own mistakes or problems, and frequent behaviors associated with Attention Deficit Hyperactive Disorder.

Possible Least Restrictive Educational Setting. Children with this condition may be educated in a special class within a regular school if the condition is mild. However, the majority of students with this disorder are educated in a more restrictive program housed within special schools, residential schools, or institutions if the antisocial behavior is extreme.

DSM—III-R Diagnostic Code. 313.81.

ANXIETY DISORDERS OF CHILDHOOD

Separation Anxiety Disorder

Description. A disorder characterized by extreme anxiety associated with separation from someone with whom the child views as a significant other. While this reaction may be common with very young children on their first day of school, continuation of the anxiety for more than two weeks indicates a problem that needs to be addressed. This separation anxiety is frequently exhibited at school and at home. It should be noted that if symptoms of separation anxiety occur in an adolescent, other factors such as social or academic pressure may be the contributing cause.

Age of Onset. This condition may be seen in children as early as preschool age, while onset in later developmental stages around adolescence is rare.

Educational Implications. Children with this disorder may require a great deal of the teacher's attention. The child may cling, be afraid to try new things, require a great deal of reassurance, and cry frequently. Panic attacks are common and the teacher may find that reason does not reduce the anxiety. Physical complaints are common and should never be ignored. However, in cases of separation anxiety, these "physical" symptoms are usually manifestations of the anxiety once medical causes are ruled out.

Possible Least Restrictive Educational Setting. Children with this disorder can usually be maintained in the regular class setting through the help of the school psychologist working with the child and parents. If the condition persists and the diagnosis changes, for example, major depression, then outside professional help may be required. A more restrictive program, sometimes even homebound instruction if attendance at school is not possible, may have to be instituted.

DSM—III-R Diagnostic Code. 309.21.

Avoidant Disorder of Childhood or Adolescence

Description. A disorder that results in the child withdrawing from social contact or interaction with an unfamiliar peer or adult to the point of becoming a significant factor in social development.

Symptoms. Symptoms of this disorder include a lack of assertiveness, low self-esteem, frequent embarrassment, narrow *safety zone* (areas or situations in our lives in which we safely and comfortably operate), and a need to be socially involved only with family members or peers known to the child.

Sex Ratio. This disorder may be found more commonly in females than males.

Educational Implications. Children with this disorder can maintain regular class placement as long as achievement levels do not present problems, possibly signifying some other condition. Teachers with this type of student should be aware of social isolation, withdrawal from activity-based assignments, and a complete unwillingness to try new situations involving social interaction with unfamiliar peers. Trying to force the child into new social interaction situations may only result in further withdrawal socially as well as verbally. Work alone with the child or along with familiar peers only for awhile. Once a trusting relationship is developed, your influence may be more rewarding. Referring the child to the school psychologist is also highly recommended. Individual outside counseling with a slow lead into small-group counseling should be explored. However, this transition may result in a great deal of resistance on the part of the child.

Possible Least Restrictive Educational Setting. Children with this disorder can usually be maintained in the regular class setting through the help of the school psychologist working with the child and parents. However, children with other disabilities may also exhibit this disorder.

DSM—III-R Diagnostic Code. 313.21.

Overanxious Disorder

Description. A disorder in which an excessive level of anxiety or worry extends over a six-month or longer period of time.

Symptoms. Children with this disorder exhibit such symptoms as the constant need for reassurance, inability to relax, unrealistic worry about present or future events, frequent physical concerns, and preoccupations with self-consciousness. Physical concerns are common but should always be checked out first by a medical professional. In most cases of overanxious disorder, somatic (bodily) complaints are manifestations of inner tension and conflict.

Educational Implications. Teachers who have students with this disorder should be aware of the possibility of poor academic performance because of the child's preoccupation with worry. The teacher should also try to reassure and compliment the child as much as possible when he or she is not drawing negative attention to himself or herself.

Possible Least Restrictive Educational Setting. Most children with this disorder can be educated within a regular class placement unless the condition is coupled with more serious disabilities that require a more restrictive setting. Referral to the school psychologist is highly recommended.

DSM—III-R Diagnostic Code. 313.00.

Obsessive Compulsive Disorder

Description. A disorder characterized by persistent obsessions (persistent thoughts) or compulsions (repetitive acts) that significantly interfere with the individual's normal social, educational, occupational, or environmental routines.

Symptoms. Typical obsessive symptoms include persistent thoughts, impulses, or images. Typical compulsive symptoms include repetitive and intentional behaviors. While the individual is aware that these behaviors and thoughts are irrational, he or she is unable to control the outcome.

Educational Implications. Children or adolescents with this disorder will have difficulty concentrating and maintaining consistent academic performance. These individuals may also experience depression as a result of their difficulties, and medication may be instituted to relieve the anxiety associated with this disorder.

Possible Least Restrictive Educational Setting. A child with this disorder can usually be maintained in the regular educational setting as long as sufficient performance levels are met. However, if the child's academic performance becomes discrepant, and/or social and intellectual factors interfere in performance, then a more restrictive placement may have to be explored.

DSM—III-R Diagnostic Code. 300.30.

EATING DISORDERS

Anorexia Nervosa

Description. A condition characterized by a marked disturbance and unwillingness to maintain a minimal body weight for their age and height. An extreme distorted sense of body image exists, and intense fears and worries about gaining weight become obsessive. It is not uncommon for bulimia nervosa (discussed later) to be an associated feature. In more severe cases, death may occur.

Etiology. Studies seem to indicate that anorexics are usually perfectionistic, high-achieving females.

Sex Ratio. Ninety-five percent of the cases of anorexia nervosa are found in females.

Symptoms. Children with this disorder may also exhibit self-induced vomiting, use of laxatives, increased reduction of food intake, preoccupation with becoming fat, and noticeable increase in the frequency and intensity of exercise. In females, absence of menstrual cycles is common as the child's weight decreases and the body chemistry changes.

Educational Implications. Teachers should be aware of frequent absences because of medical complications. These children are usually high-achieving individuals, but because of their medical conditions academic consistency may be difficult.

Possible Least Restrictive Educational Setting. Children with this type of disorder can be maintained in the regular school setting unless the condition becomes severe enough to warrant hospitalization. In some cases where the child is at home and unable to attend school, homebound instruction is utilized.

DSM—III-R Diagnostic Code. 307.10.

Bulimia Nervosa

Description. A condition characterized by recurrent episodes of uncontrolled consumption of large quantities of food (binging) followed by self-induced vomiting (purging) and use of laxatives or diuretics over a period of at least two months.

Etiology. Some research indicates that obesity during the teenage years might be a predisposing factor for bulimia in later life.

Symptoms. The individual with bulimia nervosa exhibits symptoms characterized by binging and purging, use of laxatives and diuretics, obsessive preoccupation with body shape and weight, and a feeling of lack of control over food consumption during binge episodes.

Educational Implications. Most teachers might not even know that a student is bulimic. Individuals hide this "secret" well and may not divulge the problem to anyone, not even a best friend. This is usually a private disorder until the person feels so out of control that he or she seeks help and support. Consequently, teachers should be aware of frequent trips to the bathroom, especially in the morning after breakfast or after lunch. Changes in skin color and look may give some indications of problems. However, if you suspect anything, let the nurse investigate this further.

Possible Least Restrictive Educational Setting. Unlike anorexia nervosa, children with bulimia nervosa seldom suffer incapacitating symptoms except in rare cases when the eating and purging episodes run throughout the day. Consequently, in most cases these children can be maintained in the regular school setting unless the condition becomes severe enough to warrant hospitalization.

DSM—III-R Diagnostic Code. 307.51.

TIC DISORDERS

Tourette's Syndrome

Description. A disorder characterized by motor and vocal ticking, which may be exhibited in the form of grunting, coughs, barks, touching, knee jerking, drastic head movements, head banging, squatting, and so on.

Symptoms. The foregoing symptoms may change as the child develops but the course of the disorder is usually lifelong. Associated features include OCD and ADHD (discussed earlier). The condition is more common in males and family patterns are also common. Coprolalia (vocal tic involving the expression of obscenities) is an associated symptom in about 33 percent of the cases.

Educational Implications. Teachers of students with Tourette's syndrome should be aware of and sensitive to the social difficulties and confusion exhibited by the student's peers. Social rejection, isolation, and victimization may be common, and the teacher needs to step in to prevent these situations from occurring. In older students with this disorder, teachers should be aware of the child's use of a great deal of energy in an attempt to control the tics because of social pressure at the cost of attention and consistent academic performance. If you have a student with this condition, contact the local Tourette's Association in your area for further literature.

Possible Least Restrictive Educational Setting. Children with mild forms of this disorder can easily be maintained in a regular educational setting with supportive services. Since the condition does affect performance in many cases, children with this disorder are usually classified as disabled and do receive special education services, including modifications. More severe cases which do not respond to medication may require a more restrictive setting. Medication, counseling, and special education services provide a good treatment plan. However, the child may have to try many medications before finding one that relieves the ticking. Medications are also taken if OCD symptoms are associated.

DSM—III-R Diagnostic Code. 307.23.

ELIMINATION DISORDERS

Functional Encopresis

Description. A disorder whose major symptom is repeated involuntary or intentional passage of feces into clothing or other places which deem it inappropriate. The condition is not related to any physical condition, must occur for a period of six months on a regular basis, and be present in a child over the age of four for diagnosis to take place.

Educational Implications. Children with this disorder may experience social ridicule if the occurrences take place in school. The teacher needs to be sensitive to the condition and involve the school psychologist and parents. Try to intervene as quickly as possible if a pattern exists to avoid further embarrassment for the child and secondary complications such as avoidance.

Possible Least Restrictive Educational Setting. Children with this condition should have no problem maintaining a regular educational setting unless the condition is associated with other disabilities that require special education placement. However, this condition may create social pressures and isolation for the child.

DSM—III-R Diagnostic Code. 307.70.

Functional Enuresis

Description. A disorder characterized by repeated involuntary intentional elimination of urine during the day or night into bed or clothes at an age at which bladder control is expected. A frequency of at least two times per month must be present for the condition to be diagnosed between the ages of five and six and at least once a month for older children.

Familial Pattern. In at least 75 percent of the cases, the child has a first-degree biologic relative who has, or has had, the condition.

Educational Implications. This condition may create social pressures and isolation for the child in the regular education setting. The teacher needs to be sensitive to the child's condition and involve the child's parents and school psychologist in dealing with this disorder.

Possible Least Restrictive Educational Setting. Children with this condition should have no problem maintaining a regular educational setting unless the condition is associated with other disabilities which require special education placement.

DSM—III-R Diagnostic Code. 307.60.

OTHER DISORDERS OF CHILDHOOD AND ADOLESCENCE

Elective Mutism

Description. A disorder characterized by persistent refusal to talk in one or more major social situations, including school, despite the ability to comprehend spoken language and speak. The resistance to speak is not a symptom of any other major disorder.

Etiology. The possible causes for such a condition vary from maternal overprotection, immigration, mental disabilities, and hospitalization to trauma before the age of three.

Symptoms. Some symptoms associated with this disorder besides the refusal to speak include excessive shyness, social isolation, compulsive behavior, temper tantrums, negativism, clinging, and withdrawal.

Educational Implications. This condition may create a difficult situation for the classroom teacher. The teacher will not be able to measure certain language or social levels, will have to deal with social concerns and comments from classmates, and will have a difficult time encouraging the child to participate in necessary class activities or group projects. A teacher with such a child in the classroom should contact the school psychologist as soon as possible. Individual and family counseling is highly suggested for such a disorder.

Possible Least Restrictive Educational Setting. This type of child can usually be maintained in the regular educational setting as long as the child maintains sufficient performance levels. However, if the child's academic performance becomes discrepant, and/or social and intellectual factors interfere in performance, then a more restrictive placement may have to be explored.

DSM—III-R Diagnostic Code. 313.23

SPECIFIC PERSONALITY DISORDERS

Cluster A

SCHIZOID PERSONALITY DISORDER

Description. A disorder in which the child exhibits a restrictive range of emotional experiences and expressions and indifference to social situations.

Symptoms. Individuals with this disorder do not seek out or enjoy close relationships with either family or peers. These individuals usually appear cold and aloof and are indifferent to praise or criticism. They do not seem to have goals in life, are indecisive and self-absorbed, and rarely date.

Educational Implications. In the classroom, this type of child will be considered unapproachable. He or she will be resistant to group projects or group experiences. If they are involved, they will remain on the outside and not participate in discussions. Other children will eventually ostracize the child. The teacher will also have a very difficult time establishing any meaningful relationship. Therapy and/or medication may be suggested by an outside professional or agency.

Least Restrictive Educational Setting. Children with this disorder eventually wind up in a special education setting. However, some remain in the normal mainstream because their academic performance is sufficient but are viewed as "loners" by their classmates.

DSM—III-R Diagnostic Code. 301.20.

Cluster B

ANTISOCIAL PERSONALITY DISORDER

Description. A disorder characterized by a pattern of irresponsible and antisocial behavior. The condition is usually first seen in childhood or early adolescence and continues throughout the child's development. This diagnosis is usually made after the age of eighteen, and the individual must have had a history of symptoms before the age of fifteen indicative of a conduct disorder.

Symptoms. It is common for these individuals to exhibit symptoms such as lying, stealing, truancy, fighting, vandalism, and physical cruelty to animals or people. They usually do not honor their financial obligations, repeatedly perform antisocial acts that are grounds for arrest, and fail to conform to social norms.

Educational Implications. The situation for the classroom teacher can be serious with students exhibiting this type of disorder. Since the individual has little or no regard for the personal rights of others, any antisocial act can occur, even ones that may place the teacher in danger. Medication may help reduce tension while therapy may have limited success.

Possible Least Restrictive Educational Setting. Children or individuals with this disorder may have aged out and may no longer be part of the educational system. They are usually classified as disabled and would probably be placed in a very restrictive educational setting until the age of twenty-one if they had not been arrested by that time.

DSM—III-R Diagnostic Code. 301.70.

BORDERLINE PERSONALITY DISORDER

Description. A disorder characterized by instability of self-image, inconsistent and unfulfilling interpersonal relationships, instability of mood, and persistent identity disturbance.

Symptoms. Besides those features just mentioned, individuals with this disorder exhibit recurrent suicidal threats, gestures, or behavior; engage in self-mutilation (carving their arm or wrist with a razor); experience extreme mood swings, intense anger, or lack of control of their anger; exhibit impulsivity that may be potentially self-damaging; engage in casual sex and substance abuse; and recklessly endanger self and others.

Educational Implications. In the classroom, this individual will have a hard time maintaining any consistent academic performance. Frequent outbursts, truancy, hospitalization, legal problems, or school disciplinary actions may provide an inconsistent pattern of attendance and involvement.

Possible Least Restrictive Educational Setting. The individual with this condition will usually be placed in a more restrictive special education setting, hospital program, or institution.

DSM—III-R Diagnostic Code. 301.83.

Cluster C

PASSIVE AGGRESSIVE PERSONALITY DISORDER

Description. A disorder characterized by a pervasive pattern of passive resistance to the requests or requirements placed upon these individuals in school, social, or occupational performance.

Symptoms. Typical characteristics include procrastination, stubbornness, intentional inefficiency, selective forgetting, and dawdling. These individuals strongly resent any request to increase production.

Educational Implications. Teachers will find that working with this type of student can be very frustrating. These students may become irritable, sulky, or argumentative and often blame external causes for their lack of production. Assignments may have to be readjusted so that some sense of accomplishment can be obtained. Counseling is strongly suggested.

Possible Least Restrictive Educational Setting. Most students with this disorder can be educated within the normal setting. However, they exhibit a pattern of constant underachievement. In some cases where the discrepancy becomes significant, a referral for a more restrictive setting may be suggested. A history of severe academic discrepancy resulting from this disorder may result in the child being classified as emotionally disabled.

DSM—III-R Diagnostic Code. 301.84.

MOOD DISORDERS

Dysthymia

Description. A chronic disturbance of the individual's moods involving chronic depression or irritable mood for a period of one year for children and adolescents.

Symptoms. Vegetative signs of depression include poor appetite, difficulty sleeping, lack of energy, general fatigue, low self-esteem, difficulty concentrating, and feelings of hopelessness.

Educational Implications. Teachers who experience this type of student need to work closely with the school psychologist or private therapist, if the child is in treatment. The teacher should also be aware that medication may be involved and an understanding of the side effects should be investigated.

Possible Least Restrictive Educational Setting. Students with this disorder can usually be maintained in either a regular setting or a more restrictive special education program, if the symptoms become more intense. The chronicity of this disorder rather than the severity usually accounts for a mild or moderate impairment. Consequently, hospitalization is rare unless suicide is attempted.

DSM—III-R Diagnostic Code. 300.40.

CONCLUSION

These disorders represent only a cross-section of the conditions that you may encounter in the classroom. While expertise is not required, an understanding and awareness of such disorders can only increase your effectiveness with these children. As previously stated, a more elaborate explanation, as well as further disorders associated with certain developmental periods, can be found in DSM—III.

Section 24

What Special Educators Need to Know About Being a Mandated Reporter of Child Abuse and Neglect

All states have laws governing the identification and reporting of suspected child abuse. Most states now mandate teachers and other education and health professionals to take a course on child abuse and neglect to receive or renew their licenses. As a special education teacher, you are considered a mandated reporter. Other mandated reporters are psychologists, psychiatrists, nurses, doctors, teachers, and principals. Reporting possible abuse or neglect need only be suspected prior to making a report. Any person required to report a case of suspected abuse or neglect who willfully fails to do so may be found guilty of a misdemeanor and be subject to civil penalties.

Several terms are used in laws governing child abuse and neglect. They include an abused, maltreated, or neglected child.

AN ABUSED CHILD An abused child is usually defined in the law as someone under the age of eighteen whose parent, legal guardian, or other person legally responsible for the child's care *inflicts or allows to be inflicted upon the child*

- ◆ Physical injury by other than accidental means
- ◆ A substantial risk of physical harm or injury that is created or allowed to be created which could result in serious injury or death
- ◆ Disfigurement
- ◆ Prolonged impairment of emotional or physical health

or commits or allows to be committed

- ◆ Sex offenses against the child including incest, prostitution, or obscene sexual conduct
- ◆ Engagement in sexual performance

A MALTREATED OR NEGLECTED CHILD A maltreated or neglected child is usually defined in the law as someone under the age of eighteen who

204

◆ Has had serious physical injury inflicted upon him or her or
◆ Has been impaired physically, mentally, or emotionally or is in imminent danger of becoming impaired as a result of the failure of his or her parent or other person legally responsible for his or her care to exercise a minimum degree of care in supplying the child with

Adequate food

Adequate clothing

Adequate shelter

Adequate and required educational opportunities and exposure

Adequate medical care when required

Adequate dental care when required

Adequate optometrical care when required

Adequate surgical care when required

These conditions apply when the parents or guardians are financially able or are offered assistance to seek assistance from professionals.

Further indications of maltreatment or neglect are present when the parents or guardians

1. Do not provide the child with proper supervision or guardianship
2. Unreasonably inflict or allow to be inflicted harm, or a substantial risk, including the infliction of excessive corporal punishment
3. Misuse drugs or alcohol
4. Misuse alcoholic beverages to the extent that they lose control of their actions
5. Have abandoned the child

You may want to keep in mind that the terms *maltreated* and *neglected* are often interchangeable, although some interpretations of the laws list them separately.

PROCEDURES TO FOLLOW IF YOU SUSPECT ABUSE OR NEGLECT

Remember, you need only to suspect abuse or neglect to report the case. If you suspect possible abuse or neglect, follow these steps:

1. Gather all the information you can about the suspected incident or incidents and write it up in *factual* and *behavioral terminology* (this means no opinions, interpretations, assumptions, or guesses, just factual observations or information such as "The child said…," "I directly observed…," "There were black and blue marks on his/her legs.")

2. Notify your direct administrator (usually a building principal) of the information you have that caused you to suspect abuse or neglect. Here again verbalize only facts. At this point the administrator will usually call the child abuse hotline or assign someone to call. If you are assigned to call keep the following in mind:

   a. Make sure you call the mandated reporters' hotline. Many states have two lines, one for the public and one for mandated reporters. The numbers can be found in the phone book or by calling 800-555-1212 and asking for the State Child Abuse and Neglect Hotline for Mandated Reporters since most of these hotlines are 800 numbers.

   b. Once you have a counselor on the phone, immediately ask for his or her name and note the time and date of your call.

   c. Inform the counselor that you believe you have a suspected case of abuse or neglect. You will be asked some basic questions, including what evidence you have to suspect that something has taken place.

   d. Again, report only facts and direct observations. At this point the counselor may indicate that it is either reportable or not a reportable case.

   e. If the case is reportable, the counselor will ask you more questions, so be prepared with the following information:
- The child's full name
- The address of the child
- The child's birthdate
- The parent's/guardian's first and last names (if different)
- The dominant language of the child and the parents
- The child's telephone number
- The parent's/guardian's work number if known
- Other siblings in the house and their ages
- The child's grade level
- The child's school and school district
- Number and nature of any previous reports

3. After the counselor gathers all the information, a case number may be assigned, so be prepared to jot it down. The counselor will then inform you that the case will be given to a local case worker who will contact the school.

4. Ask the counselor if the child can go home or if the school should retain the child until the case worker appears. The school has this right, especially if the child's health or safety will be compromised in any way by returning home after school. Many times the case worker will come immediately if it is deemed a serious case and will speak with the child before the end of the school day. A home visit is usually made within twenty-four hours or less if the case is considered serious.

5. The school nurse under the direction of the building administrator may photograph any obvious marks or contusions for evidence.

6. Once the case is reported, you will probably receive a Report of Suspected Child Abuse or Maltreatment form from the Department of Social Services. The school must fill this out and return it within twenty-four hours. Here, again, the person who made the original contact with the state counselor may be the one who fills out the form. An example of this type of form appears at the end of this chapter. Keep in mind that this is a legal requirement.

7. In some instances, the counselor may indicate that a case does not sound reportable as abuse or neglect, but that it does represent poor judgment on the part of parents. At this point you can ask why and ask their advice for the next step. However, if it is not reportable, write your administrator a letter indicating the time, date, and the name of the counselor to whom you spoke, and the reasons why the case was not accepted as reportable. Your legal responsibilities are now covered. However, your moral responsibilities have just begun.

8. If the administrator listens to the facts and does not see it as a reportable case, you should ask the reasons why and suggest that the case be presented to the child abuse counselor for his or her input. However, if the administrator continues to indicate that he or she does not feel it needs to go any further, inform the counselor that as a mandated reporter, you feel a responsibility to call the child abuse hotline and ask the counselor on call if he or she feels it is a reportable case. If an administrator does not want to report a case and you go along, and it is later determined that abuse or neglect was taking place, you may find yourself in very serious trouble. It is not acceptable to use the excuse, "I told my administrator...." Remember, you are a mandated reporter and are directly responsible for actions taken or not taken.

CLINICAL AND BEHAVIOR CLUES TO POSSIBLE ABUSE

Since special education teachers are mandated reporters, you need to be aware of clinical and behavioral clues indicating possible abuse.

Physical Abuse

SOME POSSIBLE BEHAVIORAL SIGNS OF PHYSICAL ABUSE

1. Fears or resists going home
2. Has past history of self-injurious behavior
3. Exhibits extreme neurotic conditions, for example, obsessions, compulsions, phobias

4. Constantly wears clothing that is inappropriate for the season such as long pants, skirts, and sleeves in the summertime possibly to cover up bruises

5. Exhibits extreme mood changes and periods of aggressive behavior

6. Seems apprehensive or afraid of adults

7. Flinches or reacts defensively to adult gestures or behavior not considered dangerous

8. Communicates that he or she is constantly falling or hitting into things as an excuse for their injuries

SOME POSSIBLE PHYSICAL SIGNS OF PHYSICAL ABUSE

1. Unexplained marks, welts, bites, or bruises on the body

2. Unexplained burns

3. Unexplained injuries to the head area

4. Unexplained burn marks

Sexual Abuse

SOME POSSIBLE BEHAVIORAL SIGNS OF SEXUAL ABUSE

1. Acts in an infantile manner and exhibits frequent withdrawal and fantasy

2. Has difficulties maintaining peer relationships

3. Engages in sexual activities with other children

4. Exhibits frequent latenesses or absences from school

5. Exhibits resistance to physical examinations

6. Has a history of running away

7. May have a history of self-injurious behavior

8. Expresses sophisticated, bizarre, or unusual knowledge of sexual acts or behavior and expresses these to other children or adults

SOME POSSIBLE PHYSICAL SIGNS OF SEXUAL ABUSE

1. Presence of bruises in genital areas

2. Difficulty walking or sitting for long periods of time because of pain

3. Bruises to the mouth area

4. Extreme pain, itching, or discomfort in the genital area

5. A history of urinary tract infections

6. Sexually transmitted diseases especially in the preadolescent period

Neglect or Maltreatment

SOME POSSIBLE BEHAVIORAL SIGNS OF NEGLECT

1. Is frequently caught taking food from other children
2. Arrives at school much earlier than the other children
3. Seems to hesitate going home at the end of the day and is seen wandering the halls
4. Exhibits constant fatigue
5. Frequently falls asleep in class
6. Develops habit disorders such as tics and other signs of tension
7. Exhibits symptoms typical of conduct disorders such as antisocial behavior
8. Frequently uses drugs or alcohol
9. Develops clinging behavior patterns toward other adults

SOME POSSIBLE PHYSICAL SIGNS OF NEGLECT

1. Medical or physical conditions that go untreated
2. Severe lags in physical development as a result of malnutrition
3. Consistent hunger
4. Poor hygiene
5. Inappropriate clothing for the particular weather conditions
6. Mentions that he or she is often left home alone
7. Chronic absences from school
8. A history of latenesses to school

Try to keep in mind that you should use common sense and good judgment prior to reporting suspected abuse. Such reports are a serious matter. On the other hand, never hesitate if you suspect abuse believing that "Such a family could never do such things." Remember that as a mandated reporter you are really an advocate for children in cases of suspected abuse or neglect. Never assume that something is so obvious that someone must have called it in. It is always better to be safe than sorry.

EXAMPLE OF A REPORT FORM OF SUSPECTED CHILD ABUSE MALTREATMENT

Subjects of Report

List all children in household, adults responsible for household, and alleged perpetrators

Last Name	First Name	M.I.	Aliases	Sex M or F	Birthdate or age	Ethnic Code	Suspect or Relationship Code	Check if alleged Perpetrator Code
1—								
2—								
3—								
4—								
5—								
6—								
7—								

If known, list addresses and telephone numbers:

Basis of Suspicions

Alleged consequences or evidence of abuse or maltreatment. Place the above line numbers next to the appropriate children, write "ALL."

_____ Sexual Abuse

_____ Emotional Neglect

_____ Abandonment

_____ Lack of Supervision

_____ DOA/Fatality

_____ Fractures

_____ Lacerations, Bruises, Welts

_____ Excessive Corporal Punishment

_____ Drug Withdrawal

_____ Child's Drug/Alcohol

_____ Lack of Medical Care

_____ Malnutrition

_____ Failure to Thrive

_____ Educational Neglect

_____ Lack of Food, Clothing, Shelter

_____ Internal Injuries

_____ Other, Specify _____

State reason for suspicion. If possible, include type and extent of the child's injury, abuse or maltreatment in each case. Further, if known, list any evidence of prior injuries, abuse or maltreatment to the child or any siblings. Also list suspicions of any behavior on the part of the parent/s which may contribute to the problem.

If known, give the time and date of alleged incident:

Month _____ Date _____ Year _____

Time _____ AM _____ PM _____

Sources for the Report

Person making this report

Name:
Address:

Telephone:

Agency/Institution

Source of this report if different

Name:
Address:

Telephone:

Agency/Institution

Relationship (mark X for reporter and * for source)

— Medical Examiner/Coroner   — Physician   — Hospital Staff   — Law Enforcement
— Neighbor   — Relative   — Social Services   — Public Health
— Mental Health   — School Staff   — Other (specify) _____

This Section for Physicians Only

Medical diagnosis on child:

Signature of physican who examined or treated child:

Telephone number:

Hospitalization required: —None   —Under one week   —1–2 weeks   —Over 2 weeks

---

Actions taken or about to be taken

— Medical examiner   — Hospitalization   — Notified D.A.   — Notified medical examiner

— Notified coroner   — Returned home   — Removal/keeping   — X-ray

— Photographs

Signature of person making this report: Title: Date submitted:

Section 25

Diagnosing the Learning Disabled Child

Learning disabled (LD) children account for approximately 3–6 percent of the student population. Consequently, there is a very good chance that you will come in contact with these children somewhere in your career. You should keep in mind that the LD population is a very specific population characterized by certain characteristics. There are a number of academic, intellectual, and social and emotional behaviors that describe a student with possible learning disabilities. However, many students may exhibit any number of these characteristic behaviors and may not be learning disabled for reasons to be explained later. In either case, a closer investigation is warranted. Understanding the symptoms will help identify the child earlier and offer the appropriate help so that further frustration and secondary problems can be avoided.

INTELLECTUAL CRITERIA

The first set of criteria used in identifying a learning disabled child is usually potential intellectual ability. Since one criterion for identification as LD is average intelligence, one needs to review the child's intellectual profile. The average range of intellectual ability falls within the 90–109 range. However, there may be times when you will find a child scoring below this level who exhibits all the other criteria for classification. One needs to look at the profile of scores for the presence of what is called "scatter or variability." (This factor was previously mentioned in an earlier section on "Indications of Greater Potential on the Wechsler Scales.") The key phrase with this factor is "potential average intelligence." You may find that a child scores below 90, but upon investigation you notice a great deal of fluctuation in his or her scores. Variability or scatter usually indicates that the resulting score should only be considered a minimal indication of the child's ability and the real level of potential is higher. So it is possible that a child scoring an 83 on an IQ test and because of scatter has at least average potential and meets the intellectual criteria. On the other hand, if a child scores an 83 but there are no indications of any greater potential and past tests show consistent results, then limited intellectual capacity may be the reason for low academic performance and not a true learning disability. The psychologist is usually the one who determines true intellectual potential, but you should be aware of what procedures are used to determine this result.

ACADEMIC CRITERIA

A history of low academic performance is usually a key factor in the identification of a child with a learning disability. A learning disability does not occur in grade 5 with high levels of achievement in past grades. An LD child usually has a history of academic difficulties in one or several areas. Test scores may reflect this pattern and generally a deficit of six months to one year below grade level is considered mild, one to two years moderate, and a deficit of more than two years a severe academic deficiency.

PROCESS CRITERIA

Many batteries of tests used to identify a learning disability will rely on perceptual tests to identify possible difficulties in the child's learning process. The underlying assumption with all learning disabilities is that subtle neurological difficulties contribute to process impairment and consequently difficulties in learning. These perceptual tests can tell us if a child's receptive, associative, memory, expressive, and other areas are intact or in need of repudiation. This process factor usually sets the LD population off from the underachieving population whose main reason for lack of performance is usually based on emotional criteria rather than limitations in the learning process.

EXCLUSION CRITERIA

The identification of a learning disabled child also includes certain other conditions that must be ruled out as primary factors contributing to the child's inability to learn. These include primary emotional factors, mental disabilities, visual or hearing handicaps, poor teaching, cultural deprivation, inconsistent attendance, or other environmental factors such as abuse.

BACKGROUND CRITERIA

While it is not mandatory for identification, many children with learning disabilities may come from families with a history of this condition. Second, the child's history indicates a pattern of problems in learning dating back to primary grades. Third, some behavioral indications during development (language delays, motor difficulties, problems listening, etc.) may be observed in the intake history.

BEHAVIORAL CRITERIA

Other "typical" behaviors are commonly exhibited by a number of LD children and may include

1. Variability in performance and not succeeding in school in one or more of the following areas:
   a. Basic reading skill (decoding)
   b. Reading comprehension
   c. Mathematics calculations
   d. Mathematics reasoning
   e. Written expression
   f. Oral expression
   g. Listening comprehension
2. Attention problems, for example, inability to concentrate for even short periods of time, distractibility, attention to irrelevant details.
3. Organization problems, such as
   a. Poor organization of information
   b. Poor organization of school materials such as notes, homework, and so on
   c. Poor organization involving productive use of time
4. Perceptual problems—many are confused by words or numbers that look or sound alike. They may have trouble differentiating similar sounds.
5. Poor motivation or attitude mainly because they have experienced repeated failure.
6. Memory problems
   a. Problems retrieving information or concepts
   b. Problems with short-term memory
   c. Problems with sequential memory
   d. Problems with long-term memory
7. Language deficits—listening, speaking, and vocabulary
8. Poor motor abilities—fine and gross motor coordination
9. Inappropriate social behavior—social perception, emotional behavior, establishing social relationships

WHO IS NOT A STUDENT WITH A LEARNING DISABILITY

A student with a learning disability is not a student whose learning problems are primarily due to
1. Other handicapping conditions such as
   a. Mental disabilities
   b. Emotional disabilities
   c. Visual or hearing loss
   d. Motor handicaps
2. Limited learning opportunities because of
   a. Prolonged absences from school
   b. Lack of consideration for language differences
   c. Inadequate instructional practices

3. Limited learning potential in all areas (e.g., slow learners whose achievement is commensurate with their potential).

4. Sociological causes, including environmental, cultural, or economic disadvantages, limited proficiency in English language, or other such conditions that may result in, but are not the result of, a learning problem.

SEVERE LEARNING DISCREPANCY

Many state definitions of learning disabilities may include a statement indicating that for a learning disability to exist there must be a severe discrepancy between achievement and intellectual ability. This has been interpreted to mean achievement which falls at or below 50 percent of an individual's expected achievement level when intellectual ability, age, and previous educational experiences are considered.

Initially, a formula was derived that appeared in P.L. 94–142 or the 1975 Federal Guidelines for the Education of the Handicapped. The formula used was

$$\frac{\text{C.A. (IQ} + .17) - 2.5}{300} = \text{severe discrepancy level}$$

The following table uses this formula for different IQs and C.A.s. The scores represent half of the child's potential when IQ and age are factored in. For example, a child with an IQ of 120 at chronological age 10-0 (fifth grade) has a potential *grade level* performance of 6.4. Half that would be 3.2, which represents that child's severe discrepancy grade level. This means that if the child scored below this level on a standardized test in an achievement area, the child would be considered severe enough to be classified as having a learning disability.

CHRONOLOGICAL AGE (YEARS-MONTHS)

	9-0	9-3	9-6	9-9	10-0	10-3	10-6	10-9
135	3-1	3-2	3-4	3-6	3-7	3-9	4-0	4-2
130	2-9	3-1	3-2	3-4	3-5	3-7	3-8	4-0
125	2-8	2-9	3-1	3-2	3-4	3-5	3-7	3-8
120	2-6	2-8	2-9	3-1	3-2	3-3	3-5	3-6
100	2-0	2-1	2-3	2-4	2-5	2-6	2-8	2-9
80	1-4	1-5	1-7	1-8	1-9	2-0	2-1	2-2
75	1-3	1-4	1-5	1-6	1-7	1-8	1-9	2-0
65	1-0	1-1	1-2	1-3	1-4	1-5	1-6	1-7

This formula will help to quantify the definition of learning disabilities, since a word "definition," interpreted differently by different committees, may have caused increased numbers of identified students and resulted in significant costs to state and federal governments. However, this formula was soon dropped and did not appear in the state definitions. Yet the concept of "severe discrepancy" did and the interpretation was left up to the individual Committees on Special Education.

In conclusion, identification and diagnosis of a learning disabled child should include the following:

1. Average or above-average potential intelligence
2. A history of mild, moderate, or severe academic deficiencies
3. No indications of primary emotionality, mental disability, poor teaching, lack of motivation, and so on
4. A background history that supports an historical pattern of difficulties in development or achievement
5. Behavioral indications such as difficulties in attention, distractibility, coordination, memory, and so on
6. A significant discrepancy between ability and achievement

Part

Practical Parenting Tips for Parents

Section 26

How Special Educators Can Help Parents Work with Their Children on Homework

Every night in millions of homes across the country you can imagine the scenario—the age-old story of children and their homework. The scene may have different characters, but the script is usually the same.

Parents have always attempted to help their children with homework. This help ranges from a short occasional explanation to total completion of the task by the parent. Whatever the case, numerous problems exist. In an attempt to cope, parents will use trial and error, bribery, threats, reasoning, and anything they hope will work.

There seems to be little doubt that the motives of the parents are genuine. Who could find fault with the motive of concern. However, it is not the motive that creates the anxiety and tension for both parents and children, but the techniques employed.

For some children, school can be a stressful place. When one takes into account work demands, social pressures, concern over parental approval, fear of failure, and so much more, children may need the home as a haven to unwind. If they encounter stress in the form of parental agitation during homework, then where can they "hang their hat"? For those of us who work, it might be comparable to working all day at a job that has its share of stresses and coming home to a tense environment. Think of how long you might be able to handle such a situation. Also keep in mind the alternatives that we have as adults if the pressure gets to be too great. Children do not have the same options.

The following techniques are provided to facilitate the process of homework and prevent frustration, anger, and disappointment.

TRY TO SET UP A HOMEWORK SCHEDULE Many children benefit from a set homework schedule. For some, the responsibility of deciding when to sit down and do homework is too difficult. These children may decide to do their homework after school or after dinner. This is a personal choice and has to do with *learning style*. However, once the time is determined, the schedule should be adhered to as realistically as possible. This will also relieve the problem of having to "hunt down" or "corral" children to get them to do their homework. After a while, this will become a natural part of their schedule. It should be noted that during this time, no interruptions should be allowed. Phone calls, TV, and everything else can wait until the work is completed.

RANK THE ASSIGNMENTS For some children, the decision about what to do first becomes a major chore. They may dwell over this choice for a long time. Other children use *horizontal perspective*. This occurs when everything takes on the same level of importance and no priority is seen.

If you choose to rank order, suggest which assignment to do first and so on. Many children tend to use a *quantity orientation* (number of assignments left) rather than a *qualitative orientation* (difficulty of assignment). This means that if they have five things to do, have them finish the four easy ones first. In their eyes, they have only one assignment left even though it may be a more difficult task.

AVOID SITTING NEXT TO YOUR CHILD DURING THE HOMEWORK SESSION This is usually a very big problem for some parents. All I can say is that parents employing this technique are not only setting themselves up for tremendous frustration and anger, but they are also creating "learned helplessness."

Many parents will say that their children cannot work unless they are sitting next to them. It is not that many children are unable to work, but that they choose not to work. The work stoppage on the part of children occurs when a parent attempts to break away and no longer provides them with undivided attention. This "dependency" is very unhealthy because it is not imitated in the classroom. Consequently, such children may put off doing their classwork and bring the unfinished work home. In this way they may gain mommy or daddy's full attention. After a hard day's work, parents are tired, and the thought of sitting down with children for up to three hours doing homework can only lead to problems.

If you are already locked into this type of situation, you should not break away all at once. You should *desensitize* children a little at a time. Sit at the end of the table for a few days. Then slowly increase the distance between yourself and the child's work until he or she is working alone.

CHECK CORRECT PROBLEMS FIRST Parents sometimes have a habit of "zeroing in" on the incorrect problems. Next time your child brings you a paper to check, focus first on how well he or she did on the correct problems, spelling words, and so on. For the answers that are incorrect say, "I bet if you go back and check these over you may get a different answer." Now the child will go back and redo the problems without any animosity or feelings of inadequacy. If you focus first on the incorrect problems and become angry, when the child returns to the work area he or she will likely be more involved in dealing with the loss of parental approval rather than finishing the task.

NEVER LET HOMEWORK DRAG ON ALL NIGHT Sometimes parents will allow a child to work on homework for several hours or until they finish. This is fine if the performance of the child is consistent or the assignment realistically calls for such a commitment of time. However, in the event that a child is no farther along after one or two hours than after ten minutes into the assignment, you should stop the homework activity. The only thing accomplished by allowing a child to linger on hour after hour with very little performance is increased feelings of inadequacy. The parent may choose to end the work period after a reasonable amount of time and write the teacher a note explaining the circumstances. I am sure that such concerns can be worked out at a meeting with the teacher.

There may be several reasons for such a behavior pattern. First, the child may not have understood the concept in class and therefore will not be able to finish the assignment at home. Second, the child may already have feelings of helplessness. Consequently, waiting long periods of time may result in the completion of the assignment by the parents. Third, the child may have serious learning difficulties, especially if this is a pattern, and may be overwhelmed by a series of assignments.

DISCUSS HOMEWORK QUESTIONS BEFORE YOUR CHILD READS THE CHAPTER Most textbooks, except for the newer ones, have the chapter questions at the end. When this procedure occurs, many children are not aware of what they should be looking for while reading. Discuss and talk about the questions before children begin reading. By using this strategy, they will know what important information to look for in the chapter.

Some children have a tendency of trying to remember everything. You may want to give them a pencil and suggest that they lightly note a passage or word that sounds like something in one of the questions. This will help many children when they have to skim back over the many pages in the chapter.

CHECK SMALL GROUPS OF PROBLEMS AT A TIME Many children benefit from immediate gratification. Have your child do five problems and then come back to you for checking. Zero in on the correct ones, and after they are checked send the child back to do the next group. In this way the child gets immediate feedback and approval and the necessary motivation for the next assignment. Additionally, if the child is doing the assignment incorrectly, the error can be detected and explained, preventing the child from having to redo the entire assignment.

PLACE TEXTBOOK CHAPTERS ON TAPE Research indicates that the more sensory input children receive, the greater the chance the information will be retained. Therefore, tape record some science or social studies chapters so that children can listen while they read along. This will allow both auditory and visual input of information. From time to time you may want to add a joke, a song, or a message to keep the interest of the child.

DARKEN PAGE LINES FOR CHILDREN LEARNING HOW TO WRITE Sometimes, when children are first learning how to write, they will experience problems with control. While this can be a normal developmental problem, it is suggested that parents darken top and bottom lines so that the children have a reinforced boundary. This boundary can help maintain control and help them focus on letter formation. This technique can also be used for older children who have visual-motor problems that are manifested in their handwriting.

CHECK HOMEWORK ASSIGNMENTS AT THE END OF THE NIGHT Anxiety is exhibited by some children over the thought of possibly bringing incorrect homework to school. Therefore, it is very important for parents to take time each night to check homework. This offers children a feeling of accomplishment, a source of positive attention, and a sense of security that the work is correct. This sense of academic security may carry over to the classroom and offer children a greater sense of confidence with classwork. However, if it is clear that the child did not understand a particular concept, the teacher should be made aware of it.

BE AWARE OF NEGATIVE NONVERBAL MESSAGES Parents will often say to me that they never get frustrated or yell while working with their children on homework. However, if all communication were verbal, then these parents would have a good case. But as we know, nonverbal communication is a large part of overall communication. Since this is possible, many messages, especially negative ones, can be communicated easily without your awareness. Grimaces, body stiffness, sighs, raised eyebrows, and other types of body language are all nonverbal responses. If children are sensitive, they will pick up these messages, which can only add to the tension of the homework relationship. This is extremely important with younger children who cannot distinguish between loss of parental approval and loss of love. Such a state can only add stress to their ability to perform.

AVOID FINISHING ASSIGNMENTS FOR YOUR CHILD Some parents will complete an entire assignment for their children. While the parents' motivation may be helping their child finish a difficult assignment, the end result may be very destructive. Children tend to feel inadequate when a parent finishes homework. First, they feel a sense of failure. Second, they feel a sense of inadequacy since they can never hope to do the assignment as well as mommy or daddy. I have seen parents do an entire social studies term paper. This can only foster increased dependency and feelings of helplessness on the part of children.

If children cannot complete an assignment, and they have honestly tried, write the teacher a note explaining the circumstances. Most teachers will understand the situation.

To recap, before you sit down to work with your children, make sure that they are not exhibiting symptoms that may reflect more serious concerns. When parents attempt to work with children who have severe learning problems or a high tension level, they may be faced with tremendous frustration, anger, and disappointment. Following basic guidelines when helping with homework can result in a more rewarding situation for both parents and children.

Section 27

How Special Educators Can Help Parents Use Effective Discipline

Many parents find the use of discipline and reward very difficult. What makes it difficult is the parent's confusion over what is either too strict or too lenient. The added pressure of confrontation with its built in unpopularity further adds to this discomfort. Certain techniques and attitudes are basic when it comes to this area of child rearing. It is very important that parents develop a healthy mental set about this area so they can be realistic, consistent and supportive. The following techniques are offered as "tools" for the parent. Not all these techniques may work for all people, and some may take several tries before results are observed. However, the following tools may represent conservation of energy and reduce the possibility of "parent burnout."

NECESSARY LIMITS AND GUIDELINES FOR A CHILD'S EMOTIONAL DEVELOPMENT For children, limits and guidelines represent a "safety net" within which they can behave. Children will know that any act of poor judgment will be brought to their attention if limits are well defined. Consequently, they will be led back to the safety net. If children are not bound by well-defined limits, there is no buffer between them and the outside world. The result may be a high level of tension and frequent inappropriate behavior.

ALL BEHAVIOR MUST HAVE A CONSEQUENCE This means appropriate behavior is rewarded and negative behavior punished. However, the consistency of such rewards and punishments from day to day is also crucial. Consistency of consequence, whether reward or punishment, will aid the child in developing a frame of reference.

REWARDS NEED NOT BE MONETARY Although this is one possibility, rewards can also be verbal praise, written notes of thanks, extended playtime or bedtime, and so on. They should be natural and not mechanical. Variety is also nice in dealing with rewards.

PUNISHMENT ONLY WILL NOT BE EFFECTIVE IN CHANGING NEGATIVE BEHAVIOR Punishment tells children what not to do, but rewards tell children what behavior is acceptable. If long-term changes in behavior are desired, then reward must be included. Many parents shy away from rewards because they feel that doing what is expected should not be rewarded. However, all human beings need positive stroking regardless of whether or not the behavior is expected. Rewarding children for cleaning a room without having been told to do so reinforces the continuation of that behavior. This type of reward may come in the form of a positive comment of appreciation. I am not saying that every behavior should be verbally rewarded. The key to any system is discrimination. It would be very nice if one's boss thanked them for being on time every day, even if it were an expected behavior.

LIMIT PUNISHMENTS TO SOMETHING THAT YOU CAN CONTROL Quantity is not always important. For very young children with no concept of time, five minutes in a "time-out" chair (controllable) rather than fifty minutes (uncontrollable) is just as good. On the other hand, delaying a teenager's departure for two hours on a Friday or Saturday night can be just as effective and more easily controlled than being grounded for a week. The most important thing to remember with discipline is that the parent begin it and end it. Maintaining both boundaries is crucial. Consequently, parents should avoid very harsh "You are grounded till you get married" punishments at first. This will only confuse children and distort their frame of reference. Even worse, the parent will most likely be the one punished if long unrealistic consequences are chosen.

NEVER TRADE A PUNISHMENT FOR A REWARD If children do something inappropriate and then something appropriate, the two incidents should be treated separately. You may want to say that while you appreciate their appropriate behavior and feel good about their choice, the poor judgment they had shown with the other incident cannot be overlooked. If you begin to trade off, children will learn to avoid punishment merely by doing something appropriate.

TRY TO PROJECT A UNITED FRONT WHEN USING DISCIPLINE If one parent disagrees with the other's tactics or reasoning, discuss it at a private moment. Open disagreement concerning a disciplinary action can confuse children and place them in the uncomfortable position of having to choose between parents.

FOCUS ON THE INAPPROPRIATE BEHAVIOR, NOT THE PERSONALITY Remember, children are not stupid; it is their inappropriate behavior that is unacceptable. You may want to use phrases such as "poor judgment" and "inappropriate behavior," when confronting the act. Focusing on the act allows children to save face. It may also allow them to understand better and accept more appropriate options for the next time. Children who grow up in a home where personalities are attacked tend to model that behavior in their social relationships. They tend to be less tolerant and more critical of their peers.

CHOOSE YOUR BATTLEGROUNDS WISELY Try to view energy like money. In this way you will be deciding whether an issue is worth a $2.00 or $200.00 investment. Overinvesting can only lead to parent burnout.

Parents should sit down with each other and discuss what they feel are the more important issues. As long as children are not verbally abusive or destructive, statements of frustration or healthy anger should be tolerated. However, if these statements become loudly vocalized to the point of screaming at the "top of their lungs," then limits must be set and they should be taught more appropriate ways of venting feelings. It is very destructive to allow children to use verbal abuse in any form because a parent "feels" that they must be allowed to vent feelings.

For the purposes of this particular section, verbal abuse should be defined as any verbal act directed at the parent using cursing, vulgar comments or attacks against the parent's personality, such as jerk, idiot, and so on. There are healthy ways to communicate anger rather than verbal abuse.

NEVER ALLOW TEMPER TANTRUMS AN AUDIENCE   Children will sometimes choose the most inopportune place to throw a tantrum, for example, in a supermarket or while visiting a relative's house. Regardless of the location, you should not allow them control of the situation. Removal of the audience is crucial.

Further, the more one tries to reason with children when they are in this state, the more control you are relinquishing. Tell them that you will be more than happy to discuss their concerns when the tantrum is over. But remember, no audience. Removal to a room, a car, or some isolated area may be necessary.

When the child is in a more rational state, teach him or her other ways to discuss concerns. Further inform him or her that if a tantrum is chosen over communication, there will be a consequence. Remember to reward any behavior that approaches verbal communication.

TRY NOT TO CONCEAL PROBLEMS WITH CHILDREN FROM THE OTHER PARENT   Some parents will choose this direction to "protect" children. Parents may actually increase a child's anxiety level if this approach is used. Children tend to lose a frame of reference in regard to the other parent when it comes to anger. The message is that the other parents should be feared. If many incidents are held back, children begin to ponder the other parent's reaction if they find out. This fear may increase internal tension and preoccupy their mind with unbased fears.

In most cases, it is better for children to gain a sense of reality rather than fantasize about what might happen. The only exception occurs when one parent is prone to violence and abuse. In this case, such protection is a form of survival.

TRY NOT TO RELINQUISH POWER TO THE OTHER PARENT   Relinquishing power, for example, saying "Wait until Daddy gets home," gives off a negative message to children. It implies that you cannot control the situation. What may be the real issue is that you have run out of techniques and are feeling frustrated. If this is the case, delay dealing with your children. Send them to their room and tell them that you will deal with this later. Regroup your own control rather than pass it off to the other parent. Further, relinquishing power tends to reduce feelings of self-esteem both as a parent and as a person.

TRY TO USE A FORCED CHOICE TECHNIQUE WHENEVER POSSIBLE Choose two options that are both acceptable to you. Then, say to children, "You may do...or...Which do you prefer?" This technique is more realistic than an open-ended "What would you like to do?" In this case you may either get no response or one that is not acceptable to you. Using a forced choice technique allows children to feel that they are making the decision. Either choice will be acceptable. If children reply, "Neither," remind them that "neither" is not an option and they may only choose either of the two presented. After a few minutes of testing most children will make a choice.

DON'T BE AFRAID TO DELAY A CONSEQUENCE WHEN YOU ARE VERY ANGRY The use of delay allows for a different perspective than that viewed at the height of anger. There is nothing wrong with saying, "I am so angry right now that I don't want to deal with this situation. Go to your room and I'll deal with you in fifteen minutes." The use of delay will also reduce impractical consequences.

In conclusion, be aware that parenting is not a popularity contest but a responsibility. The opportunity to select from a variety of tools when confronted with a positive or negative situation can only enhance the difficult but rewarding job of child rearing.

Section 28

How Special Educators Can Help Parents Communicate Better with Their Children

Communication is a major factor behind any good relationship, whether between friends, spouses, siblings, or parents and children. However, many parents are at a loss when it comes to communicating with their children. What may start out as communication may wind up as a lecture, argument, or worse.

Communication comes in many forms and knowledge of certain techniques can greatly enhance a relationship. The following guidelines should be kept in mind to allow positive interaction with children.

COMMUNICATION IS A TWO-WAY STREET The technique of "I'll talk and you listen, and then you talk and I'll listen" is a first step and should be taught to children as soon as possible. Many people think they are communicating but in a sense they never listen. The technique of active listening is a first step in the development of communication skills.

TRY NOT TO ATTACK WHEN COMMUNICATING Communication will tend to deteriorate if either party feels they are being attacked. This feeling can come in many forms, but the most usual way is through the use of the word "you." This word more than any other creates a defensive structure and interrupts the flow of communication. When communicating feelings, try using the words "I," "we," or "me" as often as possible. Even if someone has done something to hurt you, focus on your feelings rather than their behavior. Inform the individual on how the behavior affected you.

TEACH CHILDREN TO LABEL FEELINGS PROPERLY There are many times when the only difference between communication and an argument is the choice of words. Many arguments could be avoided if either party used more appropriate labels. The ability to label one's feelings is an important factor in communication. Nowhere is that more evident than in the case of children. Children may have a very hard time communicating because they lack the experience in labeling their feelings. When children are unable to correctly label an internal feeling, the feeling becomes trapped and the frustration may be become manifested in behavior problems, physical symptoms, and so on. When such feelings are manifested in these forms, they are usually misunderstood or misinterpreted. Therefore, it is crucial for parents to assist their children in correctly labeling a feeling or emotion. You may want to say, for example, "While the feeling you are expressing sounds like anger, it is really frustration, and frustration is...." It is also helpful to have children develop an emotional vocabulary so that feelings and communication can flow more easily.

USE CONNECTIVE DISCUSSION WHENEVER POSSIBLE Parents will often use direct communication such as, "Tell me what is wrong," or "Tell me what you feel," or "Tell me why you did that." It is this line of questioning that has the least chance of obtaining a response from the child. Since most children do not possess the labels or experiences in communication necessary for such an answer, what parents may want to use instead is *connective discussion.* This technique assumes something and offers children reasonable labels for what they may be experiencing. For example, parents may say, "It seems to me that you are feeling upset over your new baby brother. I think you may be feeling somewhat jealous because you feel he gets more attention than you." Another example may be to say, "I get the feeling from your behavior that you are trying to say something. I think what you may be trying to say...." If you are in close physical proximity, you may observe some nonverbal reaction, an intense denial, crying, or some other similar response. At this point, children should have an easier time expressing themselves since they have a foundation from which to work.

ALL BEHAVIOR HAS A TRIGGER Sometimes this trigger may be unconscious and not available for identification. However, in many cases, the trigger is conscious, and the knowledge that an intense response will always follow some incident or feeling, and soon, can be helpful. If parents can trace back children's responses to the source or trigger, they will have a very good chance of identifying the real problem. In fact, it may be good practice to have children do just that if they become upset or show inappropriate behavior. Ask them to think about what took place immediately prior to the behavior. If they cannot remember and you are aware of the "trigger," use connective discussion to make the bridge.

BE AWARE OF NONVERBAL MISINTERPRETATIONS Children are very prone to nonverbal misinterpretations. They may, for instance, misread the look on a parent's face and personalize it into something negative. This is very typical of younger children.

If parents are upset, angry, or frustrated with some situation other than their child, they should let the child know that fact in a verbal way. You do not have to go into detail, but merely say, "I am very upset right now with something. But I wanted to tell you that it has nothing to do with you, and after I think for awhile, we will get together."

This small piece of communication may prevent some very anxious moments for children.

USE WRITTEN COMMUNICATION WHENEVER POSSIBLE Another useful form of communication is writing. The use of writing to communicate feelings is an excellent tool since it allows parents and children to phrase thoughts as desired for the best results. Notes thanking a child for some positive behavior are great. Notes telling children to have a nice day, that you love them very much or you appreciated their cooperation are all examples of written communication.

Notes can also be used to register a complaint without nose-to-nose confrontation. This is nice to use when the issue at hand is not a major one.

Spontaneity with written communication is also a very nice message. Notes in a lunch box, notebook, slipped into a textbook are excellent. Of course, discrimination with any technique is suggested.

TRY TO USE DIRECT LOVE AS OFTEN AS POSSIBLE Many clients in therapy will often talk about the way their parents expressed love to them. The need to feel loved and cared for is a primary need for any individual at any age. Many of these clients, as well as other adults with whom I have spoken, express the indirectness on the part of their parents when it came to communicating feelings of love and caring.

For instance, when asked the question, "How did you know your father or mother loved you?" some will respond by saying, "Because they used to take care of me when I was sick." Other responses included "bringing home things when they were good...being kept neat and clean...being helped with homework...." All these messages are fine except they all represent *indirect love*.

If indirect love is the only "game in town," then the individuals receiving it from parents must utilize interpretation and assumption. These individuals have all assumed the fact that because of "A," "B" must be true. Such a need for assumption when dealing with indirect messages of love can be dangerous. The same assumption can be made and is often made that such love is conditional. The individual assumes that illness, injury, and other situations are the conditions for love and caring.

Be aware of this factor and utilize as many direct messages of love as you can. Direct messages of love require no interpretation or assumption by children. Even teenagers, who on some verbal level will reject such expressions of love, need to hear it anyway. Direct messages include verbal statements like, "I am a very lucky parent to have a son/daughter like you," or "You mean a great deal to me," or "There may be times when I am angry with you, but I want you to know I always love you." Don't assume your children know that you feel this way. Communicate to them directly.

Another very necessary and important example of *direct love* is through the use of physical demonstration of feelings. When dealing with children, demonstrating love by hugging, kissing, cuddling, holding, allowing to sit on your lap, and other expressions should be an everyday part of communication. While not every adult has "learned ability" to use such direct messages, the absence of this form of communication in a parent-child relationship may have adverse effects for the child in later life.

The higher the *approachability factor* on the part of parents, the easier it is for children to express and show direct love to them. In later life, the individual may have an easier time using direct forms of love in relationships. The lower the approachability factor, the more difficult it is for children to communicate love to their parents. In later life, these individuals may have unproductive relationships.

EXAMPLES OF ALTERNATE RESPONSES

Avoid	*Try*
Use of the word "you"	Use the words "I," Me," or "We"
"Tell me what you feel."	"I get the feeling that . . ." "It seems to me . . ." "I get the feeling from your behavior that you are trying to say . . ."
"You listen to me!"	"I'll talk and you listen and then you can talk and I'll listen."
"What would you like?"	"You can choose between . . . and . . . Which do you prefer?
"Speak with me later."	"Let's get together in 10 minutes."
"Clean your room!"	"Please clean your room and by clean I mean the following . . ."
"Be home early."	"Please be home between . . . and . . ."
"I don't trust you . . ."	"Trust is not the issue. It's your sense of judgment that concerns me."
"You are grounded forever."	"I am so angry. I'll deal with you later."

In conclusion, the ability to communicate using proper labels will relieve both children's and parents' emotional turmoil and benefit the relationship in the long run.

Section 29

How Special Educators Can Help Parents Improve Their Child's Self-esteem

Self-esteem is feeling good about yourself. Because it is a feeling, self-esteem is expressed in the way that people behave. However, success is important for the growth of positive feelings about oneself. High self-esteem will allow children to keep failure situations in proper perspective. Whether or not a failure situation is perceived as a learning experience, or as a self-punishment, depends on one's level of self-esteem.

Children as well as adults will vary in the type of self-esteem exhibited. We all feel more confident on some days than others. Feeling low self-esteem from time to time is not a problem. However, a pattern of low self-esteem should be observed in order for there to be a concern. Parents can easily observe children's self-esteem by seeing what they do and how they accomplish it.

CHARACTERISTICS OF A CHILD WITH HIGH SELF-ESTEEM

- ◆ Feels capable of influencing other's opinions or behaviors in a positive way
- ◆ Communicates feelings and emotions in a variety of situations
- ◆ Behaves independently
- ◆ Approaches new situations in a positive manner
- ◆ Exhibits a high level of frustration tolerance
- ◆ Takes on and assumes responsibility
- ◆ Keeps situations in proper perspective
- ◆ Communicates positive feelings about himself or herself
- ◆ Tries a new situation without major resistance

Such children will possess an *internal locus of control*. Consequently, they feel that whatever happens to them is a direct result of their own behavior or actions. These children will therefore feel a sense of power over their environment.

CHARACTERISTICS OF A CHILD WITH LOW SELF-ESTEEM

- ◆ Communicates self-derogatory statements
- ◆ Exhibits a low frustration tolerance
- ◆ Becomes easily defensive
- ◆ Listens to another's judgment rather than his or her own

- Resists new situations and experiences
- Constantly blames others for his or her failures and problems
- Has very little feeling of power and control
- Loses perspective easily (blows things out of proportion)
- Avoids any situation that creates tension
- Is unwilling to reason

Such children will possess an *external locus of control*. Consequently, these children feel that what ever happens to them is the result of fate, luck or chance.

FACTORS ASSOCIATED WITH SELF-ESTEEM

To understand self-esteem fully, one must consider the factors involved. Self-esteem occurs when children experience the positive feelings of satisfaction associated with feeling:

Connected—A child feels good relating to people, places, and things that are important to him or her and these relationships are approved and respected by others.

Unique—A child acknowledges and respects the personal characteristics that make him or her special and different and receives approval and respect from others for those characteristics.

Powerful—A child uses the skills, resources, and opportunities that he or she has to influence the circumstances of his or her own life in important ways.

HOW TO BUILD A CHILD'S SELF-ESTEEM

The following suggestions are offered to enhance children's positive feelings about themselves. These recommendations require consistency, genuineness, and discrimination on the part of parents. No one suggestion by itself will have long-lasting effects. A combination of techniques will have greater impact. However, parents should always keep in mind that many other factors, not within their control, for example, peer group, school success or failure, perception, and so on, will also contribute to children's self-esteem. However, the role of parents is a crucial one and can offset difficulties in other areas.

BE SOLUTION ORIENTED An important step in building children's self-esteem is to teach solutions rather than blame. Some families are very "blame oriented." When something goes wrong, everyone is quick to "point the finger" at each other. Children who grow up in this type of environment not only become easily frustrated, but never learn how to handle obstacles. Teaching children solutions begins with simple statements like, "Who's at fault is not important. The more important question is what can we do so that it doesn't happen again." Being solution oriented allows children a sense of control and resiliency when confronted with situations that could be ego deflating.

ALLOW CHILDREN THE RIGHT TO MAKE DECISIONS While the statement, "No one promised them a democracy" may hold true in some parental situations, allowing children the right to make decisions that affect their daily life can only enhance their self-esteem. Decisions about clothing, room arrangement, friends to invite at a party, menu for dinner, and so on can make children feel some sense of control in what happens to them. Coupled with solution orientation, mistakes can be used as a positive learning experience.

OFFER ALTERNATIVE WAYS WHEN HANDLING A SITUATION Some people know only one or two alternatives in handling situations. After these fail, frustration occurs. Teaching children to see many alternative ways of handling a situation or obstacle can also enhance their self-esteem. Asking children what they have tried, and offering them options to other possible solutions, increases their "tool box." The more "tools" we have at our disposal, the easier life becomes. Individuals with limited "tools" tend to use avoidance and flight.

TEACH CHILDREN THE PROPER LABELS WHEN COMMUNICATING FEELINGS The ability to label one's feelings correctly is a factor in self-esteem. Children have a very difficult time communicating because they lack the proper labels for their feelings. Children who are unable to label an internal feeling become trapped, and their frustration may become manifested in behavior problems, physical symptoms, and so on. When such feelings are manifested in other forms, they are usually misunderstood or misinterpreted. Parents can offer children the correct labels. For example, you may want to say, "While the feeling you are expressing sounds like anger, it is really frustration and frustration is...." Now that you know this, is there anything that is causing you frustration?"

Building an emotional vocabulary allows communication to flow more easily and reduces a child's unwillingness to deal with situations.

ALLOW CHILDREN THE OPPORTUNITY TO REPEAT SUCCESSFUL EXPERIENCES Whenever possible, allow children the chance to handle any job or responsibility in which they have proven success. A foundation of positive experiences is necessary for self-esteem. Since the child has mastered skills required for the job, any opportunity to repeat success can only be ego inflating. Jobs such as cooking dinner, cutting the lawn, fixing something around the house, and making the shopping list are examples of repetitive experiences.

ALLOW AVENUES FOR DISAGREEMENT Children with higher self-esteem will always feel they have an avenue to communicate their concerns. Even though the result may not go in their favor, the knowledge that a situation or disagreement can be discussed allows the child to feel some involvement in his or her destiny. This factor becomes important when one sees that many children with low self-esteem feel a loss of power in affecting change.

HELP YOUR CHILD SET REALISTIC GOALS This is a crucial issue in helping children improve their self-esteem. Some children will set unrealistic goals, fall short, and feel like a failure. Over time, the child begins to feel a sense of urgency, leading to more unrealistic goals. This circular behavior sometimes results with children becoming unwilling to venture out or take chances. The more limited children become in their experiences, the less chance there is for success. Avoidance, passivity, rejection of an idea or experience will only reinforce feelings of inadequacy. Help children by defining their goals. You may want to ask them what they want to accomplish. After this, try to help them define the steps necessary to accomplish the task. Each step becomes a goal in itself. Children should not see one final goal, but a series of smaller goals leading to a final point. In this way they will feel accomplishment at every step.

USE A REWARD SYSTEM TO SHAPE POSITIVE BEHAVIOR Punishment tells a child what not to do, while rewards inform them of what to do. Rewarding positive behavior increases self-esteem. Children enjoy winning the approval of parents, especially when it comes to a job or task. You may want to use rewards such as notes indicating how proud you feel about what the child has accomplished. Rewards can also be special trips, special dinners with one parent, extra time before bed, or a hug and a kiss. The use of monetary rewards can also be utilized every so often at the parents' discretion.

DON'T PAVE ALL YOUR CHILDREN'S ROADS Some parents make the mistake of reducing frustration for children to the point where the child receives a distorted view of the world. Children with high self-esteem get frustrated. However, they tend to be more resilient because they have previously handled frustrating situations and have worked out the solutions themselves. When parents rush to the aid of their children, or change the environment to prevent them from becoming frustrated, they are unwittingly reinforcing children's low self-esteem. After awhile, children become so dependent upon their parents to "bail them out" when they are confronted with frustration. The need to master the environment and find solutions to challenges is crucial to positive self-esteem. The old saying, "Catch me a fish and I'll eat today, teach me to fish and I'll eat forever," seems to apply.

In closing, parents need to evaluate their own feelings of self-esteem. If they are experiencing feelings of inadequacy, changing children's feelings about themselves will be more difficult. Improving children's self-esteem is a process that needs to be viewed in a positive way. Altering feelings of low self-esteem offers children a more positive future.

Section 30

What Parents Need to Know About Retention

Retention of a student's grade placement is a very difficult decision for both parents and educators. In some cases the decision is based on a single factor such as classroom performance. In other cases several factors are considered. Whatever the input, it is a decision that should not be taken lightly. The implications for the student and his or her family can have long-lasting effects.

When parents are first presented with this suggestion by the school, they may become very overwhelmed and confused. Instead of looking into the possible reasons, some parents will get angry and exert more pressure on the child. They may see this action as a social stigma rather than an educational recommendation. In other cases, parents agree to the school's recommendation without question. If parents are presented with this option, then great care should be taken in examining all the variables that will effect the outcome.

We have all heard stories from friends, neighbors, teachers, and family on the results of grade retention. Some adults will say that the decision was a positive step and gave them the opportunity to "catch up." However, others express negative feelings surrounding the ridicule, family pressure, loss of self-esteem, social problems, and continued difficulties in school even after retention.

Present research seems somewhat divided about the use of such an educational alternative. Some studies have shown that the greatest success for such an action occurs in kindergarten and first grade. The chances for success dramatically decrease as children become older. Other studies seem to indicate that if retention is exercised as an option in kindergarten and first grade, boys seem to benefit most. This result seems to support the developmental pattern of a more advanced social and academic maturity in girls. Some parents decide to wait an extra year before enrolling their sons in school. Since most referrals to psychologists, resource rooms, and special education class elementary school are boys, this "waiting period" should be further explored. However, the emphasis with today's education is to begin earlier, around age four, not later. Consequently, more research is needed.

Since parents should be involved in the decision of retention, it is important that they become educated in this area. The following factors should be taken into consideration prior to the final action.

PRESENT GRADE PLACEMENT As previously mentioned, the greatest chance for retention to work is in kindergarten and first grade. By the time children are in fourth or fifth grade, the chances for success decrease dramatically.

IMMATURE BEHAVIOR PATTERNS The level of interpersonal relations exhibited by children is also a factor to consider. If they tend to play with children much younger than themselves, retention will have fewer consequences. However, if children choose peers who are equal or older in age, retention may have more negative results.

AGE OF THE CHILD Children who are younger than their classmates will experience fewer problems with retention. However, children who are one or two years above their classmates may have more serious adjustments to this action, especially if they are retained in the upper grades.

BROTHERS AND SISTERS Children without siblings seem to make a better adjustment when repeating a grade. Others with brothers or sisters in the same grade or one year below find retention much more difficult. Children in this category find the experience ego deflating and feel a loss of familial status.

ATTENDANCE The more times a child is out from school, the greater the reason for retention. Children who are ill and miss over 25 days of school are prime candidates. This is especially important in the early grades where the foundations of reading and basic skills are taught. Some children with excellent attendance are less suitable candidates.

INTELLECTUAL ABILITY Children with average intelligence have the better chance of success with retention. However, those with below-average (lower 2–10 percent) or superior ability (upper 2–10 percent) tend to have more difficulty. Children who fall into these categories may be having difficulties in school for other reasons that would not be addressed by retention, for example, emotional and mental disabilities.

PHYSICAL SIZE Children who are smaller in stature make better candidates. Those who are physically larger than their present classmates will have more problems when retained.

GENDER As previously mentioned, boys in kindergarten and first grade make the best candidates. After fourth grade both boys and girls will have little chance of success when it comes to retention.

PRESENT CLASSROOM PERFORMANCE Students who are performing one year behind in most academic subjects may find retention a help. Those who are more than two years behind may need an alternate type of program such as special education class or resource room help. Children who are functioning on grade level or above should be reviewed carefully.

PRESENT EMOTIONAL STATE Children who do not exhibit any signs of serious emotional difficulties, for example, impulsivity, nervous habits, distractibility, unwillingness to reason, and tantrums, have a better chance when retained. Children who exhibit serious emotional concerns should not be considered for retention. However, other educational options should be explored.

PARENT'S ATTITUDE This factor is crucial. Children will have the best chance of adjusting to retention when their parents see it as a positive step. Frustrated, angry, and disappointed parents will negate any chance of success.

STUDENT'S ATTITUDE Children who see retention as an opportunity to "catch up" will have a better chance of success. Children who become very upset, exhibit denial about poor performance, or show indifference may have greater difficulty.

NUMBER OF SCHOOLS ATTENDED Children who have attended several schools within their first two years of school will have less success with retention. This results from a lack of other factors to ease the transition, i.e. peer connections, prior teacher relationships, environmental frame of reference, and so on.

EVIDENCE OF LEARNING DISABILITIES Children with intact learning skills and processes have a greater chance for success when it comes to retention. Children who have been diagnosed as having learning disabilities should receive alternate educational support. In such cases, retention should not be considered as an option.

The foregoing factors are offered as a general guide for parents. There may be other factors that should be considered as well. Regardless, parents' input into this decision is crucial.

Section 31

LD Organizations and Information Services

It is very important that parents of learning disabled children have every opportunity to gain further knowledge about groups, organizations, legal services, publications, and other resources that can help them to understand better the issues being faced by their children. The following list was prepared with this motive in mind. Parents are urged to write or contact these organizations so that they can receive excellent resource material. Such material includes practical readings, suggestions, parent's rights, and so on. The Institute for Practical Parenting is providing the following list as a service and in no way advocates one organization's services over another.

Association for Children and Adults with Learning Disabilities (ACLD)
National ACLD
4156 Library Road
Pittsburgh, PA 15234
(412) 341-1515

This is a membership organization for professionals and parents. The literature inventory lists over three hundred publications on learning disabilities which may be purchased.

Closer Look
1201 16th Street, N.W.
Washington, D.C. 20036
(202) 833-4160

A national information center for handicapped people. This organization provides information on federal legislation affecting the handicapped, legal rights, bibliographies, and other materials. Closer Look offers a free booklet, "Steps to Independence for People with Learning Disabilities."

Closer Look L.D. Teenline
(800) 522-3458

This is toll free for information and referral services for parents of LD teens, educators who serve them, and LD teens themselves.

The Council for Exceptional Children (CEC)
Division for Children with Learning Disabilities (DCLD)
1920 Association Drive
Reston, VA 22091
(703) 620-3660 or Toll Free (800) 336-3728

This organization provides services for teachers, therapists, parents, administrators, and students.

LD Hotline
(212) 409-2233

This service provides free information and referral services to parents of LD/neurologically impaired children, adolescents, and adults, as well as service providers who work with these problems.

National Easter Seal Society
2023 W. Ogden Avenue
Chicago, IL 60612

This organization provides information on publications concerning the learning disabled child.

National Information Center for Handicapped Children and Youth
Box 1492
Washington, D.C. 20013

This organization provides an informational newsletter on projects, progress, and good things happening to handicapped youth in your area.

The Orton Society, Inc. (Main Branch)
8415 Bellona Lane
Towson, MD 21204

Public Affairs Pamphlets
381 Park Ave. South
New York, NY 10016

This organization provides valuable information covering social and personal concerns for the handicapped as well as health and mental health issues.

Your State Education Department
Office for Education of Children with Handicapping Conditions

State Education Departments provide a great deal of information. Just list your needs. Make sure you send for *A Parent's Guide to Special Education—Your Child's Educational Rights in New York State.*

Besides gathering information from the foregoing sources, several excellent publications are available on the topic of learning disabilities. These are wonderful sources of information, comfort, and reassurance for parents and children.

Academic Therapy
20 Commercial Boulevard
Novato, CA 94947

This journal, published six times a year, emphasizes methods of identification, diagnosis, and remediation.

ACLD Newsbriefs
4156 Liberty Road
Pittsburgh, PA 15234

This newsletter, printed six times per year, emphasizes current research on learning disabilities.

Bulletin of the Orton Society
8415 Bellona Lane
Towson, MD 21204

This is the official bulletin of the Orton Society. It is issued once a year and tends to focus on the study, treatment and education of children with specific language disability (dyslexia).

Exceptional Children
Publication of the Council for Exceptional Children
1920 Association Drive
Reston, VA 22091

This publication includes articles that cover all exceptionalities in children.

The Exceptional Parent
P.O. Box 101
Boston, MA 02117

This journal contains detailed articles on all aspects of exceptionality. It is issued six times a year.

The Journal of Learning Disabilities
101 East Ontario Street
Chicago, IL 60611

This journal, which is issued ten times a year, contains information applicable to all children with learning disabilities. It is very practical in its approach.

The Journal of Special Education
Buttonwood Farms
3515 Woodhaven Road
Philadelphia, PA 19154

This journal, which is issued four times a year, contains relevant material for remedial reading approaches for handicapped children.

Learning Disability Quarterly
Council for Exceptional Children
1920 Association Drive
Reston, VA 22091

The content of this publication includes educational articles with an applied emphasis that focuses on learning disabilities.

Perceptions: The Newsletter for Parents of Children with LD
P.O. Box 142
Millburn, NJ 07041

Published monthly, this newsletter contains practical suggestions and reports on the field of learning disabilities.

If you feel the rights of your learning disabled child are not being addressed or feel you have been denied due process, call the local child advocacy center or organization. They are usually listed in your phone book.

Section 32

How Special Educators Can Help Parents Improve Their Child's Study Skills

Many children experience difficulty in school because they have weak study skills. This section suggests various strategies that promote efficient study habits and thereby enhance a child's chance for academic success. However, these strategies are not intended as a solution for children who have severe learning problems.

When you have decided which strategies might be beneficial, introduce one at a time as a helpful hint or in a game format. Some of these activities will be used on a trial-and-error basis. Be flexible in following each strategy. If it works, that's great! If not, abandon it.

It is important to keep in mind that not every strategy will work with every child. Success will depend upon the child's individual learning style and needs, motivation, and willingness to accept parental guidance. At all times, your relationship with your child is of primary importance. It should be relaxed and stress free. Offer praise and encouragement frequently. If implementation of any of these strategies creates anxiety or resentment (on the part of either parent or child), it is advisable to discontinue.

HOW TO KEEP YOUR PLACE If your child loses his or her place, skips lines, or mixes up words in successive lines, use a placemarker. If a pencil or fingertip doesn't suffice, try using a blank unlined index card as a marker. The index card can also be effectively used on a page of questions to expose one question at a time. This technique will help the child focus on each question without becoming confused or overwhelmed by all the writing on the page.

USE A BOOKSTAND Using a bookstand is helpful to many children when reading or copying from a textbook. The diagonal position the bookstand provides makes it easier to read the material because the viewing angle is better. Positioning the bookstand directly above the paper also makes for easier copying. Since children can raise and lower their eyes without moving their head sideways, it becomes simpler to shift from the book to the writing paper and back again.

A SPECIAL WAY TO READ TEXTBOOKS Just think of all the information one gets from watching a movie or television preview. Similarly, children can gather much information by previewing and surveying textbook material. It is advisable to do this to know when to cue into important content as one goes along.

Strange as it may seem, do not have the student start at the beginning and read through to the end of the chapter. First, survey the chapter by looking at the title and paragraph headings in bold print. Suggest that your child think of these as "road signs" to help find the way through the chapter. Also look at graphic material (pictures, charts, and maps) and read captions.

Next, read the summary and the questions at the end of the chapter. That's the preview! By now, your child should have some idea of what the chapter will be about and what information to look for.

RESTATE THE MAIN IDEA This strategy is particularly effective when reading content area material (social studies, science, etc.). After the child has read a paragraph, ask him or her to think about what was read and tell you the most important idea or facts in his or her own words. It may be necessary for the child to reread the paragraph. If difficulty persists, you may have to discuss several paragraphs and provide appropriate responses for each of them until the child is able to do so independently.

Be sure to stress that the overall main idea must be followed from paragraph to paragraph. Students in the upper grades will find this strategy helpful and wish to write down the main ideas or tape them. This will provide an excellent review format for tests.

CORROBORATE ANSWERS If your child works quickly and/or carelessly and makes errors when answering comprehension questions, try this strategy. Encourage the child to "prove" his or her answers by locating supporting information in the text. When demonstrating, point out that the words in dark print will help find the section that is most likely to contain the information.

Again, think of the words in dark print as road signs to help you find the way.

This strategy discourages "guessing" and promotes accuracy in locating information. The next time a similar assignment is given, remind your child that you expect him or her to be able to "prove" the answers.

DEVELOP MEMORY USING WORD STRATEGIES Mnemonic strategies (memory aids) can be effectively used to help individuals recall information. Letters and words can be arranged in a variety of ways to enhance memory.

1. **First letter of each item to be remembered forms a word.**

Example: To recall the names of the Great Lakes, think of the word "HOMES":
        Huron Ontario Michigan Erie Superior

2. **Group items by first letters.**

Example: For the seven continents, six begin with the letter "A" and one begins with the letter "E": Asia, Australia, Antarctica, Africa, N. America, S. America, Europe

3. **Put key words in a sentence.**

Example: "Spring forward and fall back" (to recall time changes)

Remembering the key word or clue will help organize the material to be retrieved. Gradually, encourage the child to make up his or her own clues.

USE GAMES TO ENHANCE LEARNING When a child has to learn new vocabulary and factual information, the use of game formats can take the chore out of study…and can actually be fun. The games are easy to make and individualize for specific tasks.

Write new vocabulary words on a set of 3-inch by 5-inch index cards and the corresponding definitions on another set of cards. Your child can help create the games.

1. **Matching**—Mix up each set of cards. Place both sets of cards on the table (writing side up). See if your child can match the words to the correct definitions. Then review any words the child is unsure of. When the child can match all the pairs correctly, he or she is ready to proceed to the next game.

2. **Concentration**—Turn about six or seven pairs of cards face down on the table. (The number of cards used can be adjusted to suit the child's capabilities.) Player 1 turns over any two cards, reading them aloud. If they match, he or she keeps the pair and takes another turn. If not, the cards are replaced, face down, in the same position and player 2 takes a turn. The game proceeds until all the cards have been matched. The player with the most pairs wins.

3. **Password**—Place the set of vocabulary words face down. Player 1 picks the top card, reads the word to himself, then gives clues to the other player. Player 2 must guess the word from the clue. (Both players must be familiar with the definitions in order to play.)

An advanced form of this game involves selecting a card and writing the definition with points awarded for correct answers and bonus points for correct spelling.

The games are not limited to vocabulary. They can be used to study different kinds of information, such as explorers and places of exploration, famous men and women, discoveries, and states and their capitals. The game formats and rules can be varied to meet each child's functional and motivational needs.

RESEARCH If research is assigned on a topic that is totally unfamiliar to your child and/or if reading skills are weak, ask the librarian to suggest simple books that deal with the topic. Explain to your child that if you, as an adult, were taking a first course in something you had never studied before (chemistry or physics), a good place to start might be in a middle school or high school book. This type of book supplies some really basic information in simpler language and builds a foundation for understanding the harder material.

REPEAT INFORMATION ALOUD For many children, silently reading material is often an ineffective method of study. Verbalizing or repeating information aloud is an important aid to retention. Encourage your child to read a small segment (verbalizing softly) from a chapter. Then, covering the material, quietly say to himself or herself or repeat aloud what he or she wishes to remember. This kind of "verbal rehearsal" is a beneficial strategy for many children.

HOMEWORK HINTS It is helpful for a child to have a set place and time for doing schoolwork. The place the child works in should have adequate lighting and be quiet enough for concentration. Materials (paper, pencils, etc.) should be organized and easily available. School papers should be secure from younger siblings and pets. But remember, needs vary. Your child may not wish to be isolated or may rely on some adult support while completing tasks.

When the child participates in determining his or her daily homework schedule, he or she is more likely to adhere to it. It should be flexible, allowing for changes due to special events. You may wish to vary it with the seasons to allow for outdoor play in good weather. Consideration might also be given as to whether one lengthy session or two or three shorter sessions are more suitable to the child's work style and attention span.

It should be agreed that during the planned time, there will be no interruptions (telephone, television, etc.).

If your child spends an excessive amount of time doing homework, making up classwork, or struggling with assignments, consider scheduling a conference with your child's teacher to discuss the matter.

Please keep in mind that your patience, praise, and support are integral components of all the suggestions herein.

Section 33

How Special Educators Can Help Parents Improve Their Child's Reading

Not all children develop the ability to read at the same rate. To read competently, one must be able to decode (sound out or recognize) words and comprehend the meaning of the material being read. The emphasis in this section will be on decoding. Some of the strategies suggested have been successfully used in classrooms, while others are basic hints that will help you foster a positive attitude toward reading in your home.

It is important to keep in mind that not every strategy will work for every child. Success will depend upon the child's motivation, particular learning style, and willingness to accept parental guidance. Your relationship with your child is of primary importance—it should be relaxed and stress free. If implementation of any of these ideas creates anxiety or resentment (on the part of either parent or child), it is advisable to discontinue immediately.

Introduce one strategy at a time, either as a helpful hint or in a game format. Some of these suggestions may be used on a trial-and-error basis. If a suggestion works, that's great! If not, abandon it. Be flexible in following them. If you can expand a successful idea, or find a better way to use it, that's wonderful.

Finally, the purpose of these strategies is to help mild reading problems and promote positive reading attitudes. Although many of the following suggestions may be applicable, this material is not intended as a solution for children who have severe learning problems.

IMPROVING WORD RECOGNITION A technique that has been very successful with many children who have difficulty reading certain words (and who possess some phonic skills (knowing the sounds letters make) is to enlarge those words on 3-inch by 5-inch index cards in dark ink or marker. The words can be taken from textbooks, directions, workbooks, and other resources.

Show the child the card, say the word and/or sound it out, and say the word again. (If the word cannot be sounded out, just say the word while pointing to it.) Then have the child do it. Provide help if necessary. After several tries, put the cards away in an envelope or a small box. Mark them "WORDS TO BE LEARNED."

You are now ready to construct a game format with the child. Every day, you will show him or her each card. If he or she knows the word, a check is earned (right on the card). If not, repeat the introductory steps again. When three checks have been earned for three consecutive responses on different days, the card goes into another group marked "MASTERED WORDS." Set up a reward system for every set number of mastered words (a sticker for every five new words). A larger reward may be set for mastery of every group of twenty-five or fifty words, at which time the mastered words would be reviewed. Of course, the real reward will be the satisfaction the child feels when the number of cards representing learned words grows larger and larger. Do not introduce more than three or four new words at a time. There should be no more than ten words in the "learning" pack at one time. (You can keep your own list of difficult words and add them as the child progresses.) It is important to praise your child when he or she is successful and avoid showing disappointment when he or she is not.

For children who need additional help with word recognition, use picture clues when you can. Have the child draw the picture or you can give word clues, such as "not smooth, but _____." Try using the word in a sentence, or encourage the child to make up the sentence, such as "My steak is tough (tough)."

When the child has learned the word, award credit and transfer the word to another card without the clue. You will be surprised at the number of words learned in a school year with only five or ten minutes of daily practice.

VARIATIONS ON IMPROVING WORD RECOGNITION If your child is meeting with success using these strategies, you may wish to try the following variations. Some are more suitable with younger children, while others are geared toward use with older children.

For Younger Children

1. Word "families" can be placed on a single card.

Examples:

at	**ew**
hat	new
bat	few
cat	drew
fat	grew

Pointing to "at," pronounce it carefully. Then say to the child, "What does this say?" Then pointing to each word, pronounce it and have the child repeat it.

2. Another variation is to write a "root" or "base" word, and the same word with suffixes or endings.

Examples:

walk	**fast**
walks	**fast**er
walked	**fast**est
walking	

Take care to line up all the root words. You may even wish to write the root words in black and the suffixes in another color. This will help the child to see more clearly how new words are formed. It is also beneficial for children who consistently omit word endings when reading.

For Older Children

1. If the word is multisyllabic, use dots to separate the syllables.

Example

un. der. stand

This will allow the child to view each syllable as a smaller unit and make reading the word easier. Of course, explain the strategy to the child. Pronounce each syllable while pointing to it. Have the child repeat the syllable after you. Then say the whole word and let the child repeat it. If the word is particularly difficult, you may have to do this each time you review the word for several days.

2. If the dots don't do the trick, draw a loop under each syllable. This will increase the child's ability to visually separate the word into syllables and make it more manageable.

Example

un der stand

Use the same procedure as above. For both variations give the child credit after he or she has mastered the word. Then write the word on another card, without clues, to include in the learning pack.

USE CONTEXT CLUES When a child comes across a word he or she can't read, encourage him or her to read the entire sentence. Often the meaning or context of the sentence, in combination with the first letter of the word, will provide a good clue.

Example: I saw my friend riding a h_____ when we went to the ranch. (horse)

Also, thinking about the meaning of the sentence may give the child a clue about which word has been read incorrectly.

Example: I took a slip of milk.

Since "slip" doesn't make sense, the child will go back and look at the word again.

HOW TO KEEP YOUR PLACE When children lose their place, skip lines, or mix up words from different lines, have them use a marker. If a finger or pencil tip is not sufficient, try using an unlined 3-inch by 5-inch index card as a marker. The index card can also be effectively used on a page of questions, to expose one question at a time. By doing this, the child can focus on each question, without becoming confused or overwhelmed by all the writing on the page.

USE A BOOKSTAND Using a bookstand is helpful to many children when reading or when copying from a textbook. The angle the bookstand provides makes it easier to read the material on it. Having the bookstand directly above the writing paper also makes for easier copying.

MAKE READING AN IMPORTANT ACTIVITY IN YOUR HOME Children tend to model adult behavior. If your child observes family members reading during leisure time (books, newspapers, magazines), he or she will learn to imitate that behavior. Conversely, if little or no reading takes place, (with television occupying much leisure time), there will be little reading initiative derived from the home environment.

VISIT THE LIBRARY Your child should visit the library regularly and become a cardholder when permitted. The more familiar he or she is with the library, the more comfortable he or she will feel there. In addition to books, libraries offer records, magazines, videotapes, reference material, and more.

You may wish to ask the librarian to recommend "high-interest" books for the reluctant reader. "High-interest–easy-reading" books may also be available for the youngster whose chronological interests do not correspond with his or her reading level.

ABOUT RECREATIONAL READING LEVELS When your child is selecting books for recreational reading, he or she may select material that appears to be too simple. It may be easier than the instructional material being used in the classroom. That is perfectly all right (as long as the discrepancy is not too great), since the object of this type of reading is to relax and develop an appreciation of books. On the other hand, if a child has a very strong interest in a particular subject or hobby, he or she may select books that are rather difficult, but his or her high level of motivation will act as a compensating factor.

RULE OF "5" IN SELECTING BOOKS FOR ENJOYMENT In the absence of a particularly motivating topic (see discussion earlier), how can a parent judge if a book is too difficult for a child? A general rule that may be helpful is

1. Open the book to any page.
2. Have the child read the page out loud.
3. Count the number of words missed.
4. If there are more than five words that the child had difficulty with, the book is probably too hard.

Once you've explained it, the child can use this method independently to make appropriate selections.

WRITE TO READ A creative and motivating way to stimulate reading is to actually write a personalized book. The book should be about the child, a family pet, the child's hobby, a vacation, or any special topic. Once a blank book is purchased, there are several ways to go about this. For example, following a vacation, snapshots can be pasted in the book and accompanying "text" written by the child and/or parent describing the pictures. Action shots are great for this purpose. The text can vary from several words per page for a young child to several sentences or paragraphs for the older child. An alternative to snapshots is having the child illustrate the story. He or she can even make up a story and illustrate it. If the child has difficulty writing or spelling, he or she can dictate and the adult can write, or the adult can provide the text, using words geared toward the child's reading level. When completed, read the book aloud several times. The child will probably pick up any new reading words from the context. In any case, the child is usually thrilled, and the most reluctant reader will want to read and share his or her unique book.

READING IS ALL AROUND US In addition to reading books, there are many opportunities for your child to read every day. Here are some suggestions:

◆ Write notes to your children. Try slipping one into a lunch box or leaving a note in their room.

◆ During vacations or camp time, write more often and call fewer times.

◆ When you go marketing, have your youngster read the shopping list to you and help you check the ingredients on labels. Point out sizes on food containers and signs in the store.

◆ Reading a television schedule has its own built-in reward.

◆ Let your child read road signs, license plates, and maps when traveling.

◆ Have your child read directions to games, model-making kits, and other activities.

◆ Have him or her read recipes when baking or cooking together.

◆ Encourage your child to read the menu to make selections when eating in restaurants.

◆ Buy word games as gifts.

◆ Give a subscription to a children's magazine as a gift. (Check with the librarian for suggestions.)

This is only a partial list of ideas. I'm sure you will think of other ways to extend it. By taking advantage of these opportunities, you will provide your child with many valuable learning and reading experiences.

Please keep in mind that your praise, encouragement, and support are integral components of all the suggestions herein.

Section 34

How Special Educators Can Help Parents Improve Their Child's Comprehension

To read competently, one must be able to decode (sound out or recognize) words and comprehend the meaning of the material being read. Since comprehension depends on the ability to recognize words, refer to the word recognition and context clues information found in Section 33 of this book. Other activities focus on improving comprehension when more formal reading begins to predominate in schoolwork as the grade levels progress.

It is important to keep in mind that not every strategy will work for every child. Success will depend upon the child's individual learning style and needs, motivation, and willingness to accept parental guidance. At all times, your relationship with your child is of primary importance. It should be relaxed and stress free. Offer praise and encouragement frequently. If implementation of any of these strategies creates anxiety or resentment (on the part of either parent or child), discontinue immediately.

When you have decided which strategies might be beneficial, introduce one at a time as a helpful hint or in a game format. Some of these activities will be used on a trial-and-error basis. Be flexible in following each strategy. If it works, great! If not, abandon it. Perhaps you can expand an idea that works for you or find a better way to use it.

Although many of the following suggestions may be applicable, this section is not intended as a solution for children who have severe learning problems.

LISTENING STRATEGIES FOR PROMOTING COMPREHENSION

If word recognition presents a real problem for your child but his or her listening comprehension is good, you may wish to consider the following strategies:

READ ALOUD TOGETHER: CHORAL READING Read aloud orally with your child. This usually removes stress. If the child doesn't know the word, you will provide it and reduce embarrassment and/or frustration. He or she will hear it correctly and possibly recognize it after several repetitions. You will also set a model for good oral expression, and you are there to discuss the material or answer any questions that your child may have.

ALTERNATE READING PARAGRAPHS When an assignment is lengthy and word recognition problems exist, you may choose to alternate reading paragraphs. When it is the child's turn to read, tell him any unknown words. This will reduce the stress created when the child has to struggle with the words and free energy for comprehension.

USING A TAPE RECORDER Pretape a reading assignment. Encourage the child to read the text while listening to the tape. This may be particularly useful if the parent is not available during homework sessions or if working together produces anxiety. If your child is an auditory learner (learns more easily by listening), he or she can use the tape again prior to a test to review material.

GENERAL STRATEGIES FOR INCREASING COMPREHENSION

"SET THE SCENE": A PREREADING ACTIVITY Before a child reads a story or factual passage, discuss any information or experiences related to the content of the material. In this manner, you can heighten awareness and interest levels. You will also establish "associative hookups," that is, form a basis or foundation for assimilation of new knowledge. The child will find the material more meaningful and easier to understand and retain.

PREVIEW NEW VOCABULARY After you have "set the scene," preview difficult words or new vocabulary terms that appear on a worksheet or in a story. In textbooks, these words usually appear in boldface. Discussing the meaning of the words may also be helpful. If the child cannot read the word or does not understand what a word means, this will interfere with comprehension. Try to keep the number of words limited to four or five. If there are too many words, reduce the reading assignment to smaller segments. When one segment has been completed, you can introduce the words for the next part.

BE AWARE OF SEQUENCE When working with questions following a reading selection, it may be helpful for the child to be aware that the order of the questions usually follows the sequence of the material in the story. For example, the answer to the first question will often be located at the beginning of the passage, the second after that, and so on. This is particularly true of reading comprehension worksheets used in the earlier grades.

UNDERSTAND KEY QUESTION WORDS To understand material and answer questions competently, your child must understand exactly what is being asked. Focusing on the key word in a question will help him or her to do this.

Example: "**Who**" asks for a person or a group of people.

"**When**" refers to a time (hour, day, date, era, before or after another event, etc.) Other key words are "**Where**," "**What**," "**How**," and "**Why**."

Familiarity with these words can be reinforced in everyday situations. You can use these words when discussing a television program, movie, or any personal, family, or newsworthy event. Experience in talking about "Why"something happened establishes an understanding of cause and effect. Similarly explaining "How" something is done emphasizes the importance of sequencing statements and explaining things clearly. These experiences establish a basis for responding appropriately to school-related tasks.

HIGHLIGHT IMPORTANT INFORMATION Highlighting is an effective technique for increasing comprehension since the child must focus on the text and decide what is important. He or she must learn to look for topic sentences and important details. The idea of using a highlighter appeals to many youngsters. Additionally, when reviewing material or looking for answers to questions, the highlighted words or sentences make for easy skimming.

The first few assignments should be done with you, since many children tend to highlight too much, thus defeating the purpose. Highlighters can generally be purchased anywhere that school supplies are sold. Of course, they can only be used on worksheets, consumable workbooks, or copies of textbook pages, never in the textbook directly unless it belongs to the child.

In summary, comprehension skills are a very necessary part of a child's academic "tools." Both the ability to decode and accurately comprehend material are requirements for successful reading. If you plan to work on these skills with your child, be patient and include as much positive reinforcement as possible.

Part

Appendixes

Section 35

Parent Conference Handouts

It is always helpful for parents to leave a conference with some practical material that will assist them in helping their child. We should never leave the responsibility for the creation of techniques up to parents. Some teachers may notify parents of a problem, but not assist them with practical suggestions for resolving it. This type of approach only heightens the anxiety levels of parents and causes a great deal of turmoil in their relationship with their child. This anxiety also increases when the parent tries a "shotgun approach" to resolving the problem but fails because they lack guidance from professionals.

The following Parent Conference Handouts should alleviate some of the obstacles parents face and help them become a resource for their children's learning.

HOW TO IMPROVE A CHILD'S SELF-ESTEEM

Be Solution Oriented

An important step in building self-esteem is to teach solutions rather than blame. Teaching children solutions to problems or frustrating situations begins with statements like, "Who's at fault is not important. The more important question is what can we do so that it doesn't happen again."

Allow Children the Right to Make Decisions

Allowing children the right to make decisions that affect their daily life can only enhance their self-esteem. Decisions about clothing, room arrangement, friends to invite to a party, menu for dinner etc. can make children feel some sense of control in what happens to them.

Offer Alternate Ways of Handling a Situation

Conditioning children to see many alternate ways of handling a situation, obstacle etc. can also enhance a sense of power and self-esteem. Asking children what they have tried and offering other options to possible solutions increases their "tool box."

Teach Children the Proper Labels When Communicating Feelings

When children are unable to label an internal feeling they become frustrated more quickly. When such feelings go unlabeled, they may become manifested in some negative behavior which will only reduce self-esteem. Parents can offer children the correct labels, i.e., "While the feeling you are expressing sounds like anger, it is really frustration and frustration is . . . Now that you know this, is there anything that is causing you frustration?"

Allow Children the Opportunity to Repeat Successful Experiences

A foundation of positive experiences is necessary for self-esteem. Since the child has mastered skills required for the job, any opportunity to repeat success can only be an ego inflating experience.

Allow Avenues for Disagreement

Children with high self-esteem feel they have an avenue to communicate their concerns. Even though the result may not go in their favor, the knowledge that a situation or disagreement can be discussed with their parents allows the child to feel a sense of power in their destiny rather than feel like a victim.

Help Your Child Set Realistic Goals

Some children will set unrealistic goals, fall short and feel like a failure. Repeated over a period of time, the child begins to develop a sense of urgency for success and this in turn may lead to more unrealistic goals. Parents can help children by assisting them in defining their objective and determining the steps necessary to accomplish the goal. Children should not see one final goal, but a series of smaller goals leading to a final point.

Use a Reward System to Shape Positive Behavior

Punishment tells a child what not to do, while reward informs a child of what is acceptable behavior. Rewarding positive behavior increases self-esteem. Rewards can be in the form of special trips, extra time before bed, special dinners with one parent, a hug, kiss, or a note in their lunchbox.

Don't Pave Every Road for Your Child

Some parents make the mistake of reducing frustration for children to the point where the child receives a distorted view of the world. Children with high self-esteem get frustrated. However, they tend to be more resilient since they have previous success in handling frustrating situations themselves. Teaching children alternate solutions, proper labels for their feelings, to set realistic goals, solution orientation and techniques to verbalize their disagreements are more productive than "bailing them out" when they are confronted with frustration.

HOW TO DETECT LEARNING PROBLEMS IN CHILDREN

Some Possible Causes of Learning Problems

Intellectual Reasons
Limited intelligence—slow learner
Retardation

Social Reasons
Peer pressure
Peer rejection

Emotional Reasons
Consistent school failure
Traumatic emotional development
Separation or divorce
High parental expectations
Sibling performance
Health-related problems
Change in environment—moving

Academic Reasons
Learning disabilities
Poor academic skills—math, reading
Style of teacher vs. style of student
Language difficulties

Be Aware of Avoidance Symptoms Indicating Possible Learning Problems

- Selective forgetting
- Child takes hours to complete homework
- Child can't seem to get started with homework
- Child frequently brings home unfinished classwork
- Child complains of headaches, stomachaches, etc.
- Child forgets to write down assignments day after day

Be Aware of Other Symptoms Reflective of Tension, Stress or Difficulties with Learning

At School
Child may exhibit:
- inability to focus on task
- disorganization
- distractibility—impulsiveness
- poor memory
- inflexibility
- irresponsibility
- poor judgment
- denial

At Home
Child may exhibit:
- over-sensitivity
- tantrums
- forgetfulness
- restlessness
- daydreaming
- unwillingness to venture out
- unwillingness to reason
- denial

Social Interaction
Child may exhibit:
- social withdrawal
- finds faults with other children
- low peer status
- unwillingness to try new relationships

Sleep
Child may exhibit:
- trouble falling asleep
- restless sleep
- resistance to rising
- frequent nightmares

While many of these symptoms may not by themselves indicate a major problem, several guidelines should be used in determining the severity of the problem:

1) FREQUENCY OF SYMPTOMS—Consider how often the symptoms occur. The greater the frequency, the greater chance of a serious problem.

2) DURATION OF SYMPTOMS—Consider how long the symptoms last. The longer the duration, the more serious the problem.

3) INTENSITY OF SYMPTOMS—Consider how serious the reactions are at the time of occurrence. The more intense the symptom, the more serious the problem.

If you suspect serious problems contact the school psychologist, special education teacher or a private mental health clinic for an evaluation.

HOW TO HELP CHILDREN WITH HOMEWORK

Try to Set Up a Homework Schedule

For some children, the responsibility of deciding when to sit down and do homework may be too difficult. Children may decide to do their homework after school or after dinner. This is a personal choice and has to do with learning style. However, once the time is determined, the schedule should be adhered to as closely as possible.

Rank Order Assignments

For some children, the decision as to what to do first becomes a major chore. They may dwell over this choice for a long period of time because everything takes on the same level of importance. Rank ordering assignments means that the parent determines the order in which the assignments are completed.

Try Not to Sit Next to Your Child While He/She Does Homework

Employing this technique may create learned helplessness because the same "assistance" is not imitated in the classroom. Parents serve their children better by acting as a resource person to whom the child may come with a problem. After the problem is solved or question answered, the child should return to his/her work area without the parent.

Check Correct Problems First

When your child brings you a paper to check, mention to him/her how well he/she did on the correct problems, spelling words, etc. For the ones that are incorrect say, "I bet if you go back and check these over you may get a different answer."

Never Let Homework Drag On All Night

The only thing accomplished by allowing a child to linger on their homework hour after hour with very little performance is increased feelings of inadequacy. If this occurs, end the work period after a reasonable period of time and write the teacher a note explaining the circumstances.

Discuss Homework Questions Before Your Child Reads the Chapter

Discuss the questions to be answered before the child reads the chapter. In this way he/she will know what important information to look for while reading.

Check Small Groups of Problems at a Time

Many children can benefit from immediate gratification. Have your child do five problems and then come to you to check them. Additionally, if the child is doing the assignment incorrectly, the error can be detected and explained, preventing the child from doing the entire assignment incorrectly.

Place Textbook Chapters on Tape

Research indicates that the more sensory input children receive, the greater the chance the information will be retained. For instance, parents can place science or social studies chapters on tape so that the child can listen while reading along.

Be Aware of Negative Nonverbal Messages During Homework

Many messages, especially negative ones, can be communicated easily without your awareness. If children are sensitive, they will pick up these messages which can only add to their tension, i.e., raised eyebrows, inattentiveness.

Avoid Finishing Assignments for Your Child

Children tend to feel inadequate when a parent finishes their homework. If children cannot complete an assignment, and they have honestly tried, write the teacher a note explaining the circumstances.

Be Aware of Possible Signs of More Serious Learning Problems

Parents should always be aware of symptoms indicating the possibility of more serious learning problems. Many of these symptoms may show up during homework. If these symptoms present a pattern, contact the psychologist or resource room teacher for further assistance. Such symptoms may include constant avoidance of homework, forgetting to bring home assignments, taking hours to do homework, procrastination of classwork, low frustration tolerance, labored writing, poor spelling, etc.

Check Homework Assignments at the End of the Night

This will reduce the child's concerns over the thought of bringing incorrect homework to school. This also offers children a feeling of accomplishment, a source of positive attention and a sense of security that the work is completed.

HOW TO HELP CHILDREN WITH READING AT HOME

Help the Child Use Context Clues

When a child comes across a word he/she can't read, encourage him/her to read the entire sentence. Often the meaning or context of the sentence, in combination with the first letter of the word, will provide a good clue. Also thinking about the meaning of a sentence may give the child a clue as to which word has been read incorrectly.

Have the Child Use a Bookstand

Using a bookstand is helpful to many children when reading or when copying from a textbook. The angle the bookstand provides makes it easier to read the material on it. Having the bookstand directly above the writing paper also makes for easier copying.

Make Reading an Important Activity in Your Home

Children tend to model adult behavior. There is a greater chance that children will be motivated to read if they observe other family members reading during leisure time (books, newspapers, magazines).

Encourage Recreational Reading

When your child is selecting books for recreational reading, he/she may select material that appears to be too simple. It may be easier than the instructional material being used in the classroom. That is perfectly alright (as long as the descrepancy is not too great), since the object of this type of reading is to relax and develop an appreciation of books.

Learn the Rule of "5" in Selecting Books for Enjoyment

In the absence of a particularly motivating topic, a parent can judge if a book is too difficult for the child by using the Rule of 5. This includes the following steps:

   a) Open the book to any page

   b) Have the child read the page outloud

   c) Count the number of words missed

   d) If there are more than 5 words the child has difficulty with, the book is probably too hard.

Do Not Allow Your Child to Struggle Over a Word When Reading Outloud

Be aware of the concern that some children may have over making a mistake while reading in front of their parents. If your child is reading out loud to you and comes across a word that is too difficult, do not let him/her struggle for long periods of time in hopes of sounding it out. If you see that his/her skills are not working in figuring out the word, assist him/her and allow them to continue. A sense of completion and parental approval is more important at this time.

Write To Read

A creative and motivating way to stimulate reading is to actually write a personalized book. The book should be about the child, a family pet, the child's hobby, a vacation, etc. Once a blank book is purchased, there are several ways to go about this. For example, following a vacation, snapshots can be pasted in the book and accompanying "text" written by the child and/or parent describing the pictures. Action shots are great for this purpose. An alternative to photographs is having the child illustrate the story.

Reading Is All Around Us—Suggestions

There are many opportunities for your child to read everyday in addition to reading books. Some examples are as follows:

- Write notes to your children. Try slipping one into a lunch box or leaving a note in their room.
- During vacations or camp time, write more often and call fewer times.
- When you go marketing, have your youngster read the shopping list to you and help you check the ingredients on labels.
- Reading a television schedule has its own built-in reward.
- Have your child read road signs, license plates and maps when traveling.
- Have your child read directions to games, model making kits, etc.
- Have him/her read recipes when baking or cooking together.

HOW TO COMMUNICATE WITH CHILDREN

Communication Is a Two Way Street

Many people feel they are communicating but in a sense, they never listen. Therefore, use the technique of, "I'll talk and you listen and then you talk and I'll listen" as a first step in developing communication with your child.

Try Not to Attack When Communicating Your Feelings

When communicating feelings, try using the words "I," "We" or "Me" as often as possible and stay away from the word "You." Even if someone has done something to hurt you, focus on your feelings rather than their behavior. Inform the individual on how the behavior affected you.

Teach Children to Label Feelings Properly

Children may have a very difficult time communicating because they lack the experience in labeling their feelings. Therefore, it is crucial for parents to assist their children in correctly labeling a feeling or emotion. You may want to say for example, "While the feeling you are expressing sounds like anger, it is really frustration and frustration is. . . ."

Use Connective Discussion Whenever Possible

When faced with a direct question concerning a feeling or a reason for some behavior, most children will shrug their shoulders in confusion or immediately respond, "I don't know." Instead of this direct communication, try connective discussion. This technique assumes that the parent may be aware of the trigger and connects the feeling and resulting behavior for the child. For example, parents may say, "It seems to me that you are feeling jealous over the attention your new baby brother is getting and that may be the reason for your behavior." At this point children may have an easier time responding since the foundation and labels have been presented.

Remember That All Behavior Has a Trigger

If parents can trace back children's responses to the source or trigger, they will have a very good chance of identifying the real problem. Remember that all behavior is a message and for many children their behavior is the only means of communicating their frustrations or feelings. The problem is that such behavior is frequently misunderstood and misinterpreted, resulting in more problems.

Be Aware of Nonverbal Misinterpretations

Children are very prone to nonverbal misinterpretations. They frequently misread a look on a parent's face and personalize it into something negative. If you are upset, angry or frustrated with something other than your children, let them know that fact in a verbal way. Try, "I am very upset right now about something. But I wanted to tell you that is has nothing to do with you and after I think for awhile we will get together."

Use Written Communication Whenever Possible

The use of writing to communicate feelings is an excellent tool in that it allows parents and children to phrase thoughts as desired. Notes thanking a child for some positive behavior or telling them how proud you are of them are just some examples. Notes can also be used to register a complaint without nose to nose confrontation.

Try to Use Direct Love as Often as Possible

The need to feel loved and cared for is a primary need for any individual at any age. Direct messages of love require no interpretation or assumptions on the part of the child and should be viewed on the same level of importance as gasoline to a car. Examples of direct love include hugging, kissing, cuddling, holding, stroking, etc.

Make Yourself as Approachable as Possible

The higher the approachability factor on the part of parents, the easier it will be for children to express and show direct love. Parents may want to evaluate just how easy their children feel in approaching them with feelings or problems and make adjustments if necessary. In later life, such individuals may have an easier time using direct forms of love in relationships.

HOW TO SPOT POSSIBLE LEARNING DISABILITIES

Intellectual Requirements

Children with learning disabilities usually exhibit intellectual potential within the average range and above. This usually translates into a score of 90 or better. Such potential should only be measured by an individual intelligence test like the Wechsler Intelligence Scale for Children-Revised.

Academic Requirements

Children with learning disabilities usually exhibit mild academic deficits (6 months–1 year below grade level), moderate academic deficits (1–2 years below grade level) or severe academic deficits (more than 2 years below grade level). These deficits may exhibit themselves in any one of the following areas:

Decoding (word attack skills)	Reading Comprehension	Mathematical
Computation	Written Expression	Oral Expression
Mathematical Reasoning	Listening Comprehension	

Exclusion Requirements

Children with learning disabilities are not retarded, primarily emotionally disturbed, hearing impaired, visually impaired, slow learners or the result of inadequate instructional practices, cultural or economic disadvantages.

Background Requirements

Children with learning disabilities usually exhibit a history of learning, social and developmental difficulties dating back to early grades.

Behavioral Requirements

Children with learning disabilities usually exhibit several of the following:

- Variability in performance across subject areas
- Attention problems—i.e., distractibility, poor concentration
- Organizational problems with information, space or time
- Poor motivation and attitude due to repeated academic failure
- Memory problems
- Language deficits in listening, speaking or writing
- Poor motor abilities in fine motor (small muscle) or gross motor (large muscle)
- Inappropriate social behavior—i.e., making friends, poor reactions to social situations

Processing Requirements

Children with learning disabilities usually exhibit deficits in the learning process. The strengths or weaknesses in this process are usually measured by process (perceptual) tests such as the Slingerland, Woodcock Johnson, Detroit Tests of Learning Aptitudes or the ITPA. However, the following list indicates some difficulties exhibited by children with processing problems in the following areas:

Visual Motor Disability

- poor motor coordination
- poor perception of time and space
- gets lost easily
- poor handwriting, artwork, drawing

Auditory-Vocal Disability

- appears not to listen or comprehend
- responds with one word answers
- may emphasize wrong syllables in words
- offers little in group discussions

Auditory Association Disability

- fails to enjoy being read to
- has difficulty comprehending questions
- slow to respond, takes a long time to answer tasks

Visual Association Disability

- unable to tell a story from pictures
- unable to understand what he/she reads
- fails to handle primary workbook

Manual Expressive Disability

- handwriting and drawing are poor
- poor at game playing, can't imitate others
- clumsy, uncoordinated
- poor at acting out ideas or feelings

Verbal Expression Disability

- mispronounces common words
- uses incorrect word endings
- difficulty in sound blending
- omits correct verbal endings

Auditory Memory Disabilities

- fails to remember instructions
- can't memorize nursery rhymes, poems
- doesn't know alphabet

Visual Memory Disabilities

- misspells own name frequently
- inconsistent word identification
- frequent misspellings, even after practice

If you suspect that your child may have a learning disability, contact the school psychologist, special education resource teacher or nearby mental health clinic for an evaluation.

FREQUENTLY ASKED QUESTIONS CONCERNING
LEARNING DISABILITIES

The term "learning disability" is an umbrella covering a multitude of learning problems. Some learning disabilities are mild (child may require minimal support for remediation), moderate (child may require more support coupled with special placement), or severe (child may require a special setting involving smaller and more extensive help). Regardless of the educational program, parents play an important role in assisting children with this type of disability.

Consequently, it is necessary for you to have an adequate understanding of this type of learning problem to help your child positively. You have probably been troubled for some time by your child's frustrations over learning. The term "learning disabled " may have been used by professionals, but you are not quite sure what that means. Other terms like Committee on Special Education or least restrictive environment may have also been mentioned. This handout provides some very important information concerning your child's present situation and answers any questions you may have.

Q: What is a learning disability?

A: In general, a learning disability is a problem in acquiring and using skills required for listening, speaking, reading, writing, reasoning, and mathematical ability. Such problems in the acquisition of skills cannot be traced to inadequate intelligence, school environment, emotional problems, visual or hearing defects, cultural deprivation, or lack of motivation.

Q: How many children have learning disabilities?

A: The answer to this question depends in part on the definition used. The U.S. Department of Education reports approximately 5 percent of a school's population may be learning disabled. According to their statistics taken in 1984, this represented 1,811,451 students throughout the country.

Q: What causes learning disabilities?

A: Several theories have been proposed concerning the cause of learning disabilities. Some of the more widely held theories center on heredity, complications of pregnancy, lag in nervous system development (sometimes referred to as a maturational lag), or some subtle neurological impairment, sort of like crossed wires in a telephone line.

Q: Can a true learning disability show up in later grades with no earlier indications?

A: This is a widely held misconception. In most cases a true learning disability has an historical pattern with symptoms appearing as early as a child's first school experience or sooner. A fifth grade student who is referred by a teacher for suspected learning disabilities and has no prior educational difficulties should be considered a low-risk LD child.

Q: Are dyslexia and learning disabilities the same?

A: No. Dyslexia is a specific and severe form of a learning disability. Dyslexia refers to a severe problem in learning how to read. All learning disabled children are not dyslexic. However, all dyslexic children are learning disabled.

Q: Are reversals an indication of a learning disability?

A: This symptom has been greatly inflated by the media. Parents should keep in mind that reversals of letters, numbers, and so on may be very common in children up to grade 3 and may not by themselves indicate any learning disability. However, if a child frequently reverses letters and/or numbers along with other symptoms or continues to do so after age eight, you should discuss this with a professional as soon as possible.

Q: Can a child be learning disabled in only one area?

A: Yes. Some children may have a learning disability in the area of short-term memory, mathematical computations, spelling, or reading comprehension. Of course, the more areas affected, the more serious the disability.

Q: What kinds of symptoms signal a possible learning disability?

A: There are a variety of symptoms that may signal the presence of such a problem. Some of the more common include disorganization, poor muscle coordination, impulsivity, distractibility, short attention span, trouble in completing assignments, poor spelling, poor handwriting, poor social skills, low reading level, difficulty in following directions, discrepancy between ability and performance, and language difficulties.

Q: What is the first thing to do if I suspect that my child may have a learning disability?

A: It is hoped that the school has already identified this possibility. However, if this is not the case, immediately contact the school psychologist, or head of the school's child study team, and make them aware of your concerns. If you do not wish to go through the school, then contact a qualified professional in the field, or a clinic that specializes in learning disabilities. They will be happy to evaluate your child. However, keep in mind that such an evaluation can be very expensive while it is free through the school.

Q: Must my child be referred to the committee on special education if he or she has a learning disability?

A: The answer in most cases will be yes. It is the legal and moral responsibility of every school district to refer such a child for a review before the Committee on Special Education. A review does not mean immediate classification. It just means that enough evidence exists to warrant a "look" by the district. If the child has a learning disability and is encountering frustration in school, then the services he or she will receive should greatly reduce such problems.

Section 36

Examples of Psychoeducational Reports

The following report is of an elementary school–aged child referred by his teacher for a suspected learning disability.

REPORT FOR A STUDENT IN THE PRIMARY GRADES

IDENTIFYING DATA

Name: John Carson

Address: 15 Williams Street
Newton, NY 11687

Phone: 546-9864

School: Benton Ave.

Teacher: Mrs. Grissom

Grade: 4

Date of Birth: August 10, 1984

Chronological Age: 9-10

Date of Testing: June 7, 1993

Date of Report: June 18, 1993

Referred by: Teacher

Parents' Names: Jane/Robert

REASON FOR REFERRAL John was referred for a psychoeducational evaluation as a result of a suspected learning disability.

BACKGROUND HISTORY John is a nine-year-old boy presently living in an intact household with his mother, a teacher; father, an engineer; older brother age fifteen; and younger sister age seven. At the present time no other relatives reside within the home.

According to parent intake, John was the result of a full-term pregnancy and normal delivery. According to the mother, John was operated on for a hernia, but there were no complications. Developmental milestones seem to have been within normal limits except for talking, which the parent indicated was later than expected. Early history indicates normal childhood illnesses, no traumatic experiences, and no long hospital stays. However, John had frequent middle ear infections within the first three years. The mother indicated that he has not had his eyesight or hearing checked since last year.

Academic history indicates that John seems to have been experiencing difficulties since the early grades. Concerns have been expressed by several teachers indicating weaknesses in the language arts areas. According to his present and past

273

teachers, John's overall performance in the classroom was and is poor, despite above-average potential intelligence.

His past and present teachers have reported that he does not participate in class, is verbally resistant, has problems remembering and following through on directions, has a short attention span, procrastinates handing in written assignments, and has difficulty working independently.

His present teacher reports that his organizational skills seem weak and that he needs step-by-step instructions from the teacher. She also reported that John is having social difficulties and is being isolated by his peers.

Socially, his parents reported that John does not seem to have many friends and that the ones he does have are much younger. He enjoys collecting stamps and baseball cards and is very involved with the computer.

BEHAVIORAL OBSERVATIONS John, a thin, frail-looking, nine-year-old, entered the testing situation in a relatively guarded manner. He wore a baseball cap pulled down over his forehead and made very little eye contact with the examiner. John did not initiate conversation, but remained cooperative throughout the sessions. His pattern of performance seemed labored on written tasks, and he frequently asked to have the questions repeated.

John did briefly comment that he did not like school and wished he didn't have to come. He indicated that he had "a lot of friends" and kept asking how long the testing would take.

John is right handed and holds his pencil with an awkward grasp. He seemed resistant to changing the grip and kept his head fairly close to the paper when writing, slightly tilting his head to the right.

TESTS ADMINISTERED

> Wide Range Achievement Test—Revised
>
> Beery Test of Visual Motor Integration
>
> Woodcock-Johnson Achievement and Cognitive Battery—Revised

TEST RESULTS On the Wide Range Achievement Test—Revised, John achieved grade score equivalents of 2B in spelling, placing him at the ____percentile, 4E in math (computation), placing him at the ___ percentile, and 2B in reading (decoding), placing him at the ___ percentile.

Analysis of the spelling subtest indicated below-grade-level performance. In looking at the spelling results, one sees adequate spacing and size relationships but very poor letter formation characterized by difficulty with sequencing and closure such as "spla" for spell. Further analysis indicated letter omissions ("liht" for light), erratic use of capitals, and low frustration tolerance as the words became more difficult.

Analysis of the math section indicated more than adequate skills.

Analysis of the reading section indicated good sight word vocabulary. When it came to multisyllabic words, John did not decode by a sequential blending of isolated sounds, but rather by maneuvering all or some of the sounds until he got a recognizable word. However, in many cases the wrong word was pronounced. He seemed to take a great deal of time decoding, which will impact on his reading rate in class.

John's performance on the Woodcock Johnson Battery—Revised placed him in the average range with respect to cognitive ability. Strength areas were noted in the areas of Processing Speed, which involved the rapid performance of relatively trivial cognitive tasks; Visual Processing, the capability to perceive and think with visual patterns; and Comprehension-Knowledge, a measurement of the breadth and depth of knowledge and its effective application. John's scores on tasks measuring short-term memory were within the average range. However, his effectiveness in storing and retrieving information over extended periods of time was in the low-average range.

The area of greatest concern seemed to center on comprehension and synthesis of auditory patterns involved in auditory processing (fourth percentile). The skills of auditory closure and sound blending which comprise this cluster would impact directly on John's word attack skills, which were measured at the thirty-first percentile on this battery.

John's performance in reading on this battery indicated an achievement score which exceeded his estimated aptitude. However, upon closer analysis John's word attack skills were at the 2.6 grade level and were considerably lower than his reading vocabulary grade score of 4.3 and reading comprehension of 4.6.

In the area of written language, John's achievement was significantly below his measured aptitude, resulting in a grade score of 2.4. This places him within the twelfth percentile when compared to his peers and would impact on his willingness and ability to complete written assignments, especially those with time constraints. His most notable difficulties involved capitalization, punctuation, and spelling. His encoding problems were consistent with the decoding deficits indicated throughout the testing.

CONCLUSIONS John is a nine-year-old boy presently functioning in the average range of intellectual ability.

Results of testing seem to indicate that John presently exhibits adequate skills in areas involving mathematics, reading comprehension, and reading vocabulary. However, his most significant weakness appears to be in the area of auditory processing, which has impacted significantly on his decoding skills in reading and on his ability to spell. Visual-motor integration skills also appear to be of concern and were evident in John's written work.

Other factors may also be contributing to John's overall lack of performance in school. His overall high level of distractibility, avoidance, procrastination, low self-esteem, and resistance may be symptomatic of secondary tension arising from school frustration.

Overall analysis of the test results seem to indicate that John's difficulties should be considered moderate in nature and his overall pattern is similar to students with learning disabilities.

RECOMMENDATIONS Results of testing, observation, and intake suggest the following recommendations:

To the School

1. Considering the profile of scores, John's test behavior, and dates since last exam, a new vision and hearing test are suggested to rule out any possibility of these factors contributing to his present situation.

2. In view of the nature and severity of John's school-related difficulties, a review by the Committee on Special Education is recommended. The CSE may want to explore the possibility of resource room assistance.

3. The school may want to consider placing John in remedial reading to increase his ability in decoding.

To the Teacher

1. John's spelling difficulties may result in resistance to written assignments. The teacher may want to allow John the use of a word processor with a spelling checker for written tasks.

2. To help John gain some confidence in spelling, oral tests or spelling tests that require John to identify each correctly spelled word from a list of four words may be beneficial.

3. John needs assistance in the classroom identifying long vowel sounds, words with the silent "e" spelling pattern, vowel digraphs, and common endings such as "ble," "dle," "tle," "ary," "ery," and "cry."

4. The teacher may want to seat John closer to her desk to increase attention and focus.

5. Further recommendations will be addressed at a meeting with the teacher.

To the Parent

1. Mr. and Mrs. Carson may want to set up a homework schedule for John so he will have a structured time when homework needs to be addressed. In addition, they may want to check his work at the end of the night to make sure it's complete and correct. By doing this, John can feel more comfortable about the accuracy of his work when he comes to school.

2. Unison reading at home is also suggested. Unison reading means that both the parent and the child have the same book and read aloud together thereby reinforcing the correct pronunciation.

3. Further recommendations will be addressed at the meeting with the parent.

REPORT FOR A STUDENT IN SECONDARY SCHOOL

The following report is an example of a secondary school–aged child referred by his teacher for suspected behavioral and academic difficulties.

IDENTIFYING DATA

Name: Mary Wilson   **Date of Testing:** Dec. 30, 1993
Address: 110 Arnold Street   **Date of Report:** Oct. 12, 1993
Munsey, PA 11687
Phone: 947-99641   **Referred by:** PPT
School: Wilshire Middle School   **Parents' Names:** Mildred/Art
Counselor: Mr. Kirby
Grade: 8
Date of Birth: Sept. 29, 1980
Chronological Age: 13-3

REASON FOR REFERRAL Mary was referred for an educational evaluation by the pupil personnel team due to behavioral and academic difficulties.

BACKGROUND HISTORY See psychological report dated October 7, 1993, for a complete history profile.

BEHAVIORAL OBSERVATIONS Mary remained attentive and cooperative throughout the testing sessions. She demonstrated good attention to task, and her speech and verbal abilities seemed age appropriate. Mary was very engaging with the examiner, frequently initiating conversation, and was very responsive in answering questions by the examiner. At the end of the sessions, Mary indicated that she had enjoyed the testing and would like to come back.

Mary is right handed and did not wear glasses.

TESTS ADMINISTERED
Woodcock-Johnson Psycho-Educational Battery
Stanford Achievement Test—Advanced II

TEST RESULTS Mary's performance on the Woodcock-Johnson Broad Cognitive Ability Full Scale Cluster, which measures a broad set of verbal and nonverbal cognitive abilities, resulted in a score at the fifty-eighth percentile for her grade, with a confidence interval of 50–66. This performance should be considered average for her grade.

Among her cognitive abilities, strengths were indicated in Verbal Ability (eightieth percentile, 12.8 G.E.), a measure of receptive and expressive vocabulary, and Memory Ability (seventy-fourth percentile, 12.9 G.E.), a measure of auditory and symbol reorganization. Mary obtained scores within the average range in the area of Reasoning Ability (thirty-ninth percentile, 7.5 G.E.), a measure of nonverbal abstract reasoning and problem solving. Her lowest scores fell within the low-average range in Perceptual Speed (twenty-second percentile, 6.6 G.E.), a measure of visual perceptual ability.

Based on these cognitive measures, Mary should be expected to achieve academically at the following levels:

Achievement Cluster	Percentile	Grade Equivalent
Reading	75	11.4
Knowledge	56	9.4
Written Expression	39	8.2
Mathematics	38	8.1

On the Woodcock-Johnson Achievement Clusters, Mary's performance indicated high-average scores for her grade on the Knowledge Achievement Cluster (eighty-second percentile, 12.2 G.E.) and in the average range for her grade on the Written Expression (fifty-ninth percentile, 9.5 G.E.), Mathematics (fiftieth percentile, 8.6 G.E.), and Reading (forty-fourth percentile, 8.2 G.E.) achievement clusters.

When Mary's academic achievement is compared with her scholastic aptitude in knowledge, her present functioning level is in the high-average range. When her academic achievement in mathematics and written language is compared to her scholastic aptitude in both these areas, her present functioning level is within the average range. However, when her academic achievement in reading is compared with her scholastic aptitude in reading, her present functioning is in the low-average range.

Mary's test results on the Stanford Achievement Test were as follows:

Achievement Area	Percentile	Grade Equivalent
Reading Comprehension	45	8.4
Reading Vocabulary	66	11.4
Mathematical Applications	19	6.4
Total Mathematics	22	6.7

Mary's performance on the Reading Comprehension and Reading Vocabulary subtests of the Stanford are consistent with her average reading achievement on the Woodcock-Johnson.

In contrast, Mary's Total Mathematics score on the Stanford was not consistent with her average achievement score on the Woodcock-Johnson. An analysis of her math achievement on the Stanford indicates below-average achievement in Mathematical Applications, a test that measures the student's ability to apply mathematical skills to the solution of problems. This subtest contributed to the overall low Total Math score on the Stanford. However, since Applied Problems (a subtest that assesses skill in solving practical arithmetic problems) on the Woodcock-Johnson was found to be above average, the difficulty that Mary experienced on the

Stanford Mathematics Applications may have been the result of working under timed, group-administered conditions.

Mary's writing sample provided a logical sequence of ideas, and she maintained coherence throughout the story. The content was found to be both age appropriate and well focused. A definite theme was evident and mature vocabulary was employed. In addition to the fine content, Mary demonstrated good command of the mechanics of written expression. The only exception were several run-on sentences and minor spelling errors.

CONCLUSIONS Mary's test profile reveals a strength in verbal ability and a relative strength in memory. Mary also obtained scores that reflected average performance on nonverbal abstract reasoning and problem-solving tasks. Overall, there was very little variation among her cognitive abilities.

Results of achievement measures indicated that Mary possesses average to above-average skills in knowledge, written expression, mathematics, and reading. When Mary's academic achievement is compared with her scholastic aptitude, her present level of achievement is in the average range.

RECOMMENDATIONS

To the School

1. On the basis of these test results and the most recent individual IQ score indicating average ability, no significant discrepancies seem to exist in Mary's cognitive and achievement areas.
2. Other factors may be contributing to her behavioral difficulties and low class performance. As a result, a full psychological evaluation is suggested.

To the Teacher

1. Additional time may assist Mary in the completion of assignments.
2. Mary may benefit from exercises involving proofreading for run-on sentences and minor spelling errors.
3. Setting very clear and consistent boundaries is extremely important with Mary. The teacher may want to preempt Mary's behavior pattern by speaking with her alone before class and explaining what is acceptable and not acceptable when she enters the room. Clear consequences and rewards need to be expressed by the teacher.

To the Parent

The parents may wish to consult with the school psychologist for other possible factors which may be contributing to Mary's lack of production in spite of her ability.

Section 37

Abbreviations

Symbol	Meaning
ACLC	Assessment of Children's Language Comprehension
ADHD	Attention Deficit Hyperactive Disorder
A.E.	age equivalent
AUD.DIS	auditory discrimination
BINET	Stanford-Binet Intelligence Test
BVMGT	Bender Visual Motor Gestalt Test
C.A.	chronological age
C.A.T.	Children's Apperception Test
CEC	Council for Exceptional Children
CP	cerebral palsy
CSE	Committee on Special Education
DAP	Draw a Person Test
db	decibel (hearing measurement)
DDST	Denver Developmental Screening Test
DQ	developmental quotient
DTLA-3	Detroit Tests of Learning Aptitude, Third Edition
E.D.	emotionally disturbed/disabled
EMR	educable mentally retarded
FAPE	free appropriate public education
fq	frequency range (hearing measurement)
G.E.	grade equivalent
GFW	Goldman-Fristoe-Woodcock Test of Auditory Discrimination
HH	hard of hearing
HTP	House-Tree-Person Test
Hz	Hertz (hearing measurement)
IEU	intermediate educational unit
IHE	Institutions of Higher Education
IQ	intelligence quotient
ITPA	Illinois Tests of Psycholinguistic Abilities
LA	learning aptitude
LD	learning disabled
LEA	local education agency
LPR	local percentile rank

M.A.	mental age
MBD	minimal brain dysfunction
MH	multiply handicapped
MMPI	Minnesota Multiphasic Personality Inventory
MR	mentally retarded/disabled
MVPT	Motor-Free Visual Perception Test
NPR	national percentile rank
PHC	pupils with handicapping conditions
PIAT	Peabody Individual Achievement Test
PINS	person in need of supervision
PLA	psycholinguistic age
PQ	perceptual quotient
PPVT	Peabody Picture Vocabulary Test
PR	percentile rank
PS	partially sighted
PSEN	pupils with special educational needs
PTA	pure tone average (hearing measurement)
SAI	School Abilities Index
SCSIT	Southern California Sensory Integration Tests
SEA	state education agency
SIT	Slosson Intelligence Test
SRT	speech reception threshold (hearing measurement)
TACL	Test for Auditory Comprehension of Language
T.A.T.	Thematic Apperception Test
TMR	trainable mentally retarded/disabled
TOWL	Test of Written Language
TWS	Larsen-Hammill Test of Written Spelling
VAKT	visual/auditory/kinesthetic/tactile
VIS.DIS	visual discrimination
VMI	Beery-Buktenica Developmental Test of Visual Motor Integration
WAIS—R	Wechsler Adult Intelligence Scale—Revised
WISC—R	Wechsler Intelligence Scale for Children—Revised
WISC—III	Wechsler Intelligence Scale for Children—Third Edition
WPPSI—R	Wechsler Preschool and Primary Scale of Intelligence—Revised
WRAT—R	Wide Range Achievement Test—Revised

Section 38

Glossaries of Special Education Terminology

EDUCATIONAL TERMINOLOGY

Ability Grouping—The grouping of children based on their achievement in an area of study.

Accelerated Learning—An educational process that allows students to progress through the curriculum at an increased pace.

Achievement—The level of a child's accomplishment on a test of knowledge or skill.

Adaptive Behavior—An individual's social competence and ability to cope with the demands of the environment.

Adaptive Physical Education—A modified program of instruction implemented to meet the needs of special students.

Advocate—An individual, either a parent or professional, who attempts to establish or improve services for exceptional children.

Age Norms—Standards based on the average performance of individuals in different age groups.

Agnosia—A child's inability to recognize objects and their meaning usually resulting from damage to the brain.

Amplification Device—Any device that increases the volume of sound.

Anecdotal Record—A procedure for recording and analyzing observations of a child's behavior; an objective, narrative description.

Annual Goals—Yearly activities or achievements to be completed or attained by the disabled child that are documented on the individual educational plan.

Aphasia—The inability to acquire meaningful spoken language by the age of three usually resulting from damage or disease to the brain.

Articulation—The production of distinct language sounds by the vocal chords.

At Risk—Usually, infants or children with a high potential for experiencing future medical or learning problems.

Attention Deficit Hyperactive Disorder (ADHD)—A psychiatric classification used to describe individuals who exhibit poor attention, distractibility, impulsivity, and hyperactivity.

Baseline Measure—The level or frequency of behavior prior to the implementation of an instructional procedure that will later be evaluated.

Behavior Modification—The techniques used to change behavior by applying principals of reinforcement learning

Bilingual—The ability to speak two languages.

Career Education—Instruction that focuses on the application of skills and content area information necessary to cope with the problems of daily life, independent living, and vocational areas of interest.

Categorical Resource Room—An auxiliary pull-out program that offers supportive services to exceptional children with the same disability.

Cognition—The process of understanding information.

Consultant Teacher—A specialist who provides a supportive service for disabled children in the classroom.

Criterion-Referenced Tests—Tests in which the child is evaluated on his or her own performance according to a set of criteria and not in comparison to others.

Declassification—The process in which a disabled child is no longer considered in need of special education services. This requires a meeting of the CSE and can be requested by the parent, school, or child if over the age of eighteen.

Deficit—A level of performance that is less than expected for a child.

Desensitization— A technique used in reinforcement theory in which there is a weakening of a response, usually an emotional response.

Diagnosis—The specific disorder(s) identified as a result of some evaluation.

Distractibility—Difficulty in maintaining attention.

Due Process—The legal steps and processes outlined in educational law that protects the rights of disabled children.

Dyscalculia—A serious learning disability in which the child has an inability to calculate, apply, solve, or identify mathematical functions.

Dysfluency—Difficulty in the production of fluent speech as in the example of stuttering.

Dysgraphia—A serious learning disability in which the child has an inability or loss of ability to write.

Dyslexia—A severe learning disability in which a child's ability to read is greatly impaired.

Dysorthographia—A serious learning disability that affects a child's ability to spell.

Enrichment—Providing a child with extra and more sophisticated learning experiences than those normally presented in the curriculum.

Exceptional Children—Children whose school performance shows significant discrepancy between ability and achievement and as a result require special instruction, assistance, and/or equipment.

Etiology—The cause of a problem.

Free Appropriate Public Education (FAPE)—Used in P.L. 94-142 to mean special education and related services that are provided at public expense and conform to the state requirements and conform to the individual's IEP.

Group Homes—A residential living arrangement for handicapped adults, especially the mentally disabled, along with several nonhandicapped supervisors.

Habilitation—An educational approach used with exceptional children which is directed toward the development of the necessary skills required for successful adulthood.

Homebound Instruction— A special education service in which teaching is provided by a specially trained instructor to students unable to attend school. A parent or guardian must always be present at the time of instruction. In some cases, the instruction may take place on a neutral sight and not in the home or school.

Hyperactivity—Behavior which is characterized by excessive motor activity or restlessness.

Impulsivity—Nongoal-oriented activity exhibited by individuals who lack careful thought and reflection prior to a behavior.

Individualized Educational Plan (IEP)—A written educational program that outlines a disabled child's current levels of performance, related services, educational goals, and modifications. This plan is developed by a team including the child's parent(s), teacher(s), and supportive staff.

Inclusion—Returning disabled children to their home school so that they may be educated with nonhandicapped children in the same classroom.

Interdisciplinary Team—The collective efforts of individuals from a variety of disciplines in assessing the needs of a child.

Intervention—Preventive, remedial, compensatory, or survival services made on behalf of a disabled individual.

Itinerant Teacher—A teacher hired by a school district to help in the education of a disabled child. The teacher is employed by an outside agency and may be responsible for several children in several districts.

Learning Disability—A condition present in children with average or above-average potential intelligence who are experiencing a severe discrepancy between their ability and achievement.

Least Restrictive Environment—The educational setting of exceptional children and the education of handicapped children with nonhandicapped children whenever realistic and possible. It is the least restrictive setting in which the disabled child can function without difficulty.

Mainstreaming—The practice of educating exceptional children in the regular classroom.

Mental Age—The level of intellectual functioning based on the average for children of the same chronological age. When dealing with severely disabled children, the mental age may be more reflective of levels of ability than the chronological age.

Mental Retardation/Disability—A disability in which the individual's intellectual level is measured within the subaverage range and there are marked impairments in social competence.

Native Language—The primary language used by an individual.

Noncategorical Resource Room—A resource room in regular school that provides services to children with all types of classified disabilities. The children with these disabilities are able to be maintained in a regular classroom.

Norm-Referenced Tests— Tests used to compare a child's performance to the performance of others on the same measure.

Occupational Therapist—A professional who programs and/or delivers instructional activities and materials that help disabled children and adults to participate in useful daily activities.

Paraprofessionals—A trained assistant or parent who works with a classroom teacher in the education process.

Physical Therapist—A professional trained to assist and help disabled individuals maintain and develop muscular and orthopedic capability and to make correct and useful movements.

Positive Reinforcement—Any stimulus or event which occurs after a behavior has been exhibited that affects the possibility of that behavior occurring in the future.

Pupil Personnel Team—A group of professionals from the same school who meet on a regular basis to discuss children's problems and offer suggestions or a direction for resolution.

Pupils with Handicapping Conditions (PHC)—children classified as disabled by the Committee on Special Education.

Pupils with Special Educational Needs (PSEN)—Children defined as having math and reading achievement lower than the twenty-third percentile and requiring remediation. These students are not considered disabled but are entitled to assistance to elevate their academic levels.

Related Services—Services provided to disabled children to assist in their ability to learn and function in the least restrictive environment. Such services may include in-school counseling, speech and language services, and math remediation.

Remediation—An educational program designed to teach children to overcome some deficit or disability through education and training.

Resource Room—An auxiliary service provided to disabled children for part of the school day. It is intended to service children's special needs so that they can be maintained within the least restrictive educational setting.

Screening—The process of examining groups of children in hopes of identifying potential high-risk children.

Section 504—The section of the Rehabilitation Act of 1973 that guaranties the civil rights of disabled children and adults. It also applies to the provision of services for children whose disability is not severe enough to warrant classification, but could benefit from supportive services and classroom modifications.

Self-contained Class—A special classroom for exceptional children usually located within a regular school building.

Sheltered Workshops—A transitional or long-term work environment for disabled individuals who cannot or who are preparing for work in a regular setting. Within this setting the individual can learn to perform meaningful, productive tasks and receive payment.

Surrogate Parent—A person other than the child's natural parent who has legal responsibility for the child's care and welfare.

Token Economy—A system of reinforcing various behaviors through the delivery of tokens. These tokens can be in the form of stars, points, candy, chips, and so on.

Total Communication—The approach to the education of deaf students that combines oral speech, sign language, and finger spelling.

Underachiever—A term generally used when referring to a child's lack of academic achievement in school. However, it is important that the school identify the underlying causes of such underachievement since it may be a symptom of a more serious problem.

Vocational Rehabilitation—A well-designed program designed to help disabled adults obtain and hold a job.

PSYCHOLOGICAL TERMINOLOGY

Affective Reactions—Psychotic reactions marked by extreme mood swings.

Anxiety—A general uneasiness of the mind characterized by irrational fears, panic, tension, and physical symptoms, including palpitations, excessive sweating, and increased pulse rate.

Assessment—The process of gathering information about children to make educational decisions.

Baseline Data—An objective measure used to compare and evaluate the results obtained during some implementation of an instructional procedure.

Compulsion—A persistent, repetitive act that the individual cannot consciously control.

Confabulation—The act of replacing memory loss by fantasy or by some reality that is not true for the occasion.

Defense Mechanisms—The unconscious means by which individuals protect themselves against impulses or emotions that are too uncomfortable or threatening. Examples of these mechanisms include the following:

Denial—A defense mechanism in which the individual refuses to admit the reality of some unpleasant event, situation, or emotion.

Displacement—The disguising of the goal or intention of a motive by substituting another in its place.

Intellectualization—A defense mechanism in which the individual exhibits anxious or moody deliberation, usually about abstract matters.

Projection—The disguising of a source of conflict by displacing one's own motives to someone else.

Rationalization—The interpretation of one's own behavior so as to conceal the motive it expresses by assigning the behavior to another motive.

Reaction Formation—A complete disguise of a motive that it is expressed in a form that is directly opposite to its original intent.

Repression—The psychological process involved in not permitting memories and motives to enter consciousness though hey are operating at an unconscious level.

Supression—The act of consciously inhibiting an impulse, affect, or idea, as in the deliberate act of forgetting something in order not to think about it.

Delusion—A groundless, irrational belief or thought, usually of grandeur or of persecution; usually a characteristic of paranoia.

Depersonalization—A nonspecific syndrome in which the individual senses a loss of personal identity, that he or she is different, strange, or not real.

Echolalia—The repetition of what other people say as if echoing them.

Etiology—The cause(s) of something.

Hallucination—A imaginary visual image that is regarded as a real sensory experience by the person.

Magical Thinking—Primitive and prelogical thinking in which the child creates a outcome to meet his or her fantasy rather than the reality of a situation.

Neologisms—Made-up words that only have meaning to the child or adult.

Obsessions—A repetitive and persistent idea that intrudes into a person's thoughts.

Panic Attacks—A serious episode of anxiety in which the individual experiences a variety of symptoms including palpitations, dizziness, nausea, chest pains, trembling, fear of dying, and fear of losing control. These symptoms are not the result of any medical cause.

Paranoia—A personality disorder in which the individual exhibits extreme suspiciousness of the motives of others.

Phobia—An intense irrational fear, usually acquired through conditioning to an unpleasant object or event.

Projective Tests—Methods used by psychologists and psychiatrists to study personality dynamics through a series of structured or ambiguous stimuli.

Psychosis—A serious mental disorder in which the individual has difficulty differentiating between fantasy and reality.

Rorschach Test—An unstructured psychological test in which the individual is asked to project responses to a series of ten inkblots.

School Phobia—A form of separation anxiety in which the child's concerns and anxieties are centered on school issues and as a result he or she has an extreme fear about coming to school.

Symptom—Refers to any sign, physical or mental, that identifies something else. Symptoms are usually generated from the tension of conflicts. The more serious the problem or conflict, the more frequent and intense the symptom.

Syndrome—A group of symptoms that identify a condition.

Thematic Apperception Test—A structured psychological test in which the individual is asked to project his or her feelings onto a series of drawings or photos.

Wechsler Scales of Intelligence—A series of individual intelligence tests measuring global intelligence through a variety of subtests.

MEDICAL TERMINOLOGY

Albinism—A congenital condition marked by severe deficiency in or total lack of pigmentation.

Amblyopia—A dimness of sight without any indication of change in the eye's structure.

Amniocentesis—A medical procedure done during the early stages of pregnancy for the purpose of identifying certain genetic disorders in the fetus.

Anomaly—Some irregularity in development or a deviation from the standard.

Anoxia—A lack of oxygen.

Aphasia—The inability to acquire meaningful spoken language by the age of three as a result of brain damage.

Apraxia—Problems with voluntary or purposeful muscular movement with no evidence of motor impairment.

Astigmatism—A visual defect resulting in blurred vision caused by uneven curvature of the cornea or lens. The condition is usually corrected by lenses.

Ataxia—A form of cerebral palsy in which the individual suffers from a loss of muscle coordination, especially those movements relating to balance and position.

Athetosis—A form of cerebral palsy characterized by involuntary, jerky, purposeless, and repetitive movements of the extremities, head, and tongue.

Atrophy—The degeneration of tissue.

Audiogram—A graphic representation of the results of a hearing test.

Audiologist—A specialist trained in the evaluation and remediation of auditory disorders.

Binocular Vision—Vision using both eyes working together to perceive a single image.

Blind, Legally—Visual acuity measured at 20/200 in the better eye with best correction of glasses or contact lenses. Vision measured at 20/200 means the individual must be 20 feet from something to be able to see what the normal eye can see at 200 feet.

Cataract—A condition of the eye in which the crystalline lens becomes cloudy or opaque. As a result, a reduction or loss of vision occurs.

Catheter—A tube inserted into the body to allow for injections or withdrawal of fluids or to maintain an opening in a passageway.

Cerebral Palsy—An abnormal succession of human movement or motor functioning resulting from a defect, insult, or disease of the central nervous system.

Conductive Hearing Loss—A hearing loss resulting from obstructions in the outer or middle ear or some malformations that interfere in the conduction of sound waves to the inner ear. This condition may be corrected medically or surgically.

Congenital—A condition present at birth.

Cretinism—A congenital condition associated with a thyroid deficiency that can result in stunted physical growth and mental retardation.

Cyanosis—A lack of oxygen in the blood characterized by a blue discoloration of the skin.

Cystic Fibrosis—An inherited disorder affecting pancreas, salivary, mucous, and sweat glands that causes severe, long-term respiratory difficulties.

Diplegia—Paralysis that affects either both arms or both legs.

Down's Syndrome—A medical abnormality caused by a chromosomal anomaly that often results in moderate to severe mental retardation. The child with Down's syndrome will exhibit certain physical characteristics such as a large tongue, heart problems, poor muscle tone, and broad, flat bridge of the nose.

Electroencephalogram (EEG)—A graphic representation of the electrical output of the brain.

Encopresis—A lack of bowel control that may also have psychological causes.

Endogenous—Originating from within.

Enureusis—A lack of bladder control that may also have psychological causes.

Exogenous—Originating from external causes.

Fetal Alcohol Syndrome—A condition usually found in the infants of alcoholic mothers. As a result low birth weight, severe retardation, and cardiac, limb, and other physical defects may be present.

Field of Vision—Measured in degrees, the area of space visible with both eyes while looking straight ahead; measured in degrees.

Glaucoma—An eye disease characterized by excessively high pressure inside the eyeball. If left untreated, the condition can result in total blindness.

Grand Mal Seizure—The most serious and severe form of an epileptic seizure in which the individual exhibits violent convulsions, loses consciousness, and becomes rigid.

Hemiplegia—Paralysis involving the extremities on the same side of the body.

Hemophilia—An inherited deficiency in the blood-clotting factor that can result in serious internal bleeding.

Hertz—A unit of sound frequency used to measure pitch.

Hydrocephalus—A condition present at birth or developing soon afterward from excess cerebrospinal fluid in the brain and results in an enlargement of the head and mental retardation. This condition is sometimes prevented by the surgical placement of a shunt, which allows for the proper drainage of the built up fluids.

Hyperactivity—Excessive physical and muscular activity characterized by extreme inattention, excessive restlessness, and mobility. The condition is usually associated with Attention Deficit Disorder or learning disabilities.

Hyperopia—Farsightedness, a condition causing difficulty with seeing near objects.

Hypertonicity—A heightened state of excessive tension.

Hypotonicity—An inability in maintaining muscle tone or an inability in maintaining muscle tension or resistance to stretch.

Insulin—A protein hormone produced by the pancreas that regulates carbohydrate metabolism.

Iris—The opaque, colored portion of the eye.

Juvenile Diabetes—A children's disease characterized by an inadequate secretion or use of insulin resulting in excessive sugar in the blood and urine. This condition is usually controlled by diet and/or medication. However, in certain cases, control may be difficult and if untreated, serious complications may arise such as visual impairments, limb amputation, coma, and death.

Meningitis—An inflammation of the membranes covering the brain and spinal cord. If left untreated can result in serious complications.

Meningocele—A type of spina bifida in which there is protrusion of the covering of the spinal cord through an opening in the vertebrae.

Microcephaly—A disorder involving the cranial cavity characterized by the development of a small head. Retardation usually occurs from the lack of space for brain development.

Monoplegia—Paralysis of a single limb.

Multiple Sclerosis—A progressive deterioration of the protective sheath surrounding the nerves leading to a degeneration and failure of the body's central nervous system.

Muscular Dystrophy—A group of diseases that eventually weakens and destroys muscle tissue leading to a progressive deterioration of the body.

Myopia—Nearsightedness, a condition that results in blurred vision for distance objects.

Neonatal—The time usually associated with the period between the onset of labor and six weeks following birth.

Neurologically Impaired—Individuals who exhibit problems associated with the functioning of the central nervous system.

Nystagmus—A rapid, rhythmic, and involuntary movement of the eyes. This condition may result in difficulty reading or fixating upon objects.

Ocular Mobility—Refers to the eye's ability to move.

Optometrist—A professional trained to examine eyes for defects and prescribe corrective lenses.

Opthamologist—A medical doctor trained to deal with diseases and conditions of the eye.

Optic Nerve—The nerve in the eye which carries impulses to the brain.

Optician—A specialist trained to grind lenses according to a prescription.

Organic—Factors usually associated with the central nervous system that cause a handicapping condition.

Ossicles—The three small bones of the ear that transmit sound waves to the eardrum. They consist of the malleus, incus, and stapes.

Ostenogenesis Imperfecta—Also known as "brittle bone disease," this hereditary condition effects the growth of bones and causes them to break easily.

Otitis Media—Middle ear infection.

Otolaryngologist—A medical doctor specializing in diseases of the ear and throat.

Otologist—A medical doctor specializing in the diseases of the ear.

Otosclerosis—A bony growth in the middle ear that develops around the base of the stapes, impeding its movement and causing hearing loss.

Paralysis—An impairment to or a loss of voluntary movement or sensation.

Paraplegia—A paralysis usually involving the lower half of the body, including both legs as a result of injury or disease of the spinal cord.

Perinatal—Occurring at or immediately following birth.

Petit Mal Seisures—A mild form of epilepsy characterized by dizziness and momentary lapse of consciousness.

Phenylketonuria—Refered to as PKU, this inherited metabolic disease usually results in severe retardation. However, if detected at birth, a special diet can reduce the serious complications associated with the condition.

Photophobia—An extreme sensitivity of the eyes to light. This condition is common in albino children.

Postnatal—Occurring after birth.

Prenatal—Occurring before birth.

Prosthesis—An artificial device used to replace a missing body part.

Psychomotor Seizure—Epileptic seizures in which the individual exhibits many automatic seizure activities of which he or she is not aware.

Pupil—The opening in the middle of the iris that expands and contracts to let in light.

Quadriplegia—Paralysis involving all four limbs.

Retina—The back portion of the eye, containing nerve fibers that connect to the optic nerve where the image is focused.

Retinitis Pigmentosa—A degenerative eye disease in which the retina gradually atrophies, causing a narrowing of the field of vision.

Retrolental Fibroplasia—An eye disorder resulting from excessive oxygen in incubators of premature babies.

Rh Incompatibility—A blood condition in which the fetus has Rh positive blood and the mother has Rh negative blood leading to a buildup of antibodies that attack the fetus. If untreated, can result in birth defects.

Rheumatic Fever—A disease characterized by acute inflammation of the joints, fever, skin rash, nosebleeds, and abdominal pain. This disease often damages the heart by scarring its tissues and valves.

Rigidity Cerebral Palsy—A type of cerebral palsy characterized by minimal muscle elasticity, and little or no stretch reflex that creates stiffness.

Rubella—Also known as German measles, this communicable disease is usually only of concern when developed by women during the early stages of pregnancy. If contracted at that time, there is a high probability of severe handicaps of the offspring.

Sclera—The tough white outer layer of the eyeball that protects as well as holds the eye's contents in place.

Scoliosis—A weakness of the muscles that results in a serious abnormal curvature of the spine. This condition may be corrected with surgery or a brace.

Semicircular Canals—The three canals within the middle ear that are responsible for maintaining balance.

Sensorineural Hearing Loss—A hearing disorder resulting from damage or dysfunction of the cochlea.

Shunt—A tube that is inserted into the body to drain fluid from one part to another. This procedure is common in cases of hydrocephalus to remove excessive cerebrospinal fluid from the head and redirect it to the heart or intestines.

Spasticity—A type of cerebral palsy characterized by tense, contracted muscles, resulting in muscular incoordination.

Spina Bifida Occulta—A type of spina bifida characterized by a protrusion of the spinal cord and membranes. This form of the condition does not always cause serious disability.

Strabismus—Crossed eyes.

Tremor—A type of cerebral palsy characterized by consistent, strong, uncontrolled movements

Triplegia—Paralysis of three of the body's limbs.

Usher's Syndrome—An inherited combination of visual and hearing impairments.

Visual Acuity—Sharpness or clearness of vision.

Vitreous Humor—The jellylike fluid that fills most of the interior of the eyeball.